The
CLINTON
SCANDAL

and the
Future of
American Government

The CLINTON SCANDAL

and the
Future of
American Government

Edited by Mark J. Rozell
and Clyde Wilcox

Georgetown University Press
Washington, D.C.

Georgetown University Press, Washington, D.C.
© 2000 by Georgetown University Press. All rights reserved.
Printed in Canada

10 9 8 7 6 5 4 3 2 1   2000

This volume is printed on acid-free offset book paper.

Library of Congress Cataloging-in-Publication Data

The Clinton scandal and the future of American government / edited by
    Mark J. Rozell, Clyde Wilcox.
        p. cm.
    Includes index.
    ISBN 0-87840-776-6 (cloth : alk. paper).
    ISBN 0-87840-777-4 (pbk. : alk. paper)
    1. Clinton, Bill, 1946–   . 2. Clinton, Bill, 1946–   —
Impeachment. 3. Political corruption—United States—History—20th
century. 4. United States—Politics and government—1993–
I. Rozell, Mark J.
E886.C5784   2000
973.929′092—dc21   99-36836
                                                              CIP

CONTENTS

The Clinton Presidency and the Politics of Scandal

Mark J. Rozell and Clyde Wilcox

On December 19, 1998, the House of Representatives approved two articles of impeachment against President Bill Clinton. The first article, passed by a vote of 228 to 206, charged that the president had given "perjurious, false and misleading testimony to a federal grand jury."[1] The second article, passed by a vote of 221 to 212, charged that the president had committed obstruction of justice in the sexual harassment lawsuit filed against him by Paula Corbin Jones.[2] Clinton thus became only the second president in the nation's history to be impeached by Congress and the first elected president to suffer that fate.

Clinton faced the prospect of also being the first president in history to be removed from office. A two-thirds majority vote in the Senate on either article of impeachment would have required the president to vacate his office and turn the presidency over to Vice President Al Gore. Yet, on February 12, 1999, the U.S. Senate voted not to remove Clinton from office. Neither article of impeachment mustered even a simple majority in favor of removing Clinton from office.[3]

The Clinton scandal consumed the better part of a year of American public life. In January 1998, news reports revealed that the president had engaged in extramarital sexual relations with a young, former White House intern. More damaging still, the nation learned that by previously denying the affair, the president possibly had committed perjury in a legal deposition while under questioning about his past sexual relations. Many respected political observers declared that the president was finished: it was merely a matter of days or perhaps at most weeks before he would have to relinquish his office in disgrace. The public, they reasoned, would never stand for a president who committed such serious crimes and violated his oath of office.

What occurred over the course of the following year was as remarkable as it was unprecedented in American public life. A popular president during a period of peace and unprecedented national prosperity stood to possibly lose his office over lying about a sexual indiscretion. The controversy that ensued bitterly divided the nation, but nowhere more so than in Washington, D.C., where partisan positions hardened and leaders questioned one another's motives and integrity.

The president's defenders said that Clinton had done what any married man in his position would have done under the circumstances: deny a sexual indiscretion to protect his marriage and his family. The president, they said, had merely "lied about sex" and that did not merit a constitutional crisis. The president's detractors said that he had committed the serious offenses of perjury and obstruction of justice and that the nature of the act that led to these crimes is not recognized as a qualifying factor under the law. The president, they said, had knowingly and repeatedly broken the law and had therefore violated his oath of office. Defenders responded that circumstances are considered when punishment is rendered and that lying about a sexual affair did not deserve political capital punishment. Detractors replied that perjury of any kind is a serious matter for the person charged with seeing that laws are enforced.

It was nearly impossible to find a middle position on the Clinton scandal. Feelings ran deep and there was little room for compromise. Attempts in Washington, D.C., to overcome the partisan rancor and bitterness through some such middling position as a vote in Congress to censure the president failed to overcome partisan roadblocks, despite widespread public support. Many people simply wanted the investigation of the president to end and the government to return to other business, or they wanted to complete the process to the point of removing Clinton from office.[4]

Positions on the scandal divided along partisan lines. Political scientist Chris Achen remarked that for the first time in memory it was possible to learn someone's party from a single comment about the ongoing proceedings. The partisan divide was even deeper in the halls of Congress. Members of Congress were charged with the serious duty of voting on the issues of impeachment and removal from office on the merits of the case against the president and not according to party interests. To many constitutional scholars, what ensued was perhaps the most discouraging of all: When the votes were counted in the House only 5 of 228 Republicans voted against the first article of impeachment and only 5 of 206 Democrats voted in favor. On the second article, only 12 Republicans voted against and 5 Democrats voted in favor. As Michael Gerhardt points out in this volume, Republicans had thus cast over 95 percent of the votes in favor of impeachment and Democrats over 95 percent of the votes against impeachment. In the Senate not a single Democrat broke with the party to vote in favor of either article of impeachment. Members of Congress said that they voted their consciences based on the merits of the case against the president, yet coincidentally their consciences seemed to vary almost perfectly along party lines.[5]

At the center of the national crisis was the Office of Independent Counsel (OIC) and Independent Counsel Kenneth Starr. The OIC had originally been authorized to investigate the president and first lady's dealings in the controversial Whitewater land deal in Arkansas years before the Clinton administration and had since moved on to investigate a string of other matters. Starr's critics charged that he was obsessed with the goal of removing Clinton from office; his defenders argued that his investigation had considered so many issues because the Clinton administration was unusually deep in scandals. During the investigation, Starr and his team were presented with damaging information about the president's sexual life that was possibly germane to another ongoing legal matter: Paula Corbin Jones's sexual harassment lawsuit against Clinton. If true, this information meant that the president had purposefully lied in a legal deposition, thus committing the offense of perjury.

Starr brought information about this latest revelation to the attention of Attorney General Janet Reno, who then authorized the independent counsel to expand the scope of his investigation. The examination of the failed Whitewater land deal and many other matters became as well an investigation of whether the president had committed perjury and even obstruction of justice in the Jones case. Starr's investigation had thus taken the fateful turn that would lead to extraordinary divisiveness in the nation's capital and the president's impeachment. Starr's investigation culminated in a published report that made a forceful case that the president had acted illegally and violated his oath of office but also included explicit details of Clinton's sexual relations with the young intern.

Salacious details of the president's sexual activities with Monica Lewinsky had become public prior to the publication of the Starr report, but Starr's team chose to chronicle intimate details of the affair according to Lewinsky. The content of the report was the subject of much controversy: some argued that it was impossible to discuss the serious legal and constitutional issues at stake without delving into those details, whereas others believed that Starr had included the intimate details in an effort to politically weaken the president.

The president indeed had lied about his sexual relationship with a then 21-year-old White House intern named Monica Lewinsky and had done so repeatedly. He had lied not only in a deposition but also in a televised press conference and to his cabinet and White House aides who spoke in his defense and were then later embarrassed to be caught themselves in the deceit. When compelled to testify before the grand jury, the president said that in a strict, legalistic sense he actually had been truthful because he had never engaged in "sexual relations" with Lewinsky, which he defined narrowly as intercourse.

During the course of the Clinton scandal the nation turned increasingly sour toward the entire investigation of the president and the impeachment process. Although early polls during the scandal showed a public willing to consider removing from office a president who had committed perjury and obstruction of justice, over time the public came to believe that Clinton should remain in office even if he were found guilty of those crimes. Within a few months a substantial majority of Americans favored ending the investigation, and none of the events that unfolded in late 1998 or early 1999 shook that judgment. For nearly a year the public believed that its political leaders in Washington and the press corps obsessed with the scandal had all developed tin ears for national opinion. The disjunction between political Washington and the public never looked so large. While the former wallowed in scandal, the latter said it was time to focus the national dialogue on other issues.

As much as the public strongly expressed its conviction that the investigation and impeachment process end, people had little recourse for action other than to express their distaste in polls, in contacts with representatives, and in various media. That is, until election day.

For most of the public it appeared that the Republican party in particular was on a political suicide mission. The people had expressed their views to their elected representatives in Congress and the party in control simply was not listening. To some Republicans who carried the impeachment torch, public opinion had to take a backseat to the serious constitutional issues at stake. Although the representative function requires members to listen to their publics, it also carries the responsibility of trusteeship: to act according to their perception of their constitutional duty and in the public interest, even if the public disagrees.

The trustee function also anticipates that members will try to educate and therefore lead the public on important issues. The GOP took its case to the people in the election of 1998 and lost badly. The people had their first real opportunity to let the party know exactly what they thought of the case against the president and they spoke unequivocally: for the first time in sixty-four years the party out of the White House had lost seats in a midterm congressional election. This repudiation of the party was so serious that Speaker of the House Newt Gingrich (R-Ga.) faced opposition within his party for election as the next Speaker and chose to resign his seat in Congress. Gingrich had backed a controversial party-driven ad campaign that made presidential character a key issue. The GOP's anti-Clinton ads backfired, and Gingrich accepted responsibility and resigned.

For many analysts the 1998 election results signaled the effective end of the impeachment process. With such a thorough repudiation of the GOP at the polls and an increase in the Democratic membership of the House, almost no one could foresee any circumstance under which the president would be impeached.

Yet the 1998 election did not end the work of the 105th Congress. The lame-duck Congress still had authority to act. Indeed, the House Judiciary Committee led by Representative Henry Hyde (R-Ill.) had submitted a list of eighty-one questions to the president regarding their investigation of the scandal—questions that clearly antagonized the White House. Republicans had complained throughout the scandal that the president was not honest and forthcoming about his actions and that he had repeatedly tried to conceal the truth through evasive answers and legalistic "hairsplitting." When the president responded to the committee questions with technical, legalistic answers, the Republican members clearly had had enough.

Despite the election results, public opinion, and the projections of analysts that the impeachment process was dead, the committee Republicans decided to move ahead quickly to a vote on articles of impeachment. The committee hearings that followed were acrimonious and partisan. Some suggested that Congress had no right to take up the issue of impeachment during a lame-duck session, others charged that the Republicans were in a hurry to vote while their majority was larger than it would be when the new Democrats were sworn in. The committee moved forward the articles of impeachment on strict party-line votes. Republicans on the committee appeared so eager to move the process forward that they had the articles of impeachment drafted before all the witnesses had presented their testimonies. The Republican members indeed already believed that the evidence for impeachment was rock solid, but by moving so quickly before hearing all of the testimony, they lent credibility to charges that they acted in a single-minded partisan way.

During the committee hearings a number of legal scholars, including one contributor to this volume, gave testimony on the constitutional issues surrounding impeachment. With the exception of William and Mary law professor Michael Gerhardt, who appeared as a shared witness, the scholars appeared before the committee as either Democratic or Republican party witnesses. Legal opinion was divided. Many other academics became indirectly involved in the debate by signing one of two "scholars' briefs" on the issue of impeachment. Approximately 400 scholars signed the anti-impeachment brief and about 100 scholars and leading authorities signed the pro-impeachment letter. Yet it was journalists and political insiders who wrote the first draft of history's judgment of the Clinton scandal.

This book is an in-depth scholarly analysis of the Clinton scandal. There are a number of published books written by journalists and players on the events of the scandal, but the contributors to this volume instead are leading scholars on various topics germane to the events of the Clinton scandal. Like the scholars who appeared before the committee and those who signed the impeachment petitions, the contributors to this volume have different views on the events and eventual resolution of the scandal. Yet all of us have tried to write with scholarly detachment and fairness, even though we are certainly not devoid of the strong personal opinions that characterized the debate during the scandal. With the academic benefit of time and the lack of pressure to try to capitalize on the scandal with a quick and provocative book, we have striven to produce a collection of studies that will stand the tests of time and of more rigorous analysis.

Chapter Plan and Approach

This collection of essays is divided into two major themes: Institutional Perspectives and Political Perspectives. For the former, the contributors cover the major institutions and legal issues that were central to the scandal. For the latter, the contributors examine the major political factors that affected the scandal and its resolution. The volume concludes with an essay that broadly examines the implications of the scandal for governance.

Institutional Perspectives

Presidential scholar Robert J. Spitzer opens the volume with his analysis of the implications of the scandal for the institution of the presidency. He places the events of 1998 and 1999 in the proper historical context, noting the key differences between the Watergate crisis and the Clinton scandal. Like many scholars, Spitzer does not consider the president's actions to have risen to the level of "high crimes and misdemeanors." Nor does he believe the Clinton scandal has permanently "lowered the bar" for impeachment or made it more likely that future presidents will be impeached. Indeed, despite dire predictions at the time that President Andrew Johnson's highly politicized impeachment would leave all future presidents vulnerable to this sanction, no serious presidential impeachment effort was raised until over a century later.

The argument that the Clinton impeachment will precipitate future such action against presidents has to be predicated on the notion that there is some real partisan advantage to using this ultimate sanction. But as Spitzer notes, the GOP members gained nothing politically from their actions in 1998 and 1999 other than perhaps to have pleased their most ardent supporters. All evidence from the Clinton case suggests that Congress has much to lose from embarking on either a partisan impeachment or a perceived partisan impeachment.

Spitzer explodes other myths about the impact of the Clinton scandal. One such myth is that the presidency has been rendered "unimperial" because of Congress's actions and various court rulings limiting presidential privileges. Yet even under the cloud of impeachment the president continued to possess the authority to engage the U.S. military against Iraq, to threaten vetoes of legislation, and to propose a broad-based domestic policy agenda including Social Security and Medicare reform. As scholar Thomas Cronin has argued, in the end, the Congress and the courts punished Bill Clinton, not the institution of the presidency.

Congressional scholar Thomas Kazee examines in chapter 2 how the nature of the legislative process and the partisan composition of the House and Senate influenced the impeachment action and removal votes. Kazee argues that the House Republicans in particular ignored important warning signals about the likely fallout from their actions and ultimately overplayed their hand in large part because they were leaderless. Speaker Gingrich had resigned in the wake of the 1998 election disaster for the party. The GOP had thought that they had settled on a new speaker with Representative Bob Livingston (R-La.), but he suddenly resigned from Congress because of published reports that he had previously engaged in extramarital sexual relations.

According to Kazee, the lack of a major leader enabled the more strident second-level party leaders such as Majority Whip Tom DeLay (R-Tex.) to fill the vacuum and push a conservative impeachment agenda. Aiding this effort was the nature of the composition of the House Judiciary Committee. That committee was ideologically divided, with the Democratic members representing urban constituencies far more liberal than the party center, and the Republican members representing very conservative rural constituencies. Given these factors, the impeachment of the president was not surprising.

The Senate, on the other hand, had the benefit of seeing the reaction to the House's impeachment votes. As scholar Richard Fenno has pointed out, sequence is a crucial factor in congressional outcomes. Also important is the length of terms: Senators have greater insulation from public opinion than do House members. Whereas some House members from conservative districts may have worried about voter retribution if they did not support impeachment, most Republican senators had no such worries. The Republican senators also knew all along that they would never achieve enough Democratic votes for the articles of impeachment to achieve the necessary two-thirds vote to remove Clinton from office. That fact further insulated them from the political fallout of their actions. The Republicans could vote for removal without having to be held accountable for actually having removed a popular president from office.

In chapter 3 Karen O'Connor and John R. Hermann examine the legal controversies surrounding the Clinton scandal, in particular the issues of presidential immunities and privileges. They focus on the *Clinton v. Jones* Supreme Court decision that ultimately opened the way for the impeachment charges against Clinton and the consequences of the resolution of the scandal.

Had it not been for a typesetting error in a magazine story, Clinton may never have been impeached. The *American Spectator* ran a lengthy investigative story about allegations of Clinton's past sexual relations as governor of Arkansas, including the use of state troopers to facilitate keeping his activities secret. The editors of the story had decided just prior to publication to delete references to women's names, but mistakenly left in the name "Paula." The woman to whom that referred,

Paula Corbin Jones, was outraged by the story and immediately sought the assistance of an attorney. As the saying goes, the rest is history. Jones made her story public, accused the president of having sexually harassed her, and filed a suit asking for damages. These events set in motion the legal dispute that led to the important *Clinton v. Jones* decision in which a unanimous Supreme Court rejected Clinton's argument that a president must have immunity from civil suits while in office because of the potential distractions and attendant harm to the national interest.

O'Connor and Hermann analyze the implications of what they see as a terrible decision by the Court. It is now easier for private citizens to disrupt the public's business by bringing lawsuits against sitting presidents, perhaps even totally frivolous suits. The revelations of the most intimate and embarrassing details of Clinton's personal life could have a chilling effect on talented individuals in the future seeking election to the presidency or even to other high-level offices. For as James Pfiffner notes in this volume, many talented people have personal flaws, and many people with clean personal lives would never make good leaders. Perhaps most important, the whole episode contributed further to a debilitating cynicism in our country toward political leaders and institutions. Not only did the president's reputation for integrity suffer, but also an already unpopular Congress was held up to public ridicule and scorn for what most people perceived as the institution's partisan and foolish impeachment of Clinton.

Louis Fisher examines the investigation by Independent Counsel Kenneth Starr into various allegations concerning President Clinton and top administration officials, which ended in Clinton's impeachment in the House and the Senate's decision not to convict. The relentless criticism of Starr is put in the context of earlier probes by outside counsels of White House activity, including Archibald Cox's work on Watergate and Lawrence Walsh's investigation of the Iran-Contra affair. Fisher concludes that any outside probes of the White House that draw blood are naturally followed by devastating critiques of independent counsels.

Fisher regards Starr's appointment as a mistake and faults Starr for failing to reach closure on the matters initially assigned to him, particularly because Starr simultaneously pursued many outside legal interests. Yet he credits Starr with conducting an appropriate investigation, prevailing over a series of legal hurdles placed in his path by the White House, and providing detailed, credible evidence on Clinton's perjury and obstruction of justice. Given the procedure followed by the Senate on impeachment, the vote to "acquit" is not what it seems to be. Moreover, no one could have anticipated some of the problems that cropped up during House and Senate action on impeachment and removal. Fisher concludes that the Independent Counsel statute was the most effective tool for investigating White House activities.

Following Fisher's analysis of the controversial Independent Counsel statute is an examination of the controversial doctrine of executive privilege—a key legal issue in the Clinton scandal. The power of executive privilege allows the president and high-level executive branch officers to withhold information from Congress, the courts, and ultimately the public. Executive privilege is controversial in part because President Richard Nixon abused that power in his effort to conceal wrongdoing. With the exception of Bill Clinton, presidents since Watergate have been reluctant to use executive privilege because of the Nixon taint.

President Clinton used executive privilege extensively in the Lewinsky scandal. He claimed that he was protecting the principle of executive privilege, although the evidence suggests that the president instead was using that power to frustrate and delay the investigation of the OIC. In the end, Clinton's misuse of executive privilege had two major consequences: (1) The president contributed to the weakening of that doctrine because, like Nixon before him, Clinton's baseless actions gave opponents of executive privilege more reason to claim that it lacks legitimacy; and (2) although Clinton lost key court decisions on executive privilege and eventually had to drop his claims, the White House ultimately succeeded politically in buying time to delay the investigation and to build public opposition to Starr's efforts. Clinton hurt executive privilege but possibly saved his presidency by successfully drawing out the investigation and shifting blame for the long and costly independent counsel investigation from the White House to Kenneth Starr.

Is the President of the United States above the law? For many observers, that was the key question surrounding the scandal. In chapter 6 David Yalof and Joel Grossman make it clear that such slogans as "no person is above the law" do little to help us to understand the core issues involved when it is the president who is accused of wrongdoing. Any action taken against the president can have profound consequences for millions of citizens.

As the authors note, the issue of how to treat a president accused of wrongdoing is made all the more complicated by the Supreme Court having tried to create a "rigid demarcation between a president's public and private behavior." Although it is true, as Bill Clinton has protested, that presidents, like all citizens, "have private lives," the reality is that no president can have a private life that exists in a vacuum outside of the public arena. Yalof and Grossman argue that the law needs to reflect that reality. Current law not reflecting that reality is at the core of the difficulties that the nation had in coming to grips with how to resolve the Clinton scandal.

Yalof and Grossman examine how the law and the Constitution should handle unacceptable "private" behavior by presidents. They present the intriguing argument that presidents in some respects actually are "below the law" in that they have fewer constitutional protections of privacy than do ordinary citizens and are constantly scrutinized in ways that average citizens cannot even imagine. The authors offer some recommendations for reform, including a proposal to amend the Constitution to clarify the power of impeachment and another to empower Congress to use means other than impeachment to criticize presidents who misbehave (e.g., censure, formal rebuke).

The American obsession with political intrigue certainly did not begin with the Lewinsky scandal. As Paul Quirk observes in chapter 7, this scandal had a common feature: public expressions of disgust with the elites' emphasis on the whole tawdry event combined with the inability of the people to turn their attention away. The same public who complained for months they were tired of the coverage of the scandal and implored political Washington to focus on policy also turned into immediate national bestsellers postimpeachment books by scandal figures such as Lewinsky.

Quirk laments the American obsession with scandal and finds it harmful to the cause of good government. Rather than looking for ways to tear down public persons, the political system should find approaches to avoid scandal in the first place. That may require reforms of ethics, campaign finance laws, and a revised Independent Counsel statute, to name just some prominent examples discussed in recent years. Searching out wrongdoing should be a positive and productive endeavor that serves the purpose of promoting a better governing system. Our nation certainly seems farther away from that ideal than ever in the wake of the Lewinsky scandal. We need to learn how to better cope with scandals in this country.

Michael Gerhardt presents a detailed analysis of the Clinton impeachment and acquittal in chapter 8. During the impeachment process there was a great deal of confusion in the country over such matters as the procedures and the proper standards for an impeachment. As the author of the leading book on the federal impeachment process, Gerhardt is the right person to put these events in their proper constitutional and historical contexts.

For Gerhardt, the Clinton impeachment confirms the view that in our system of governance the heaviest burden is on those accusing the president of wrongdoing. If, in the process of moving forward a presidential impeachment, the country perceives such action as expedient, partisan, or unfair, there is little likelihood the Senate will remove the president from office. In this sense the Senate performs its intended constitutional role as a check on the decisions of the House. The true irony is that the constitutional framers anticipated the Senate would need to check the excesses of the House because the latter body was more likely to follow the whims of public opinion. In the Clinton impeachment the House deliberately acted against public opinion, with many Republican members claiming that it was their responsibility to do the "right" thing.

Gerhardt sees different consequences to the impeachment. The process, in his view, exposed many flaws in the Independent Counsel statute, including the inability of the independent counsel to maintain a reputation for impartiality in the face of political attacks by the president and his defenders. The impeachment proceedings did little to clarify the question of whether there indeed are different standards of impeachment for presidents and federal judges. The acquittal may have an impact on the actions of future Congresses considering whether to impeach a popular president—a completely different standard than applied to federal judges who lack popular support or even recognition.

Political Perspectives
In early 1998 when the scandal broke, the Clinton presidency looked finished, Democrats worried about the scandal's impact on their party, and Republicans looked forward to dramatically increasing their congressional majorities. A little more than a year later, the president was more popular than ever, the Democrats had actually gained seats in Congress, the GOP House speaker resigned, and public esteem for the Republican party was at one of its lowest levels in modern history.

Surely no one could have predicted that as the impeachment process unfolded the president's popularity would actually increase and support for the GOP would suffer. In early 1999, as the Senate considered removing a president from office, Clinton had a job approval rating higher than that of any previous president at this stage of the presidency.

Molly Andolina and Clyde Wilcox suggest in chapter 9 that several factors contributed to Clinton's strong public support. A strong economy coupled with improvement on many social indicators ranging from crime to teen pregnancy left many Americans reluctant to "rock the boat" and remove a president. Even with the constant media airing of tawdry details of Clinton's affair, the public stayed focused on the president's policies and the fact that economic times were good.

Further, Clinton's policies were popular, especially in contrast to those proposed by Republicans in Congress. The public indeed had to think about the alternatives should Congress remove the president from office. Many perceived the president as an important check on the potential excesses of a Republican-led Congress and believed that Clinton's removal would strengthen GOP policy influence.

Andolina and Wilcox add that Clinton had the ability to connect with average Americans and to project a concern and understanding of their problems that most citizens considered rare among elected officials. Clinton's political enemies were unpopular and, to many Americans, appeared to have acted unfairly in their effort to remove him from office. Finally, the public considered the Lewinsky matter one of private moral conduct, and, although they strongly disapproved, they considered the matter irrelevant to his job performance.

John Anthony Maltese examines the critical role of the media in the evolution of the Clinton scandal. For those who believe that the public always takes its cues about political figures from the media, the disconnect between reporting on the scandal and public perceptions of Clinton is surely eye opening. As Maltese notes, the media environment of the Clinton years is very different from even that of the Bush presidency years. The new media played the crucial role in breaking and then shaping the Lewinsky story. Mainstream media often reacted to the pressures of a hypercompetitive, fast-breaking news environment by emulating the practices of tabloid and other nontraditional news sources.

Maltese places the Clinton-media relationship in its proper perspective—and that requires an examination of how the president and his people dealt with reporters beginning in the first term. By trying to shut out the White House press corps and communicate a message through nontraditional means, the president and his staff created an atmosphere of unease with reporters. Some of Clinton's staff showed outright contempt for the traditional press corps and it took a long time to establish a more professional relationship. Clinton's attitude toward the media did him much harm and by the time the scandal occurred, he had very few sympathizers in the press corps. By underestimating the importance of the traditional media, the Clinton White House had planted the seeds for a most difficult press-presidency relationship.

The legacy of Clinton presidency may be Clinton himself. In chapter 11 Stephen J. Wayne argues that Clinton's political character, seductive style, and survivor mentality will continue to fascinate scholars long after his presidency has ended. Rarely has the office been visited by such a complex, multitalented individual who has been the focus of so much public approval and disapproval, praise and ridicule—a magnet for everyone's attention. Wayne discusses the components of Clinton's character that have fostered the president's political persona: limitless ambition, boundless energy, and intellectual prowess. He describes the roots and manifestations of his seductive style and the behavior pattern of excess and self-restraint that have enabled Clinton to survive on the brink of disaster.

The impeachment and Senate trial of President Clinton raised serious questions of character in the modern presidency. James P. Pfiffner tackles perhaps the most delicate subject of the Clinton scandal in chapter 12 with the kind of reasoned analysis that was so lacking in the overheated political atmosphere of 1998 and 1999.

In popular and public discourse, character is often limited to issues of sexual probity and truthfulness. Pfiffner takes those issues seriously, but he also argues that presidential character is much broader and includes presidents' approaches to public policy. Pfiffner examines concerns about sexual probity that surrounded different modern presidents and the effects that such issues ultimately had on other dimensions of presidential performance.

Several modern presidents have lied to the public, and Pfiffner distinguishes among more serious and less serious lies. Indeed, people who are faithful spouses and always truthful are not necessarily the most qualified to serve as president. Pfiffner concludes that character is much broader and more important than the narrow issues of sexual probity and honesty. To demonstrate that presidential character is multidimensional rather than seamless, Pfiffner examines the positive and negative aspects of President Clinton against the backdrop of some of his predecessors. Without excusing the president's behavior, Pfiffner reminds us that leaders are human beings and that it is important to place various aspects of their lives in a broader context rather than to judge them narrowly according to their conduct in any one area.

Soon after the impeachment scandal ended the United States was involved in an air war in Kosovo, Congress was debating spending issues, the parties seemed stalemated over conflicting ideas on how to "save Social Security," and the Republicans were pressing forward with investigations over security lapses in a nuclear facility. In short, politics as usual had returned to Washington. It is remarkable indeed just how quickly political Washington returned to normal after the resolution of the impeachment process. Yet there were lingering bad feelings among elected officials in both parties. In the wake of the Senate votes on removal, leading analysts predicted that the partisan acrimony from the previous year would leave political Washington stalemated. Some said that it would take years for players in the events of 1998 and 1999 to put aside their differences and work together.

Despite the return to normalcy in Washington, the Clinton scandal will have lasting implications for the political system, which most of the following chapters describe and analyze. Further, the scandal will certainly have a profound impact on history's judgement of Clinton's presidency. Not long after the conclusion of the scandal, Clinton himself told the press corps that future textbooks will contain a boxed item identifying him as having suffered the disgrace of impeachment. The president defended his record and said that history will balance that judgment with the story of his accomplishments.

Predicting history's judgment of the remarkable events of 1998 and 1999 is certainly beyond our capabilities as scholars. We hold different views ourselves as to what that judgment *should be*. We are confident nonetheless that our colleagues who have contributed to this volume have rendered valuable in-depth scholarly analyses of the scandal that dominated American politics for over a year.

Notes

1. *Cong. Rec.*, 144th Cong., 1998, H12040.
2. *Cong. Rec.*, 144th Cong., 1998, H12042.
3. Many analysts said after the Senate voted that the chamber had found the president "not guilty" of the House charges in the articles of impeachment. Strictly speaking that is not accurate. As Louis Fisher points out in "The Independent Counsel Statute," pp. 60–80, in this volume, the senators did not have the choice to make two votes on each article—one to determine whether the president was guilty and the second to decide whether he should be removed from office. Because of long-standing precedent, the senators had only one vote on each article, and the stake of each vote was whether Clinton could stay in office, not an official determination

of his guilt. Many senators who voted against the articles of impeachment declared that they considered the president guilty as charged by the House, but they also believed that the punishment of removal from office was far too great for the crimes committed.

4. For purposes of disclosure, the editors of this book reflect the division of opinion about the Clinton scandal. One of us (M.R.) favored the impeachment and ultimate removal of the president from office and was a signatory of the Robert Bork letter. The other (C.W.) neither condoned the president's behavior nor believed that his actions rose to the level of impeachable offenses. Like most of the rest of the country, neither one of us was left satisfied by the ultimate resolution of the scandal.

5. To be sure, the second article of impeachment would have failed without the votes of the handful of Democrats who broke with their party.

The Presidency: The Clinton Crisis and Its Consequences

Robert J. Spitzer

The Clinton crisis that dominated news headlines in 1998 and early 1999 yielded no dearth of emphatic pronouncements about its consequences for the institution of the presidency. While some commentators downplayed its likely adverse consequences, public debate was rife with dire predictions. Some of these predictions arose from predictable partisan sources. House Majority Whip Tom DeLay (R-Tex.), who led the impeachment charge, concluded, "Clearly, the President has done irreparable damage to the office of the Presidency."[1] Chief House prosecutor Henry Hyde (R-Ill.) asserted that if Clinton were not removed, the presidency would be "damaged."[2] On the opposing side of the partisan debate, Clinton lawyer Gregory B. Craig asserted before the Senate that a vote to convict and remove President Clinton on the basis of these allegations would render no president of the United States safe from impeachment ever again.[3]

Similar verdicts arose from others who were not as centrally involved in the case. For example, Senator Daniel Patrick Moynihan (D-N.Y.) warned that the very effort to attempt to remove Clinton might "very readily destabilize the presidency,"[4] suggesting political harm beyond any that might be visited on Clinton himself. The *New York Times* reported as fact that "*the* Presidency is a weaker office today than it was on Jan. 20, 1993, when Clinton first assumed it."[5] *Time* magazine also stated flatly that President Clinton has diminished the office of president.[6] Historian Arthur Schlesinger claimed that the post-Clinton presidency would be a weakened and wounded institution.[7] Law Professor Akhil Amar similarly concluded that "the Clinton scandals have done considerable damage to the presidency, leaving us with an office weaker in key respects than the one that the Founders envisioned."[8]

Before considering the merit of these dire predictions, three qualifications invite mention. First, in assessing the impact of the Clinton scandal on the presidency, one must separate the person from the office. Too often we define the presidency largely by the select group of individuals who have occupied the office, even though the office is a distinct entity, separate and apart from any particular president. Without doubt, presidents shape the office, but the institution, especially in its mature bureaucratic form,[9] possesses its own institutional dynamic, which is often obscured by popular as well as academic fascination with the individuals who have occupied the office.[10] Therefore, the emphasis here will be on the institution, not on Clinton or his place in history.

Second, the consequences of the Clinton crisis will be measured against the totality of the presidential institution. It is very easy to exaggerate the significance of that which is peripheral to presidential governance, so we must bear in mind that the presidency is most important for its political and policy role in governance and for its structural relationship in the constitutional separation of powers. To pick an example, John F. Kennedy was known to have multiple affairs with women in the White House during his presidency. While these dalliances are a matter of interest and concern, they are of relatively little importance in any analysis of the institution unless or until someone successfully argues that they had some measurable impact on the functioning of the office.

Third, the history of the presidency has repeatedly demonstrated the counterintuitive fact that, at least with regard to the presidency, strength may arise from weakness—what I will refer to here as a political slingshot effect. That is, one may not simply assume that a weak or failed president, however one might care to define this, automatically injures the institution after a term in office. So-called weak or failed presidents of the nineteenth century such as John Tyler, James K. Polk, Andrew Johnson, and Rutherford B. Hayes ultimately helped to extend the scope and powers of the office even as they paid a substantial political price during their presidencies.[11]

Watergate versus Monicagate

An assessment of the consequences of the Clinton crisis on the presidency draws one immediately to a comparison with the last great impeachment-tinged presidential scandal, Watergate. The two scandals are, of course, very different. If Watergate was, as President Gerald Ford famously called it, a "long national nightmare," the Clinton scandal was more like a drug-induced hallucination. Nevertheless, some limited comparisons are helpful, especially to gauge the consequences on the institution.

Even before the conclusion of the Watergate scandal, ending as it did with Nixon's resignation in August 1974, much of the discussion and analysis at the time centered on broad institutional and separation of powers questions. For example, in his introduction to a report prepared, at the behest of the Senate in the summer of 1974, by a panel assembled through the National Academy of Public Administration, Senator Sam Ervin (D-Ga.) warned of "a dangerous imbalance of power tilting away from the Congress toward the President."[12] Laced throughout this report, designed to examine "the key questions related to or behind the Watergate affair,"[13] was analysis concerning the growth of presidential power, dubbed "fundamental and disturbing"[14]; the institution's structural connection to the judicial branch; the role of congressional oversight; executive privilege; the watchdog role of the attorney general; ethics considerations; and campaign financing. This publication was by no means the only one to examine the implications of Watergate for the presidency and American governance.[15]

Obviously, most of the Watergate-related debate and analysis from the 1970s centered on Nixon's personal culpability and that of his subordinates. Even so, Watergate spawned wide-ranging examination of broader structural and institutional questions concerning the institution of the presidency. That it profoundly shaped the post-Nixon presidency as an institution (as well as the perspectives of presidency scholars) is a truism among students of the presidency. Tatalovich and Daynes, for example, noted that "Watergate had a profound impact on our view of presidential power."[16] Berman concluded that "Watergate revealed just how unbalanced our constitutional system had become. . . ."[17] Pious said that, as a result of Watergate, "the presidency was diminished morally, politically, and constitutionally."[18] And Watergate surely contributed to the legitimacy of the consciously antiimperial presidencies of Gerald Ford and Jimmy Carter. In short,

Watergate was a transformative moment for the institution of the presidency, above and beyond its consequences for Richard Nixon and his place in history—not because it ended the century-long march toward an ever-stronger presidency (it did not), but because it altered the nature of the imperial presidency debate and legitimized the wariness of executive excess, a notion that had once been the province solely of old-fashioned institutional conservatives.[19]

The Clinton crisis stands in stark contrast to Watergate in that, aside from some very specific institutional questions to be discussed later, no grand debate over the power of the presidency, or even the internal functioning of the executive branch, has arisen. Surely this reflects in part the fact that Clinton's misdeeds were unrelated to the execution of his official duties.[20] Admittedly, specific constitutional questions found parallels in both crises, questions such as the legitimacy and limits of executive privilege, the definition and applicability of impeachment, the proper role of an independent prosecutor, and the proper role of the courts in arbitrating disputes involving the presidency. Yet these matters arose directly from the nature of the investigation and prosecution of Nixon and Clinton. Starkly absent from the Clinton crisis was any broader constitutional soul-searching of the sort spawned by Watergate. This disjunction between the debate surrounding the two crises is all the more noteworthy when one recognizes that the public and academic appetite for news, analysis, and commentary was exponentially greater during the Clinton era, given the entrance of many academics into journalistic coverage and analysis and the proliferation of opinion magazines, cable news channels, and other academic and media sources frantic for Clinton-related grist. The marked contrast in the political and constitutional "auras" arising from these two events suggests that the Clinton scandal's implications for the institutional presidency are likely to be modest. Let us turn, however, to specific areas where the institution's power may be altered, including court rulings and the role of the courts, presidential-congressional relations, the impact on electoral politics, and consequences for those who seek and attain the presidential office.

Legal Questions and the Courts

The Clinton crisis generated several court actions pertaining to elements of executive power and authority. Most notable among these was the Supreme Court ruling in *Clinton v. Jones*,[21] in which a unanimous court ruled for the first time that a sitting president could be sued for private actions unconnected to presidential responsibilities.

Hoping to build on the precedent set in an earlier case, *Nixon v. Fitzgerald*,[22] in which the court ruled that presidents are immune from civil suits arising from official actions, Clinton argued that civil actions should be delayed until the president leaves office. The court rejected this argument, however, noting that only three presidents had ever been the object of suits for private actions, that "it seems unlikely that a deluge of such litigation will ever engulf the Presidency," making it "highly unlikely to occupy any substantial amount"[23] of a president's time, and that presidents may properly be subjected to the judicial process since they are not above the law (citing the 1974 case of *United States v. Nixon*).[24] The court further invited Congress to enact appropriate legislation to provide presidents with greater legal protections if it so chose.

Several lower-court rulings addressed matters pertaining to executive privilege and attorney-client privilege in a governmental context. In May 1998, U.S. District Judge Norma Holloway Johnson affirmed the right of the president to assert claims of executive privilege concerning conversations with senior aides, but also said that those claims were outweighed by the independent counsel's request to have access to such information for its criminal investigation. Judge Johnson also concluded that the first lady was a senior adviser and therefore could be covered by an executive privilege claim. Further, she ruled that the president could claim attorney-client privilege with a government-employed lawyer, but that in this case, the needs of the Starr investigation outweighed privilege claims extended to White House lawyer Bruce Lindsey. (In both of these latter claims, Kenneth Starr's office argued unsuccessfully that no such executive privilege claims existed. A federal court of appeals upheld the ruling concerning attorney-client privilege.)[25]

Two months later, a three-judge panel of the U.S. Court of Appeals for the District of Columbia Circuit ruled that secret service agents could be compelled to testify regarding what they saw or heard while on duty. In doing so, the panel rejected the effort to extend a "protective function privilege" to agents guarding the president, dismissing the argument that agents should be forced to testify only if they actually witnessed a felony. In so ruling, the court also brushed aside concerns that presidents might be endangered if they felt their actions might ultimately be reported by the agents assigned to guard them.[26]

The thrust of the executive privilege and lawyer-client rulings—that a qualified privilege does exist for the presidency but the particulars of these cases did not warrant ruling in Clinton's favor—followed the pattern of the touchstone case, *United States v. Nixon*, in that the court ruled against the president but for the presidency. Legal scholar Akhil Amar argues that the Clinton rulings, in conjunction with the 1974 *Nixon* case, have rendered the presidency "unimperial" (assuming such a change to be undesirable). The thrust of these cases, Amar asserts, has undercut Congress's constitutional watchdog role over the executive and impinged on "a zone of presidential privacy." Worse, these cases unleash an imperial judiciary that has set itself up to improperly intervene in executive affairs, disrupting the separation of powers.[27]

It is certainly true that the thrust of these cases ran against Clinton. But it is also true that the courts validated the existence of executive privilege, building on the court's initial recognition of the power in *Nixon,* and then extended the privilege explicitly to aides and the first lady. Attorney-client privilege was also recognized as legitimate. The only factor militating against these new and enhanced executive prerogatives is the wedge of a criminal investigation. In other words, absent a zealous Kenneth Starr–like prosecution or presidential criminality, the institution of the presidency emerges with clearly expanded powers. Amar writes with alarm that "proper (but politically sensitive) conversations in the Oval Office" are, according to the court, "entitled to even *less* protection than conversations between attorneys and clients."[28] If this is, in fact, an intrusion on presidential prerogative, it is an entirely appropriate one, as the presidential office is, first and foremost, a political office whose inner workings are routinely opened to public inspection even before a presidency ends. To treat routine conversations in the executive office (regardless of their political sensitivity) as sacrosanct, akin to the lawyer-client privilege attached to a civil or criminal action, would indeed put the capital "I" on the imperial presidency. The court's ruling to compel secret service agents to testify on noncriminal matters is, arguably, the most troubling ruling, in that it may indeed impel future presidents to leave agents behind to avoid observance of actions that need not be criminal, but merely embarrassing. Such an action could indeed increase the risk to the president's well-being. Still, by definition, such incidents are likely to be those most removed from the president's formal, official responsibilities and therefore are highly unlikely to have any impact on the day-to-day execution of the president's formal responsibilities.

The *Jones* case explicitly cut against the presidential institution by allowing civil suits to proceed during a presidency. While the court's confidence that few suits would ensue might be false, the court's invitations to other courts to dismiss frivolous suits against the president and to Congress to enact protective legislation could indeed be adequate barriers to properly protect the presidency. In any case, when we view the presidency as a whole, the inescapable conclusion is that these cases fortify presidential prerogative as much as, if not more than, they nibble at the margins of the institution, primarily because the affected presidential actions represent such a small proportion of formal, official duties, powers, and responsibilities. The bigger constitutional question is the relationship between the executive and legislative branches, especially with regard to the impeachment power.

Congress and Impeachment

Returning to the Watergate comparison, many noted the political dynamic of the Clinton scandal to be very different from that of the Nixon era. First, the Watergate inquiry was less partisan (as reflected in congressional debate and votes) than the particularly sharp partisan debate and party-line committee and floor votes in the Clinton case. Second, the Watergate charges were brought with far greater reluctance by those who led the charge,[29] a trait contrasted by the formal impeachment charges having been filed against Clinton in late 1997 before the actual charges that formed the basis for impeachment brought in early 1998 had even been raised. Third, the tone of the Watergate inquiry was chastened by very sincere and widespread public anguish and ambivalence among members of Congress on both sides of the aisle, whereas the tone of the Clinton inquiry in Congress was relatively void of similar anguish but was rather marked by certainty on each side.[30] Fourth, unlike Nixon's defenders in Watergate, Clinton's supporters acknowledged his misdeeds. The key disagreement was not whether misdeeds occurred (as with Nixon), but rather whether they rose to the level of impeachment.[31] Fifth, the Clinton scandal was unrelated to the execution of the powers of his office, whereas the reverse was true of Nixon. Sixth, and most significant, the Nixon impeachment inquiry, although halted by Nixon's resignation, ultimately met both the legal standard of high crimes and misdemeanors and the political standard of public support. The Clinton impeachment inquiry arguably failed to meet the minimum standard in the legal trial (certainly as judged by the Senate's verdict and by the weight of most academic commentators) and undeniably failed to meet the political minimum standard in the court of public opinion.

What these differences suggest about the future of impeachment for Congress and the institutional presidency is that the proceedings against Clinton did indeed lower the bar for subsequent congressional impeachment inquiries, as the Clinton impeachment was both more routine and more partisan, *if* one takes the Clinton case as having important value as precedent. The routine and partisan tone of the Clinton episode is especially noteworthy when compared with the prevailing attitude toward impeachment during the Nixon era, when the very mention of the word impeachment "had danger hanging from it the instant it left the mouth,"[32] and political support for Nixon in the country had ebbed before the impeachment inquiry picked up steam.

These differences underscore Alexander Hamilton's twofold warning about the downside of giving impeachment power to an elected body—to wit, that the charges brought against the president might be of insufficient legal weight, and that the impeachment process might be overtaken by the force of fierce partisanship. In Hamilton's words, "there will always be the . . . danger that the decision will be regulated more by the comparative strength of parties than by the real demonstrations of innocence or guilt."[33] Political scientist Terry Sullivan argues that Hamilton's warning has come to pass in the Clinton matter, with Congress's harder partisan edge pushing impeachment as a mechanism akin to a vote of no confidence, where Congress will in the future be tempted to pursue impeachment in order to remove a president with whom Congress has mere policy differences.[34]

I agree that the Clinton inquiry reflects an eerie realization of Hamilton's warnings. I do not agree, however, that it will result in a degradation of the impeachment power that invites its use against future presidents simply because of policy differences, even in an era of continued fierce partisanship and divided government. If the history of the presidency teaches us anything, it is that the political slingshot effect applies to the presidential institution in just such circumstances.

For example, John Tyler's turbulent, contentious presidency was the first to be confronted with a serious effort to impeach the president (a vote on articles of impeachment failed in the full House in 1843). Widely and properly touted as a failed presidency, Tyler's term nevertheless prepared the way for the completion of the movement toward executive leadership started by Andrew Jackson.[35] Despite the fiercely partisan and nearly successful impeachment inquiry against Andrew Johnson, no serious impeachment effort was launched again until Nixon was in office; this despite the roiling partisanship of subsequent nineteenth-century presidencies that should have precipitated impeachment efforts based on the Johnson precedent for such presidencies as those of Rutherford B. Hayes and Grover Cleveland. These latter two examples are particularly apt; in Hayes's case, he barely survived the controversial election of 1876 and did not seek his party's nomination four years later; in Cleveland's case, he suffered electoral defeat in his first reelection bid.

As for Andrew Johnson's impeachment, political scientists Sidney Milkis and Michael Nelson verify the presidential slingshot effect by first quoting a Senate defender of Johnson, who offered a dire warning very similar to that of Clinton lawyer Gregory Craig (quoted earlier), that no future president will be safe who happens to differ with a majority of the House and two-thirds of the Senate. . . . Milkis and Nelson then conclude, "As it turned out, the opposite precedent was established in Johnson's impeachment trial. The Senate's failure to remove him in 1868 meant that a president could not be forced from office simply because of unpopularity or disagreements with Congress. . . . The acquittal of Johnson made the impeachment article nearly a dead letter.". . .[36]

Similarly, the political lesson of the Clinton case will more likely be to keep the impeachment blunderbuss in its cabinet, precisely because of the apparent ease with which it was used against Clinton and because of its failure to drive him from office, erode public support for his presidency, or alter the direction of national policy. Sullivan's assertion that Congress's heightened partisanship, culminating in the impeachment effort against Clinton, "make[s] impeachment an attractive tool for winning the policy debate between a recalcitrant president and a hostile congressional majority" fails by the standard Sullivan sets: "The *practice* of impeaching officials, not its constitutional theory, defines the institution of impeachment."[37] The practical application of the impeachment effort against Clinton brought his opponents no immediate advantages, aside from assuaging some in the Republican Party's far right.

Beyond this, the traditional "unthinkability" of impeachment was, in its resemblance to a political nuclear weapon, the ultimate threat feared more by reputation than experience with use. Yet its full application in the Clinton case showed this weapon to be more like an errant scud missile—ineffective, erratic, off-target—a conclusion widely noted by Clinton supporters as well as by his detractors. Even if we assume that a divided government marked by sharp partisanship will be the norm in the years ahead, congressional opponents of presidents will surely turn to political devices other than impeachment (except in cases of clear criminality).

Finally, there is no reason to believe that the Clinton crisis will have any impact on the overall institutional relationship between the legislative and executive branches, especially on the usual political and policy ebbs and flows between the branches. A subsequent executive crisis that raises the specter of impeachment will, of course, harken to the Clinton case, just as the Clinton case harkened to the Nixon and Johnson impeachment episodes. The flaw in the argument raised by many—that the Clinton episode invites a partisan Congress to threaten or implement impeachment because of policy differences between the branches or because of overheated partisan animus—is that it presupposes this approach was somehow useful or successful and therefore invites imitation.[38] It was not and it does not. Its precedent value for post-Clinton congresses will more likely be avoidance rather than embrace of the impeachment option. Moreover, those who fear future partisan impeachments assume that members of Congress have not learned, or do not care to learn, the lesson that any serious impeachment inquiry must be built on both sound legal and sound political footing. By most accounts, Clinton supporters and critics seemed to have learned this lesson well.[39]

Electoral Balance and Popular Will

What of the post-Clinton presidency's institutional position with respect to the electorate and its impact on the partisan balance? The universal assumption, bursting almost immediately on the heels of the initial revelations in January 1998, was that the Democrats would be politically hurt, even crippled, as were the Republicans in the aftermath of Watergate. The upcoming 1998 midterm elections and Vice President Al Gore's presidential chances in 2000 seemed to offer only disappointment, if not doom, for the Democrats—especially for any who chose to side with Clinton in the succeeding months.

Yet the most stunning political fact to emerge from the Clinton crisis was that the Democrats not only survived, but benefited. Heading the column was Clinton himself, whose job approval rating, measured within days of the end of the impeachment effort in February 1999, stood at 68 percent—8 percent *higher* than before the Lewinsky scandal broke in January 1998.[40] To the shock of virtually every political pundit, the Democrats actually gained five seats in the House midterm elections, a feat not accomplished by any party since 1934 (the last time the president's party picked up seats in a midterm election and only then because of the rising New Deal tide). Even worse for the Republicans, public support for their party has diminished, at least in part *because* of its pursuit of Clinton, especially among swing voters.[41] Internal factional disputes intensified, and the party has found itself defined by many voters as the narrowly negative "anti-Clinton" party.[42]

In contrast, the Democrats emerged rather like Dorothy after the tornado—slightly amazed to be walking and talking and gratified to be greeted by smiling faces.[43] While the Democrats cannot assume that they will retake control of Congress or keep the presidency in 2000, they seem to hold the advantage in what has proven to be a series of missteps by Republicans following their stunning victories in 1994, which include the 1995 government shutdown (most citizens blamed the Republicans), Clinton's 1996 reelection, the 1998 Democratic House gains, the 1998 resignations of House Speaker Newt Gingrich (R-Ga.) and heir apparent Representative Robert Livingston (R-La.), and the failed impeachment effort.

To my knowledge, only one commentator correctly predicted the inability of the Republicans to capitalize on their 1994 victory and their subsequent missteps, capped by the mishandling of the Clinton impeachment proceeding. In a book published in 1995, at the very crest of Newt Gingrich's Republican revolution, political scientist Theodore J. Lowi predicted "The End of the Republican Era," arguing precisely that the reconstituted Republican Party, led by Gingrich allies and Christian populists, would self-destruct because of its rejection of pluralism and embrace of a narrow moral absolutism that generates "radicalism resulting from intense commitments [that] can destroy the discourse out of which political solutions can be developed."[44]

In the impeachment inquiry, Republican leaders were repeatedly driven away from moderate, compromise-oriented resolutions of the Clinton crisis (e.g., settling for a censure resolution) by the party's right wing and instead found themselves impelled to push the impeachment process ahead to its illogical conclusion.[45] When Lowi wrote his book, he knew he was whistling in the wind: "Even as I compose these final passages, I already know that everything said here will be disregarded." Even more presciently, Lowi predicted that "before the decade of the 1990s is over, there will be a civil war inside the Republican party, or the right wing will break out of the party altogether."[46] The impeachment process as it unfolded in Congress and its political backlash against the Republican Party are the realization of Lowi's prediction. In short, even if the Democrats fail to capture Congress or the White House in 2000, the Republicans will be unable to claim any new mandate arising from the Clinton crisis.

Presidential Recruitment and Personal Lives: Sex, Lies, and Audiotape

Concern continues that the most damaging legacy for the post-Clinton presidency will be its impact on persons seeking or occupying the Oval Office. With the unremitting, unyielding attention paid to Clinton's personal life, beginning even before his election in 1992, many worry that (1) qualified candidates will be scared off because of the intense scrutiny of their private lives, and (2) those who win election will find their private lives probed and scrutinized to such an extent that they will be distracted from governance, that public attention will be habitually diverted to the personal and the trivial, and that the institution of the presidency will suffer a generalized loss of prestige. Barbara Dafoe Whitehead, for example, argues that Clinton has transformed the presidency from the imperial presidency to the Intimate Presidency, where the personal prevails over the political.[47]

It is important to note, first, that the intense focus on presidents' personal lives, including sex-related matters, is nothing new. Thomas Jefferson was dogged throughout his presidency by rumors of his affairs with female slaves, Andrew Jackson was widely criticized for marrying a woman who was still married to another man, and Grover Cleveland admitted to fathering an illegitimate child. However, the intense focus on Clinton's personal life surely does represent a higher and more sustained degree of scrutiny; it is highly unlikely that any future president will be able to shield sexual dalliances from the media and the public in the manner of Warren Harding, Franklin D. Roosevelt, and John F. Kennedy, whose infidelities did not become known until after their presidencies. Clinton's presidency may have set the exposure bar higher, but the intense scrutiny focused on the lives of presidents is as old as the presidency itself. And the recent sea change in electronic media scrutiny of those in public life dates to the 1970s and 1980s, predating Clinton.[48]

As for the recruitment of future presidents, there is nothing new about some prospective candidates bowing out because of the feared personal toll of the campaign. Even so, at the start of 1999, the list of presidential aspirants was no less extensive than in prior years. Likely Republican challengers included Lamar Alexander, Gary Bauer, Pat Buchanan, George W. Bush, Elizabeth Dole, Steve Forbes, John Kasich, Jack Kemp, John McCain, George Pataki, Dan Quayle, Bob Smith, and Fred Thompson. Likely Democratic prospects included Bill Bradley, Al Gore, Jesse Jackson, and Paul Wellstone (Gore's huge advantage in fundraising and support among party activists having deterred other interested Democratic prospects from entering the race). In short, there is no reason to believe that presidential recruitment has been hampered.

Finally, the public's unwavering support for Clinton's job performance underscores an additional lesson about presidential sex. While the public strongly disapproved of Clinton's sexual indiscretions, it separated the private from the public as long as the president continued to function effectively as chief executive. This underscores the broader lesson, suggested by cases like Jefferson, Jackson, and Cleveland, that private moral behavior has, at most, a limited impact on the functioning of the presidency. Indeed, "the public is, within broad limits, functionally indifferent to presidential character."[49] A recent book that sets out to demonstrate that good husbands make good presidents and bad husbands make bad presidents ironically succeeds inadvertently in proving that such private conduct does not correlate with the relative success of a presidency.[50]

Conclusion

The first important clue suggesting how little the Clinton crisis will affect the presidential institution is the stark contrast between the debate in popular and academic circles swirling around it and that surrounding Watergate. No searching reassessment of the scope and consequences of presidential power and authority occurred during or immediately after the Clinton impeachment effort (except for this book), aside from analysis of the independent counsel law, the *Jones* case, and the like. The presidential institutional barometric pressure remained remarkably constant.

Much of the alarm raised about the potentially harmful consequences of the Clinton crisis was in connection with the several suits in which the president was involved. On this score, the presidency won further formal acceptance of executive privilege and its extension to aides and the first lady. Qualified lawyer-client privilege was also recognized. On the other hand, sitting presidents may now be sued in civil court for actions unconnected to the presidency, and secret service agents may be compelled to testify about what they observe. Even though the rights won by the institution were qualified by the courts, they were also extensions over what existed before Clinton.

Taken as a whole, including the likely lapse of the independent counsel law, it is difficult to see how the presidential institution is materially affected or impinged in its day-to-day operations. Amar's claim, discussed earlier, that the presidency is now "unimperial" because of these rulings is singularly unpersuasive when one notes that the claim was made at the very time the president, after having just survived two votes in the Senate to remove him from office, was engaged in a full-scale, unauthorized daily air war over Iraq, followed shortly by a full-blown military operation in Kosovo, and was offering up to Congress and the country a vast plate of domestic policy proposals that Congress was more than willing to consider.[51] If the presidency was imperial when Clinton took office, it will be no less so when he leaves.

While public trust in the government as a whole took a "heavy hit," the public's views of the presidency and Congress were little changed.[52] As to the impeachment power, there is no guarantee against a politicized process. The next best thing to a guarantee, however, is a process that reflects three traits: bipartisan support, a strong legal case, and political support in the country. Partisans on all sides acknowledged as much. Except for the application of the impeachment process to Clinton, little from that process recommends its use in a similar way in the immediate future.

On the electoral front, the drubbing taken by the Republicans can only make their assault on majority-party status and the White House that much more difficult. Admittedly, the year and a half between the conclusion of the impeachment inquiry and the 2000 presidential elections is a political lifetime—just ask George Bush, who found his record-high popularity eighteen months before the 1992 elections to be of little help in his loss to Clinton. For the Republicans, the bottom-line lesson is that they can expect no benefit from the Clinton crisis of the sort received by the Democrats after Watergate.

Finally, the Clinton crisis revealed that the parameters of public debate now allow more explicit and graphic discussion of the private lives of presidents than would have been accepted a few decades ago. Aside from that and the affirmation that any private action by future presidential contenders may become public, little has changed in the tabloid presidency.

When all is said and done, presidential scholar Thomas Cronin is one of the few commentators who, commensurate with this analysis, got it right when he observed, "The institution of the presidency will survive pretty well. . . . What is being punished here is the individual, not the institution."[53]

Notes

1. Jill Abramson, Lizette Alvarez, Richard L. Berke, John M. Broder, and Don Van Natta, Jr., "How Republican Determination Overcame President's Popularity," *New York Times,* 21 December 1998, A1, 26.

2. "Prosecutors Want Witnesses," *Syracuse Herald-American,* 17 January 1999, A12.

3. "White House Special Counsel Asserts Perjury Case Is Flawed," *New York Times,* 21 January 1999, A1, 17.

4. Richard L. Berke, "Moynihan Favors a Clinton Censure," *New York Times,* 25 December 1998, A1.

5. Adam Clymer, "The Presidency Is Still There, Not Quite the Same," *New York Times,* 14 February 1999, Sec. 4, 1.

6. Jonathan Alter, "The Fallout," *Time,* 8 February 1999, 30.

7. Clymer, "The Presidency Is Still There."

8. Akhil Reed Amar, "The Unimperial Presidency," *The New Republic,* 8 March 1999, 25.

9. The evolution of the presidency into a formidable and complex bureaucratic entity is described in Theodore J. Lowi, *The Personal President* (Ithaca, N.Y.: Cornell University Press, 1985).

10. Robert J. Spitzer, *The Presidency and Public Policy* (Tuscaloosa: University of Alabama Press, 1983), 2–3, 148. Lynn Ragsdale organizes an entire book around the distinction between the individual and the institution. See her *Presidential Politics* (Boston: Houghton Mifflin, 1993).

11. The paradox of weak or failed presidents whose actions nevertheless contributed to the expansion of the office is detailed in Robert J. Spitzer, "Evolution of the Veto Power" in *The Presidential Veto* (Albany, N.Y.: SUNY Press, 1988), 25–70; Spitzer, "The Evolving Relationship," in *President and Congress* (New York: McGraw-Hill, 1993), 17–39.

12. Frederick C. Mosher, "Foreword" to *Watergate: Implications for Responsible Government* (New York: Basic Books, 1974), ix.

13. Ibid., p. 13.

14. Ibid., p. 28.

15. Another example, also published before Nixon's resignation, was Charles Roberts, ed., *Has the President Too Much Power?* (New York: Harper & Row, 1973). Obviously, a flood of publications, both popular and scholarly, examined the constitutional and institutional consequences of Watergate in the years following Nixon's resignation.

16. Raymond Tatalovich and Byron W. Daynes, *Presidential Power* (Monterey, Calif.: Brooks/Cole, 1984), 10.

17. Larry Berman, *The New American Presidency* (Boston: Little, Brown, 1986), 285.

18. Richard M. Pious, *The Presidency* (Boston: Allyn & Bacon, 1996), 101.

19. For more on this debate, see Spitzer, "Conclusion" in *President and Congress,* 236–61.

20. This is not to suggest that a president cannot be impeached for private conduct. A president who committed a murder, for example, would certainly be open to impeachment. Some have argued that Clinton's conduct toward Monica Lewinsky was in the public realm because he had inappropriate sexual contact with her in his office, which is government property; however, because the conduct was not itself illegal and did not otherwise influence the execution of his constitutional responsibilities, their having engaged in such behavior in the White House cannot be considered a violation of his oath or public responsibilities (although my assertion is not meant to dismiss the validity of the impeachment charges brought against him, which pertained to perjury and obstruction of justice).

21. *Clinton v. Jones,* 137 L. Ed. 2d 945 (1997).

22. *Nixon v. Fitzgerald,* 457 U.S. 731 (1982).

23. *Clinton v. Jones,* 137 L. Ed. 2d 945, at 965–66.

24. *United States v. Nixon,* 418 U.S. 683 (1974).

25. These findings are summarized in Peter Baker and Susan Schmidt, "Starr's Plea Swayed Judge," *Washington Post,* 28 May 1998, A1; Joan Biskupic, "Echoes of 1974 Nixon Tapes Case," *Washington Post,* 28 May 1998, A18; *In re: Bruce Lindsey,* 98-3060 (1998).

26. Susan Schmidt, "Starr Wins Appeal in Privilege Dispute," *Washington Post,* 8 July 1998, A1.

27. Amar, "The Unimperial Presidency."

28. Ibid., 26.

29. This point is made by an often overlooked book on Watergate, Jimmy Breslin's *How the Good Guys Finally Won* (New York: Viking, 1975).

30. Breslin, *How the Good Guys Finally Won;* David E. Rosenbaum, "The Tone of a Routine Dispute without the Agonizing of 1974's Debate," *New York Times,* 11 December 1998, A29.

31. Rosenbaum, "The Tone of a Routine Dispute."

32. Breslin, *How the Good Guys Finally Won,* 163–64.

33. Alexander Hamilton, James Madison, and John Jay, *The Federalist Papers* #65 (New York: New American Library, 1961), 396–97.

34. Terry Sullivan, "Impeachment Practice in the Era of Lethal Conflict," *Congress and the Presidency* 25 (autumn 1998): 117–28.

35. Wilfred E. Binkley, *President and Congress* (New York: Vintage, 1962), 121.

36. Sidney M. Milkis and Michael Nelson, *The American Presidency: Origins and Development, 1776–1998* (Washington, D.C.: CQ Press, 1999), 169–70.

37. Sullivan, "Impeachment Practice," 127; ibid., 117.

38. For example, Christopher L. Eisgruber and Lawrence G. Sager, "Impeachment's Trickle-Down Effect," *New York Times,* 18 January 1999, A17.

39. See Steven S. Smith and Sarah Binder, "Impeachment Lessons," *Washington Post,* 13 December 1998, C1.

40. Richard Morin and Claudia Deane, "Public Blames Clinton, Gives Record Support," *Washington Post,* 15 February 1999, A1. See also John R. Zaller, "Monica

Lewinsky's Contribution to Political Science," *PS: Political Science and Politics* 31 (1998), 182–89.

41. Richard L. Berke, "Will G.O.P. Be Casualty of Its Own Bombardment?" *New York Times*, 18 December 1998, A28.

42. Thomas B. Edsall and Dan Balz, "Strategists Fear a Toll on GOP in Future," *Washington Post*, 10 January 1999, A1.

43. James Traub, "A Curse on the House," *New York Times Magazine*, 28 February 1999, 36–41.

44. Theodore J. Lowi, *The End of the Republican Era* (Norman, Okla.: University of Oklahoma Press, 1995), 210. Lowi's arguments have recently found much favor in public analysis. See, for example, Andrew Sullivan, "Going Down Screaming," *New York Times Magazine*, 11 October 1998, 46–51, 88–91.

45. I am not arguing here that the Republicans should not have, as a matter of law, pushed ahead with the impeachment effort, but, rather, as a political matter because they realized that they could not obtain a conviction and that the longer the process played out, the more it would hurt them politically. Pressure from the party's right wing blocked any effort to cut their losses before the bitter end. See Abramson et al., "How Republican Determination Overcame President's Popularity."

46. Lowi, *The End of the Republican Era*, 258; ibid., 236.

47. Barbara Dafoe Whitehead, "The Clinton Affair," *Washington Post*, 31 January 1999, B1.

48. Thomas E. Patterson chronicles this in *Out of Order* (New York: Vintage, 1993), 30–52, 147–75. The media frenzy over Jimmy Carter's relatively innocent comment during an interview in 1976 that he had "looked on a lot of women with lust. I've committed adultery in my heart many times" nearly derailed his candidacy, underscoring the media's and the country's interest in mere discussion of such matters. See Jules Witcover, *Marathon* (New York: New American Library, 1977), 603. The destruction of Gary Hart's 1988 presidential bid over an actual affair with Donna Rice, coming on the heels of Hart's denial of such an affair, also presaged public and media fascination with the personal sexual predilections of those at the presidential level. In the context of these events, the national obsession with Clinton cannot be considered qualitatively different. Many books have examined the sex lives of the presidents, underscoring popular fascination with the subject. See, for example, Michael John Sullivan, *Presidential Passions* (New York: Shapolsky, 1992).

49. Zaller, "Monica Lewinsky's Contribution to Political Science," 188.

50. Marvin Olasky, *The American Leadership Tradition: Moral Vision from Washington to Clinton* (New York: Free Press, 1999).

51. Eric Pianin, "Clinton, Hill GOP Turn to Agendas," *Washington Post*, 14 February 1999, A24.

52. David S. Broder and Dan Balz, "A Year of Scandal with No Winners," *Washington Post*, 11 February 1999, A1.

53. Broder and Balz, "A Year of Scandal," A1.

T W O

The Congress: The Politics of Impeachment

Thomas A. Kazee

Why did the U.S. House of Representatives impeach President Bill Clinton? The sequence of events leading up to that historic vote in December 1998 surely suggested that such an action was futile—at least with respect to removing the president from office—and perhaps damaging to the interests of those trying to impeach him. By December, it was apparent that not only was the two-thirds Senate vote necessary to convict the president unlikely to materialize, but also that the strident partisanship of the prolonged House proceedings had created a public climate of skepticism, dissatisfaction, and apathy. And why did the U.S. Senate, with a ten-vote Republican majority and presumably subject to many of the same ideological pressures as their House counterparts, move to a final vote in only five weeks—a vote in which the president's opponents failed to muster even a simple majority for either of the two articles of impeachment sent to the Senate by the House?

The behavior of the two legislative bodies can best be understood as a consequence of differences between House and Senate process, institutional culture, and leadership. Although influenced by a number of factors, House action was fundamentally shaped by three things: the unusual nature of impeachment as a legislative mechanism; the nature of the contemporary House, especially the extent of partisan polarization in recent years; and the failure of House leadership, most notably on the Republican side of the aisle. Absent any of those factors, the House would have been less likely to behave in ways that often seemed divorced from the broader political context of American politics. The Senate, on the other hand, was able to avoid the mistakes of the House for two reasons: differences in the nature of the Senate and stronger leadership.

The House

Warnings that House Republicans were treading on dangerous ground were voiced by many in and out of the Congress almost from the moment the allegations surfaced. In February 1998, one month after the press reported that the President had carried on, and then covered up, an affair with White House intern Monica Lewinsky, *Congressional Quarterly* noted that most House Republicans had avoided public comment on the Clintons' problems. They were "loath to be seen as piling on." At about the same time, former House member Philip Sharp, recently retired director of the Institute of Politics at Harvard, noted presciently, "[Impeachment] would be a huge mistake if they don't have something really substantial. There could be a reaction against that . . . if the hotheads [in the party] become the image of what the Republican Party is all about."[1]

In March 1998, Representative George W. Gekas and Senator Arlen Specter, both Pennsylvania Republicans, said that Independent Counsel Kenneth Starr must refer to the Congress an "open and shut case" on impeachment—anything less, they said, could be disastrous for the GOP.[2] Four months later, Rusty Paul, Chairman of the Georgia Republican Party, noted that GOP House candidates had to tread carefully on the impeachment issues to avoid negative public reaction: "Republicans will be somewhat cautious. . . . We have to look balanced and fair."[3] In September, as the House Judiciary Committee took up the matter, Chairman Henry J. Hyde (R-Ill.) said, "We all agree any impeachment cannot succeed unless it is done in a bipartisan or nonpartisan way."[4] And in October, Representative Ray LaHood (R-Ill.), later to preside over the House impeachment floor proceedings, said, "In the end, if there's going to be impeachment articles, it has to be bipartisan."[5]

These warnings were particularly noteworthy given the consistently high level of public support for the president. From the moment the scandal broke, Gallup Poll soundings of presidential approval showed about two-thirds of Americans approved of Clinton's performance;[6] these ratings scarcely wavered throughout this entire period. By contrast, public dissatisfaction with the impeachment process was widespread. In a national survey in September, for example, 54 percent of Americans disapproved of the way the House Judiciary Committee was handling the issue.[7] Moreover, a majority of Americans did not want the president impeached. An October poll showed 65 percent of Americans opposed impeachment,[8] essentially the same as the 63 percent of respondents who opposed impeachment at the time of House vote.[9]

House Judiciary Committee member Lindsay Graham (R-S.C.) noted the problems created by lack of public support: "Without public outrage, impeachment is hard to do, and it should be hard to do."[10] Then, as if the GOP needed any further convincing, in the November midterm elections the party lost five seats in the House and broke even in the Senate, thus becoming only the second out party in the twentieth century to fail to gain seats in a midterm election. More significantly, perhaps, the election results drove Newt Gingrich (R-Ga.) from the House speakership.

Nevertheless, the House careened toward the December vote with little likelihood of forcing the president from office. One observer noted, "As it was done at great political risk to the party and at great damage to House civility, the effort to impeach Clinton had an almost kamikaze element to it—as if House Republicans were so determined to bring the president down, they were willing to go down with him."[11]

Impeachment, the Constitution, and Independent Counsels

To understand the political inertia that drove the process, it is important first to see how the impeachment rules defined by the U.S. Constitution significantly give the advantage to a House faction determined to discredit the incumbent president—especially if that faction constitutes a majority within one of the two major parties. Articles of impeachment, for example, pass by simple majority vote—votes that cannot be delayed by filibustering members of the minority party, as in the Senate. Most important, in the impeachment process the House effectively acts as a unicameral body, for its vote to impeach (or not to impeach) is final; Senate concurrence is not a procedural or political requisite, and a presidential signature (for obvious reasons) is not required. As journalist Dan Carney noted, "It is accomplished through a simple House resolution, the same vehicle by which St. Louis Cardinals' slugger Mark McGwire was honored two months before the impeachment."[12] It is thus not surprising that the three presidents facing the most serious impeachment charges—Andrew

Johnson, Richard Nixon, and Bill Clinton—were all faced with House majorities of the opposing party.

Another impeachment rule that fundamentally affects House deliberation is, ironically, a requirement imposed on the Senate: the two-thirds vote for conviction. The House could operate with some impunity knowing that the likelihood of removing the president from office was remote. Indeed, this assumption became an argument offered by conservative Republicans who were pushing for impeachment. Do not worry about the consequences of your vote to impeach, they said, for the Senate will never convict. This argument took two forms: (1) Judiciary Committee chairman Henry Hyde claimed that the Founders intended for the House to act as a sort of grand jury, indicting a president based on evidence sufficient to call for a full trial, which presumably would take place in the Senate;[13] (2) others in the House called for impeachment on the grounds that this sanction, which Representative Bill McCollum (R-Fla.) called the "ultimate censure," was necessary to punish a president who would surely be acquitted by the Senate.[14] Impeachment thus became an end in itself, an outcome produced by the constitutional rules governing impeachment.

One other rule of the impeachment game contributed to the dynamics of House action: the independent counsel law used as the basis for the appointment of Kenneth Starr. The law, traceable to the Watergate scandal and enacted in 1978, states: "An independent counsel shall advise the House of Representatives of any substantial and credible information which such independent counsel receives . . . that may constitute grounds for an impeachment." Therefore, "the bar for Starr to act, and Congress to respond, is fairly low. Furthermore, the provision provides a kind of justification for Starr to take an action that might seem presumptive or overreaching to some—namely, suggesting that Congress consider impeaching the president."[15] In fact, the wide latitude given Starr allowed the independent counsel to drive the impeachment process, for he could continue the investigation, with all its attendant publicity, rumors, charges, and countercharges, while the House stood waiting for his report. Until his report was received, there were few realistic options for the House other than to permit the investigation to proceed.

The constitutional and statutory rules governing impeachment, then, helped to generate an almost insurmountable inertia at every stage of the process. The independent counsel law allowed Starr to operate from the outset with little fear of congressional interference.

The requirement that only a simple majority could pass articles of impeachment offered a great incentive for conservative House Republicans to rally the troops when interest in moving forward appeared to flag. The near certainty that the Senate could not produce a two-thirds majority for conviction gave political cover to GOP House members with little stomach for forcing the president from office.

The Nature of the Contemporary House

Rules regulating impeachment helped to keep the impeachment wave rolling but so did the generic rules and mores of the House. Walter Oleszek has written that "House rules are designed to permit a determined majority to work its will."[16] Seldom has this been more vividly demonstrated than in the impeachment deliberations, for the Republican majority in the 105th Congress was large enough and willful enough to see that the House did its bidding.

The dominant role played by partisan majorities was demonstrated perhaps most clearly rather late in the impeachment drama, when Democrats and Republican moderates offered censure motions as alternatives to impeachment. Censure of the president had been discussed as early as March; Senator Robert Byrd (D-W.Va.), noted protector of the Constitution and a strong critic of the president, was asked then if anything stood in the way of Congress censuring a president. His response? "No reason that I can think of."[17] To be sure, most Republicans rejected censure. In September Speaker Gingrich said that "to start talking about doing anything before we finish the investigative process simply puts the cart before the horse." Even moderate James C. Greenwood (R-Pa.) said that the "Constitution doesn't empower us to criticize the president or fine the president."[18] In the end, the GOP majority in the House blocked censure before it ever came up for a vote on the floor, passing 230 to 204 a procedural motion that prohibited a vote on a Democratic resolution to censure the president. Only two Republicans voted with the Democrats on the motion. Having no opportunity to consider a different type of sanction, Republicans uneasy with impeachment were left with the unpleasant alternative of letting the president escape with no formal punishment.

The ability of the Republican majority to run the show was characteristic of the partisan polarization evident in recent Congresses.[19] Summarizing a substantial body of scholarly literature evaluating the role of partisanship in Congress—especially in the House—Davidson and Oleszek conclude: "Because today's Republicans are more conservative and Democrats more liberal, the ideological gulf between them is hard to close on policy and other issues. Compounding this reality is the decline of centrists in each chamber." They note that the "rancorous partisan atmosphere" in the House escalated so dramatically that at one point Newt Gingrich and minority leader Richard Gephardt (D-Mo.) would not speak to each other for a year. Such enmities eventually led a bipartisan group of legislators to hold a weekend "civility retreat" for all House members and their families.[20]

Increasing partisan polarization is apparent from the number of partisan roll calls (i.e., votes in which a majority of Republicans line up opposite a majority of Democrats) cast in recent Congresses. The average partisan vote score was 37 percent in the 1970s, 44 percent in the 1980s, and 61 percent in the 1990s.[21] Perhaps more significantly, partisanship often is most pronounced on the most important issues. Senator Olympia Snowe (R-Maine) said to the *Los Angeles Times* that "the whole Congress has become far more polarized and partisan so it makes it difficult to reach bipartisan agreements. The more significant the issue, the more partisan it becomes. There used to be a time when you could expect some bipartisanship on major issues. Not any more."[22]

Impeachment was decidedly a major issue, and House partisanship was a dominant force shaping the debate and ultimately the outcome. Barely a week after the scandal broke (and in the wake of President Clinton's well-received 1998 State of the Union address), Republican pollster Frank Luntz said, "I think you'll see the Republicans beginning to ask questions and demanding answers."[23] In April, Senator Robert Smith (R-N.H.) chastised GOP moderates for shirking ideological appeals. "What moderates need to understand," he charged, "and what the leadership ought to understand, is we win elections because of conservatives."[24]

The Starr report was delivered to the House on September 9, 1998, and House leaders moved quickly to shape a bipartisan compromise regarding release of the report. Republicans Newt Gingrich, Henry Hyde, and Dick Armey (Tex.) met with Democrats Richard Gephardt and John Conyers (N.Y.) and, with much fanfare, "solemnly pledged to act in a bipartisan fashion."[25] Within days, however, Democrats on the House floor were condemning Republicans for reneging on the deal. House member David Obey (D-Wis.) accused the Republicans of "blatant disregard for fairness"; Henry Hyde retorted that the Democrats' "idea of partisanship is that we surrender on everything."[26]

House Democrats were equally willing to play the partisan game, recognizing that their party's—and Bill Clinton's—best defense was to charge the Republicans with overzealous partisanship. The rhetorical flourishes of Democratic House members were not particularly inhibited. Sheila Jackson-Lee (D-Tex.), a member of the House Judiciary Committee, said in the days following the release of the Starr report, "I have to say with great remorse, and great disappointment, that we have here a Salem witch hunt, and I will not participate."[27] In November, fellow committee member Maxine Waters (D-Calif.) lectured Starr: "The American people do not approve, Mr. Starr. They know unfairness when they see it. They know injustice when they feel it. They know hypocrisy when they smell it, they know partisan politics when they are victims of it. In their gut, they have figured this thing out."[28] And preceding the December House vote to impeach the president, John Lewis (D-Ga.) charged: "So bent are [Republicans] on the destruction of this president that they would knock down the very pillars which support our constitutional system."[29]

Partisan polarization was especially strong on the House Judiciary Committee. A *Congressional Quarterly* analysis concluded that it was "one of the most politically polarized panels in Congress" which, since the Republican capture of the House in 1994, had "been a platform for advancing conservative causes."[30] Interest-group ratings reveal the extent of partisanship on the committee. Americans for Democratic Action (ADA), a liberal group, rates members of Congress on a zero to one hundred (most conservative to most liberal) scale. The average ADA score for the twenty-one Republican members of the committee in 1997 was nine, and no member scored higher than twenty.[31] The fifteen Democrats, by contrast, averaged ninety-one on the ADA scale, with no member scoring lower than eighty. The ideological orientation of the committee members hints also at their partisan fealty: in 1997 Judiciary Committee Republicans voted with their party an average of 91 percent of the time; Democrats on the committee voted with their party 88 percent of the time.[32]

The partisan tendencies of the House Judiciary Committee, moreover, were little checked by fears of electoral vulnerability. Ten of the twenty-one Republican members were running unopposed in the 1998 elections, as were six of sixteen Democrats. This security gave the Republicans little reason to worry about national polls, and committee members of both parties had no need to worry that their support or opposition to impeachment might shift a precarious district balance in the direction of the other party.

In sum, the polarized nature of the contemporary House, reflected especially in the makeup of the ideologically bipolar Judiciary Committee, made avoidance of partisanship in the impeachment process virtually impossible. This fact, combined with the procedural uniqueness of impeachment itself, ensured that conservative House Republicans, having been handed a sword by a philandering Democratic president, would seize the opportunity to bring him down—or at least to damage him severely. As a minority party in a chamber fashioned to reward majorities, House Democrats could do little about it—other than to complain bitterly that the Republicans were engaged in an effort driven solely by partisanship.

This does not tell the whole story, however, for partisanship alone is inadequate as an explanation for the persistence of House Republicans in the face of rumblings within its own ranks and a stubbornly unsupportive public. Most notably, why was the impeachment train not derailed by the stunning outcome of the 1998 elections—an outcome that most observers interpreted as decisive voter rejection of the effort to impeach the president? The answer is clear: To stop the train required decisive leadership, and the Republicans not only lacked such leadership but also were in the throes of a post-election convulsion that led to the resignation of the Speaker of the House and, one month later, the Speaker-designate. The leadership vacuum formed by these surprising developments created an opportunity in which strong conservatives—a majority faction within a majority party— could (because of the efforts of the one GOP leader ready and eager to fill the breech) push the party to a final impeachment vote.

The Leadership Vacuum in the House: A Tale of Four Republicans

The problems House Republicans faced on impeachment are best illustrated by considering the roles played by four members of the House: Newt Gingrich, Bob Livingston, Henry Hyde, and Tom DeLay. Each was a leader to whom Republicans, at various points during the process, looked for guidance. Gingrich, speaker of the house and architect of the Contract with America, was the Republican most often credited with orchestrating an end to the long-term Democratic dominance of the House. After Gingrich announced that he would not seek reelection as speaker, his would-be successor, Bob Livingston (La.), refused to assume a decisive leadership role on the impeachment question during the short time he led the party. As nature abhors a vacuum, the leadership void was then filled, at first (reluctantly) by

Henry Hyde (Ill.), chairman of the Judiciary Committee, and then more energetically by Tom DeLay (Tex.), majority whip and persistent nemesis of President Clinton.

Any assessment of the role played by House leadership in the impeachment process must start with the speaker, for he is not only the legislative manager of the entire House but also the leader of his party. Uncharacteristically, Gingrich did not take charge of the impeachment issue during the months leading up to November elections—elections that proved to be his undoing. Gingrich's unusually low-key approach to impeachment was signaled early when he counseled caution in the days immediately following the public exposure of the Clinton-Lewinsky dalliance. He said that he had "no comment on what's happening, but I think every citizen ought to slow down, relax, and wait for the facts to develop." This approach, which *Congressional Quarterly* described as "eerily restrained,"[33] insulated Gingrich from charges that he was seeking undue partisan advantage from the scandal, but it did not please strong conservatives. In March, two Republican presidential hopefuls, Lamar Alexander and Senator John Ashcroft (Mo.), attacked Clinton's behavior and criticized other Republicans for not speaking out, and a number of Republican congressional candidates began using Clinton's association with their Democratic opponents in their campaigns. Some Republicans even attacked other Republicans on the issue. Jim Holcomb, a Tennessee Republican challenging Representative Bill Jenkins (Tenn.) in the GOP primary for a Senate nomination, chastised Jenkins for not defending "common decency and morality."[34] By late April, many Republicans were demanding that their party's leaders go on the offensive. "Given the passage of time and the president's intransigence," Senator Dan Coats (R-Ind.) said, "someone has to try to move this thing forward. There is a lot of frustration on the part of Republicans."[35]

Perhaps in response to this pressure, Gingrich went on the rhetorical offensive on April 27. Characteristically sweeping in his remarks, Gingrich said in a speech to GOPAC, his political action committee:

> I have decided to speak out—and I will never again, as long as I am Speaker, make a speech without commenting on this topic. . . . What you have lived through for two-and-a-half long years is the most systematic, deliberate obstruction of justice, cover-up, an effort to avoid the truth we have ever seen in American history.[36]

As the spring and summer rolled on, and as Clinton's poll numbers remained firm and Starr's (and Gingrich's) ratings fell, Gingrich moved again to a more restrained position. He said in August that widespread criminality alone could lead to impeachment but that Congress would have to find "a pattern of felonies," not simply "a human mistake."[37] As noted above, in September he met with Democratic House leaders to forge a bipartisan compromise on release of the Starr report, and he directed much of the media attention to Henry Hyde, chair of the House Judiciary Committee. Some conservatives then renewed their complaints about a lack of leadership on the issue. Tom Jipping of the conservative Free Congress Foundation worried that Gingrich was not doing enough to educate House members and the public that the standards for impeachment "need not be the same as that of indictable offenses." Others criticized House leaders for releasing Clinton's videotaped testimony to Starr's grand jury before it had been screened; since Clinton's behavior on tape was not as embarrassing as they had expected, Republicans "looked silly."[38]

In truth, the speaker was between the proverbial rock and a hard place on impeachment. David Mayhew succinctly summed up Gingrich's dilemma: "As a constitutional matter, the speaker should not be taking a partisan role on this, and for the most part, he hasn't. It's going to be hard, because he's going to be suppressing some of his urges as he does that."[39] Gingrich was never able to satisfactorily resolve this dilemma, especially for conservatives who saw Clinton slipping off the hook. Their worst fears seemed to be confirmed in the November elections, when the GOP lost five House seats. Gingrich's preelection desperation seemed palpable because he had approved an ill-fated eleventh-hour attempt to help Republican congressional candidates by producing television commercials that focused on the Clinton-Lewinsky affair. Some of his fellow House partisans were harshly critical as the dust settled from the elections. "The last couple of months," E. Clay Shaw Jr. (R-Fla.) said, "have been a giant screw up."[40] Henry Hyde of the Judiciary Committee was no more supportive: "Leadership takes credit when things go right. They ought to take blame when things go wrong." And Steve Largent (R-Okla.), announcing that he planned to challenge Gingrich for the speakership, said that "it's abundantly clear that on November 3 the Republican Party hit an iceberg. And I think the question that's before our conference today is whether we retain the crew of the Titanic or look for some new leadership."[41] The writing was most clearly on the wall, however, when Bob Livingston, chair of the powerful Appropriations Committee, announced that he too would seek the speakership. Gingrich, facing a widespread partisan mutiny, announced three days after the election that he would not seek another term as leader.

Unfortunately for the Republicans, the party's leadership vacuum—a product of impeachment and the centrifugal forces it created—was not filled by Livingston, even as he took steps to consolidate his control after his election by the Republican conference on November 18. Believing that a protracted impeachment proceeding promised to tear the party further apart, Livingston said only that he wanted the House to finish with impeachment before the end of the year, that is, before he formally assumed the speakership. On December 3, Livingston conceded he had no plan or exit strategy for impeachment. "I don't have any idea what we're going to do," he told reporters, "until the Judiciary Committee reports." The lack of leadership on impeachment frustrated many Republicans, Ray LaHood included: "We need to be able to tell the American people what the end game is and have a date certain when we're going to carry it out. And it's going to take the leadership to develop that."[42]

The lack of GOP leadership reached a new low on December 19 when Livingston stunned his colleagues and the nation with the announcement that he would not be a candidate for speaker in the new Congress and that he would resign from the House. Two days earlier, Livingston had admitted that he had "on occasion" had adulterous affairs, and he called on President Clinton to join him in resigning for the good of the nation.[43] Livingston was quickly succeeded by Representative Dennis Hastert (R-Ill.).

The House leader who was left twisting in the wind by the tumultuous events that drove Gingrich and Livingston from the leadership was Henry Hyde. The impeachment genie was out of the bottle, and Hyde, committed to fulfilling his duty as chair of the only committee considering impeachment matters, could not put it back in—assuming he had a disposition to do so—without the firm backing of party leaders. After the release of the Starr report, it was not clear to House Republicans who was shaping the party's strategy on impeachment, Speaker Gingrich or Judiciary Chairman Hyde. In September, Hyde was asked if the committee would consider accepting a motion of censure of instead of pushing for impeachment articles. "There's an old saying," Hyde said, " 'that's above my pay grade.' "[44] When White House spokesman Mike McCurry said that Hyde's remark revealed Gingrich to be running the show, Hyde retorted:

Nothing could be further from the truth. . . . All I know is every time I give advice to Newt, he nods his head affirmatively. [When he gives advice] I listen carefully, but I don't feel bound by it. Frankly, I was selected to chair this committee, presumably not as a delegate of the Speaker's office, but as a person who has some autonomy. We have tried to exercise it, and we'll continue to do so.[45]

A problem for Hyde was that although highly regarded by most members of the House, he had not built a record as a strong leader who could rally the party behind a single strategy or, alternatively, who could build cross-party coalitions to pass legislation accepted by both parties. Norman Ornstein said that Hyde was "respected by all, but feared by few. His ability to rein in his own troops is very limited. And his ability to forge relationships with key Democrats . . . may be even more limited."[46]

Hyde eventually staked out a position with the strong conservative faction of the party that was, after all, dominant on his committee and became one of the president's most vocal critics. This positioning may be understandable in terms of his own philosophical and political views and was consistent with many in his own party but allowed his committee majority to be characterized as overly partisan and uninterested in a careful assessment of the facts. Moreover, by the first week of December, Hyde was leading a committee that was isolated from the political support structure on which it would normally have depended. Gingrich had announced he would resign, Livingston was avoiding comment on impeachment, the public opposed impeaching the president, and the House was not even in session.[47] Hyde had, by this point, given up on the idea of building bipartisan support for articles of impeachment—he said, "I never really expected a lot of bipartisanship here"[48]—and his public comments on impeachment began to harden. When asked why his committee wanted to take testimony from convicted perjurers in matters unrelated (at least directly) to the Clinton-Lewinsky scandal, Hyde asserted, "We're exploring the double standard. We're exploring whether there's one rule of law for the powerful, for the rulers, and another one for the ruled."[49] And by the time Hyde was serving as a House manager for the impeachment articles presented to the Senate, he was invoking the language of cultural conflict more often heard from strong conservatives such as Pat Buchanan. In his closing arguments at the Senate trial, Hyde said somewhat bitterly, "I wonder if after this culture war is over that we're engaged in, if an America will survive that's worth fighting to defend."[50]

The Republican leader best positioned to fill the vacuum at the top turned out to be Majority Whip Tom DeLay. His attitude about the president and impeachment was unequivocal: The president had forfeited the right to hold the office and should be removed. After Clinton's August speech to the nation following his grand jury testimony, DeLay said the president "should resign for the good of the country."[51] His firm hold on a leadership position—even though he had been part of an earlier abortive attempt to remove Newt Gingrich as speaker—was made clear in November when he was unopposed for reelection as Majority Whip. This was an impressive show of strength, given Republican anxieties following the 1998 election debacle; Newt Gingrich had fallen, Majority Leader Dick Armey faced challenges from three other Republicans, two members ran for GOP conference chairman, and four members ran for conference vice chairman. Notably, of the Republican leadership hierarchy only DeLay had taken an uncompromising, steadfast, and vocal position on the impeachment issue.

DeLay's ability to rally the troops was shown most clearly in the first few weeks of December, as the House readied for its floor vote on the impeachment articles reported out of the Judiciary Committee. DeLay, working effectively behind the scenes, "unleashed a fusillade of arguments" that the impeachment vote was a political and moral test of conservative values.[52] Clinton's conduct, he and other conservatives argued, "was not just a political or legal issue, but part of a pattern of lies and a sign of a moral decline in society that had to be checked."[53] DeLay worked to block a vote on a censure motion and sought to orchestrate GOP unanimity on the articles themselves. In the end, the House passed Article I (alleging the president committed perjury in his grand jury testimony) 228 to 206 with only five Republicans opposed. Article II, which charged that the president perjured himself in a deposition concerning the Paula Jones lawsuit, failed 205 to 229. Article III, which charged Clinton with obstruction of justice, passed 221 to 212 (with twelve Republicans in opposition). Article IV, which said that the president violated his oath of office, failed 148 to 285.

DeLay's success in mobilizing Republican support for impeachment must be appreciated in light of the prevailing wisdom about what the whole House was likely to do when the impeachment articles reached the floor. The poor showing of the GOP in the November elections, leadership turmoil, the demonizing of Starr by Democrats, and continuing public opposition to impeachment of the president had appeared to take the steam out of the impeachment effort. A number of moderate Republicans had announced they would oppose impeachment, and others appeared to be leaning in that direction. Indeed, on November 20, the day after Starr's appearance before the Judiciary Committee, Peter King (R-N.Y.) asserted that many Republican House members would oppose impeachment: "Rock solid there are 15 or 20 . . . maybe 30 or 40, maybe more." Andrew Carney assessed succinctly the likelihood of impeachment: "There is little chance the articles would win majority support on the House floor."[54]

Perhaps most important to DeLay's success in the weeks preceding the floor vote was the devil's choice facing Republicans unsure about impeachment. As noted above, they could not vote to censure, for the House leadership, responding to DeLay's insistence, foreclosed a censure vote. Republicans' only option, then, was to vote to impeach or to appear to let the president off with no sanction whatsoever, an action sure to infuriate the Republican electoral base in many House districts. Henry Hyde's insistence that a vote to impeach was tantamount to indicting the president—let the Senate decide if he should be removed—gave moderate House Republicans political cover. This logic was clearly illustrated just three days after the House vote, when four moderate House Republicans—all of whom had voted for at least one article of impeachment—announced that they opposed his conviction in the Senate.[55]

DeLay's leadership role was important, as well, in the selection of Dennis Hastert as speaker. Hastert, referred to by many Republicans as a "healer," was the beneficiary of a quick and effective effort by DeLay to secure for Hastert the position that had just been vacated by Livingston. As *Congressional Quarterly* reported, "DeLay organized Hastert's sudden candidacy for speaker, returning the favor to the man who championed him for whip in 1994 . . . [Within 45 minutes of Livingston's announcement] 20 members of the whip team led by DeLay had gathered to divide up campaign duties and start making phone calls to build support for Hasert."[56]

The Senate

Senate action on the impeachment articles was, compared with the lengthy, contentious, and at times confusing House consideration, expeditious and definitive. This was due in part to the advantage the Senate had gained from having observed the House deliberations. But it would be a mistake to assume that the relatively efficient consider-

ation of the articles was foreordained by the rules regulating impeachment or by a clear consensus among Senate Democrats and Republicans
that a judgment could be rendered in short order. Indeed, in the days
following the House impeachment votes a number of members warned
that the Senate could be tied up in knots for months conducting the
president's trial. Many key issues were unresolved, including the extent
of testimony to be offered at trial, how any testimony would be
received (e.g., personal testimony, depositions, videotape, etc.), and
the breadth allowed House managers to offer evidence of other presidential misconduct.

The Constitution gave only limited guidance, and the rules written
for Andrew Johnson's 1868 impeachment trial were silent on these
questions. The Senate managed, however, to move from the January
7 trial opening to a February 12 final vote—a time span of about five
weeks. Two major factors account for the Senate's avoidance of a
protracted and agonizing trial: (1) the nature of the Senate demands
(and creates more opportunities for) bipartisan action, and (2) Republican and Democratic leaders in the Senate took more firm control of
the impeachment process than did their counterparts in the House.

The Nature of the Contemporary Senate

Traditional Senate rules were largely irrelevant to the trial of President
Clinton; their deliberations were guided by the Constitution, rules
from previous impeachment trials, and rules written specifically for
Clinton's trial. Nonetheless, the nature of the Senate, different in
crucial respects from that of the House, had a major impact on the
way in which it handled the impeachment issue. Two differences are
especially relevant to understanding why the Senate behaved differently
than the House: the design of the Senate as a representative institution
with respect to terms and constituencies, and the emphasis on bipartisanship and equality of influence of the members.

With regard to the design of the Senate, its longer terms of office
offered some insulation from the short-term forces that shaped the
House debate, especially for those senators whose new election was
in 2002 or 2004. This was especially important for Republican senators
who might have worried that conservatives would punish opposition
to impeachment in the next election. As Richard Fenno had pointed
out,[57, 58] the connection between campaigning and governing is one
that members have some ability to control, particularly if they are
afforded sufficient time to explain their votes and to do so over an

extended period. Indeed, for members not facing the electorate for two years or more, explaining the impeachment vote might not be critical; the trust that a senator can cultivate during that time might offer dispensation from voters disappointed in a vote to acquit the president.

The constituencies of senators, moreover, are generally more heterogeneous than those of House members, making it less likely that strong conservatives would constitute a critical mass of voters sufficient to punish an incumbent who did not toe the line on impeachment. In states such as Washington, Pennsylvania, Tennessee, and Virginia—states in which Republican senators voted to acquit the president on at least one article—relatively diverse state electorates offered to Republican incumbents some protection from the retribution of angry conservatives.

Second, the Senate is also an institution in which, compared with the House, power is more evenly distributed among the members, overt partisanship is more discouraged, and "traditions and practices emphasize minority rights." As Loomis notes, for example, "a leader spends countless hours on the Senate floor seeking to reconcile the interests and egos of 100 separate lords and ladies, each of whom jealously guards his or her own prerogatives."[59] In addition, many senators take seriously the adage that the Senate is the saucer where the overflowing passions of the House cool. In the days following the House vote to impeach Clinton, for example, *Congressional Quarterly* reported that "Republicans and Democrats are determined to avoid the harsh and hateful partisanship that marred the House action." These "strenuous and unusual efforts," in the words of one reporter, were designed to "resist the impulse to 'go nuclear.' "[60] To this end, Senate Democrats and Republicans caucused on January 8, 1999, the day after the trial began, and reached tentative agreement on rules regarding the calling of witnesses, issuance of subpoenas, and introduction of new evidence.[61] Notably, the plan was crafted by liberal Ted Kennedy (Mass.) and conservative Phil Gramm (Tex.), two long-time ideological adversaries. Their plan was approved 100 to 0 by the Senate and helped to speed the trial by limiting both the testimony and scope of allegations the House managers were permitted to address. Because a simple majority vote would have been sufficient to draft rules for the trial, the Republican majority in the Senate *could* have forced through regulations favorable to the House managers. They demurred, evidence of bipartisanship, to be sure, but also a recognition that the two-thirds vote necessary to convict was not achievable even if Clinton's prosecutors had been given much more latitude to make their case.

Senate Leadership: Lott and Daschle

A final important difference between the House and Senate on the impeachment question was the more assertive role played by Senate leaders. Clearly aware of the problems created by the absence of effective GOP leadership in the House, majority leader Trent Lott (Miss.) resisted pressure from conservatives in his party to allow numerous witnesses to be called or to expand the inquiry into other areas. Lott helped to orchestrate the bipartisan meeting that produced the Kennedy-Gramm compromise and worked closely with minority leader Tom Daschle to set a tone of accommodation. "We think that the best way to keep calm and cool and dignified," Lott said on January 7, "is to look at each other and talk to each other."[62] For his part, Daschle expected to be consulted on matters of procedure and process and was willing to cry foul when he thought he was being kept out of the loop. At one point in the trial, for example, he complained to a reporter that he had learned about a Lott initiative from the media: "I would appreciate it if he'd talk to me before he talked to you, frankly."[63]

This incident proved the exception rather than the rule, however, for Lott and Daschle both recognized that their interests were best served by a relatively speedy trial and an unambiguous verdict. Their motivations may have differed. Lott, for example, was opposed to censure because he thought it offered political cover to Democrats, who could claim to have sanctioned the president. Daschle's rationale for not pushing more aggressively for a censure vote may have been simply that he knew he did not have the votes or perhaps that he saw in an unqualified acquittal an opportunity to chastise the Republicans for wasting the nation's time and energy.

Whatever their motivations, these two leaders were much more effective at moving their institution to resolution of the issue than were their counterparts in the House. Without question, they benefited mightily from their spectator role during the House deliberations on the issue. As Fenno reminds us, sequence in politics is critical, a truth rarely more clearly demonstrated than on the impeachment issue.[64] Moreover, Lott and Daschle benefited from an institutional culture relatively less conducive to overt partisanship. We should not, however, assume that their jobs were easy, for the Senate could easily have spun out of control in a welter of witnesses, recrimination, and attempts to gain partisan advantage.

Conclusion

This chapter began with two simple questions: Why did the House impeach President Clinton, and why did the Senate acquit him? The point of this analysis is not, of course, to offer an exhaustive consideration of every facet of the impeachment saga or to claim a full understanding of all the motivations and goals of each member of Congress. Instead, the objective here has been to identify the institutional and political characteristics of the two chambers that shed light on the very different ways in which they handled the issue.

Three major conclusions are in order. First, the House and Senate behaved differently because an effort to impeach a president is, from a process perspective, fundamentally different than typical legislative action. An independent counsel, for example, can trigger the process by simply bringing to the House evidence that he or she considers to be sufficient to impeach the president. The House can then act unilaterally and by simple majority to impeach; no Senate or presidential acquiescence is necessary. In the Senate, on the other hand, the two-thirds vote requirement makes conviction unlikely except in circumstances of the most egregious presidential misconduct. House impeachment is thus much easier to attain than Senate conviction—a deceptively obvious conclusion that conceals its potential for partisan mischief. Impeachment, as in this case, becomes an end in itself, not simply the first step in a two-chamber process designed to assess a president's fitness for office.

Second, the Clinton impeachment demonstrates the impact of differences in the institutional culture of the House and Senate, especially as it applies to partisanship. Absence of an expectation of bipartisanship in the House, strong antipathy to Clinton on the part of conservative members, and, in the end, need for only a simple majority made it almost a certainty that partisan agendas would dominate House debate. This came quite naturally to the House, whose leaders have become accustomed to playing the game by the numbers: If you have the votes, you win. In the Senate, on the other hand, bipartisanship—at least in a relative sense—is expected and celebrated, both in its traditions and its rules. Those rules were not relevant for impeachment, of course, but the informal norms of the place, even in an era of elevated partisanship, set the context for Senate consideration of the House articles.

Finally, the critical importance of leadership is evident in both chambers. GOP leaders in the House, to put it bluntly, dropped the ball on impeachment. The baggage Newt Gingrich carried with him hamstrung his ability (and perhaps willingness) to offer decisive leadership, and the struggles of Henry Hyde and Bob Livingston opened the door for Tom DeLay. DeLay successfully mobilized Republicans in support of two articles of impeachment; however, his ability to do so depended on a strongly ideological and anti-Clinton appeal that played into the hands of those who wanted to characterize the process as a partisan jihad. By contrast, Trent Lott and Tom Daschle, conscientious students of the House proceedings, moved the Senate skillfully and expeditiously toward resolution of the issue.

In the end, the impeachment and acquittal of President Clinton offer a cautionary note about Congress and, more generally, about American politics today. When legislative rules encourage unbridled partisanship, as they do in the House on the question of impeaching a president, we should not be surprised to see ideologues exploit those rules to full advantage. Moreover, the increasing polarization of American politics means that many ideologues will be present in both the House and Senate. This time the president was a Democrat attacked by Republican adversaries, but the rules are just as likely to put at risk a future Republican president hounded by his or her Democratic enemies. The check to ensure that this legislative action is the product of fundamental concerns about a president's ability to govern—concerns shared on both sides of the aisle and by a large number of Americans—resides both in the Founders' insistence on a two-thirds Senate vote for conviction and in the selection of legislators (and legislative leaders) able to see a national interest defined more broadly than their own party's agenda.

Notes

1. Ronald D. Elving, "Early Task for '98 Candidates Is to Find New Political Footing," *Congressional Quarterly Weekly Report* (14 February 1998), 353–58; ibid., 358.

2. Dan Carney and Carroll J. Doherty, "GOP Struggles to Find Strategy to Deal with Starr Fallout, *Congressional Quarterly Weekly Report* (14 March 1998), 644–45.

3. Karen Foerstel, "Reaction to Starr's Report: Which Way Will It Swing?" *Congressional Quarterly Weekly Report* (11 July 1998), 1859.

4. Jeffrey L. Katz, "Promises of Bipartisanship Will Be Put to an Early Test," *Congressional Quarterly Weekly Report* (12 September 1998), 2392.

5. Jeffrey L. Katz, "Politically Charged Vote Sets Tone for Impeachment Inquiry," *Congressional Quarterly Weekly Report* (10 October 1998), 2715.

6. Jeffrey L. Katz and Jackie Koszczuk, "GOP's Recovery Strategy: Get Back to Legislating," *Congressional Quarterly Weekly Report* (13 February 1999), 356–57; Gary C. Jacobson, "Impeachment Politics in the 1998 Congressional Elections," *Political Science Quarterly*, 114 (1999), 36.

7. Carroll J. Doherty, "Braced for Impeachment Inquiry, Democrats Still Lobby for a Deal," *Congressional Quarterly Weekly Report* (26 September 1998), 2571.

8. Jeffrey L. Katz, "Politically Charged Vote Sets Tone," 2712.

9. David Hosansky, "Impeachment Day: Tiring, Unpredictable," *Congressional Quarterly Weekly Report* (22 December 1998), 3318.

10. Dan Carney and Andrew Taylor, "105th's Final Vote May Be Against Impeachment," *Congressional Quarterly Weekly Report* (21 November 1998), 3160.

11. Dan Carney, "The Presidency in the Balance," *Congressional Quarterly Weekly Report* (22 December 1998), 3337.

12. Dan Carney, "GOP's Case for Rule of Law Came to a Political End," *Congressional Quarterly Weekly Report* (13 February 1999), 374.

13. Dan Carney, "Hyde Leads Impeachment Drive in Growing Isolation," *Congressional Quarterly Weekly Report* (5 December 1998), 3248.

14. Carney, "The Presidency in the Balance," 3338.

15. Dan Carney, "Starr Report May Create Legal, Political Minefield in the House," *Congressional Quarterly Weekly Report* (28 March 1998), 798–99.

16. Walter Oleszek, *Congressional Procedures and the Policy Process*, 4th ed. (Washington, D.C.: Congressional Quarterly Press, 1996), 27.

17. Stephen Gettinger, "An Alternative to Impeachment," *Congressional Quarterly Weekly Report* (7 March 1998), 566.

18. Carroll J. Doherty, "Braced for Impeachment Inquiry, 2571; ibid., 2573.

19. Barry C. Burden and Aage R. Clausen, "The Unfolding Drama: Party and Ideology in the 104th House" in *Great Theatre: The American Congress in the 1990s*, ed. Herbert F. Weisberg and Samuel C. Patterson (Cambridge: Cambridge University Press, 1998), 163.

20. Roger H. Davidson and Walter J. Oleszek, *Congress and Its Members*, 6th ed. (Washington, D.C.: *Congressional Quarterly Press*, 1998), 182; ibid.

21. Burdett A. Loomis, *The Contemporary Congress*, 2d ed. (New York: St. Martin's Press, 1998), 133.

22. Davidson and Oleszek, *Congress and Its Members*, 183.

23. Jackie Koszczuk, "Clinton Succeeds in Slowing Scandal's Momentum," *Congressional Quarterly Weekly Report* (31 January 1998), 215.

24. Jackie Koszczuk, "On the Hill and at Home, GOP Is Torn by Internal Strife," *Congressional Quarterly Weekly Report* (4 April 1998), 860.

25. Katz, "Promises of Bipartisanship," 2393.

26. Sue Kirchoff, "Starr Report Hits Capitol Hill, Drawing Outrage and Trepidation," *Congressional Quarterly Weekly Report* (12 September 1998), 2389; ibid.

27. Dan Carney and Jeffrey L. Katz, "Panel Votes to Release Clinton Video after 'Vigorously Partisan' Debate," *Congressional Quarterly Weekly Report* (19 September 1998), 2469.

28. Carney and Taylor, "Final Vote," 3160.

29. Sue Kirchoff, "A Conservative Juggernaut," *Congressional Quarterly Weekly Report* (22 December 1998), 3340.

30. Dan Carney, "Along Clinton's Political Gauntlet: A Panel Noted for Both Partisanship, Civility," *Congressional Quarterly Weekly Report* (5 September 1998), 2329.

31. Twenty Republicans were rated; one Republican, Mary Bono (Calif.), had recently replaced her deceased husband and had no ADA rating.

32. Carney, "Along Clinton's Political Gauntlet," 2329.

33. Jeffrey L. Katz and Dan Carney, "Clinton's Latest, Worst Troubles Put His Whole Agenda on Hold," *Congressional Quarterly Weekly Report* (24 January 1998), 165; ibid.

34. Erika Niedowski, "Clinton Scandal, Starr Probe Trickle Down into Elections," *Congressional Quarterly Weekly Report* (28 March 1998), 835.

35. Jackie Koszczuk, "Gingrich, Leading Attack on Clinton, Takes off Gloves, Goes out on Limb," *Congressional Quarterly Weekly Report* (2 May 1998), 1131.

36. Ibid., 1128.

37. Dan Carney, "The Weighty Why and How of Punishing a President," *Congressional Quarterly Weekly Report* (12 September 1998), 2381.

38. Jeffrey L. Katz, "Gingrich's Role Is Scrutinized in Impeachment Drama," *Congressional Quarterly Weekly Report* (26 September 1998), 2577; ibid.

39. Ibid.

40. Jeffrey L. Katz, "Shakeup in the House," *Congressional Quarterly Weekly Report* (7 November 1998), 2990.

41. Dan Carney, "Impeachment: Seeking Closure?" *Congressional Quarterly Weekly Report* (7 November 1998), 2988.

42. Jeffrey L. Katz and Carroll J. Doherty, "Leaders Provide Little Guidance on Next Phase of Impeachment," *Congressional Quarterly Weekly Report* (5 December 1998), 3252; ibid.

43. Dan Carney, Karen Forestel, and Andrew Taylor, "A New Start for the House," *Congressional Quarterly Weekly Report* (22 December 1998), 3335.

44. Katz, "Gingrich's Role," 2577.

45. Ibid.

46. Jeffery L. Katz and Dan Carney, "Impeachment Inquiry Vote May Signal Level of Partisanship to Come," *Congressional Quarterly Weekly Report* (3 October 1998), 2648.

47. Dan Carney, "Hyde Leads Impeachment Drive," 3247.

48. David Hosansky and Andrew Taylor, "Judiciary's 'Fateful Leap,' " *Congressional Quarterly Weekly Report* (12 December 1998), 3294.

49. Dan Carney, "Hyde Leads Impeachment Drive," 3248.

50. Jeffrey L. Katz and Jackie Koszczuk, "GOP's Recovery Strategy," 356.

51. Karen Foerstel, "Clinton's Address Fails to Defuse Ticking Time Bomb of Starr Report," *Congressional Quarterly Weekly Report* (22 August 1998), 2282.

52. Jeffrey L. Katz and Andrew Taylor, "House Accuses Clinton of Perjury, Obstruction," *Congressional Quarterly Weekly Report* (22 December 1998), 3323.

53. Sue Kirchoff, "A Conservative Juggernaut," 3341.

54. Ibid., 3155.

55. Dan Carney, "Impeachment's Long Shadow," *Congressional Quarterly Weekly Report* (2 January 1999), 10.

56. Carney, Forestel, and Taylor, "A New Start," 3334–35.

57. Richard F. Fenno Jr., *Home Styles: House Members in Their Districts* (Boston: Little Brown, 1978).

58. Richard F. Fenno Jr., *Senators on the Campaign Trail: The Politics of Representation* (Norman, Okla.: University of Oklahoma Press, 1997).

59. Oleszek, *Congressional Procedures,* 26; ibid., 142.

60. Carroll J. Doherty, "Senate's Uncertain Course," *Congressional Quarterly Weekly Report* (22 December 1998), 3326.

61. Carroll J. Doherty, "After Historic Swearing-In, Duty Trumps the Party Line," *Congressional Quarterly Weekly Report* (9 January 1999), 40.

62. Ibid., 43.

63. Jeffrey L. Katz, "Partisan Tensions, Already High, Are Unlikely to End When Trial Does," *Congressional Quarterly Weekly Report* (30 January 1999), 239.

64. Richard F. Fenno Jr., *Watching Politicians: Essays on Participant Observation.* (Berkeley, Calif.: IGS Press, 1990), 113–28.

THREE

The Courts:
The Perils of Paula

Karen O'Connor and John R. Hermann

When President William Jefferson Clinton was accused of having a sexual affair with White House intern Monica Lewinsky, the scandal occupied a permanent home in the headlines for well over a year and a half. While his inexplicable relationship with Monica Lewinsky was ultimately to be Clinton's Achilles' heel, it is important to remember that much of President Clinton's trouble actually stemmed from an alleged encounter with another woman—Paula Jones.[1]

No one except Paula Jones and Bill Clinton will ever know exactly what happened in a hotel room at the Excelsior Hotel in Little Rock, Arkansas, on May 8, 1991. But the results of that encounter, which ultimately resulted in a major U.S. Supreme Court decision concerning the scope of executive immunity from civil law suits, also spawned several other court cases; an intensified investigation by the independent counsel; the uncovering of presidential sexual escapades in the Oval Office; more legal cases; and, ultimately, the impeachment, trial, and acquittal of President William Jefferson Clinton in the U.S. Congress. The Lewinsky affair, in particular, was rife with tales of exploits in the Oval Office that rivaled any soap opera story line of recent memory. The Jones and Lewinsky episodes also affected the institution of the presidency and are likely to have long-lasting ramifications on the entire political process as well as on Americans' view of the executive office and its occupant.

The purpose of this chapter is to try to put the Jones and Lewinsky matters in the context of their impact on the presidency, especially the nature of the relationship between the president and the judiciary and the Supreme Court's role in facilitating the impeachment of the president.

To facilitate our analysis in this chapter, we first examine the constitutional foundation of the executive's relationship with the judiciary within the separation of powers and checks and balances principles articulated by the framers. Second, we trace the development of the Paula Jones case from a murky rumor reported in the conservative *American Spectator* magazine to its resolution by the U.S. Supreme Court. Third, we examine the Court's decision in *Jones v. Clinton*. Fourth, we discuss the role of Independent Counsel Kenneth Starr and his investigation of the president, which was facilitated by the Court's ruling in that case. And last, we discuss the impact of the Court's decision on President Clinton, his aides, and on American politics more generally.

The Constitutional Foundation

Based on their experience under British monarchial rule in colonial America, the framers of the U.S. Constitution feared an omnipotent executive. Simply put, they did not want another King George even if his last name was Washington. The attendant result was the creation of a government that distributed the concentration of power between three ostensibly equal branches of government. Although there was a lively and contentious debate at the Constitutional Convention regarding the relative power of each branch of government, most in attendance seemed to agree that the legislature would be the dominant branch. *Federalist No. 51,* in fact, proclaims that "[I]n a Republican form of government, the legislative authority necessarily dominates."

Political scientist Robert Scigliano (1971) muses that it was the framers' intent to create a harmonic relationship between the Supreme Court and president to offset Congress's power. He contends that there is strong evidence for this perspective: There is a natural affinity between the powers of the executive and judicial branches and, as presidential appointees, the justices of the Supreme Court often represent the views of the executive. Today, this compatibility is underscored by the Solicitor General's office, the official representative of the executive branch before the Supreme Court, also being the single most successful party before the Court (Salokar 1992; Puro 1971).

Historically, the Supreme Court has often deferred to the wishes of the executive, especially in the area of foreign affairs. In fact, Aaron Wildavsky (1975) posits that there are really two presidencies, one foreign and one domestic. In the foreign affairs arena, the president is extremely powerful, whereas in the domestic arena the president is relatively weaker. While presidential scholars find Wildavsky's theory plagued with problems, it quite accurately describes the Supreme Court's perspective on the scope of presidential powers. The Court often defers to the president in the conduct of foreign affairs but is not nearly so acquiescent when hearing cases involving domestic issues.

In *United States v. Curtiss-Wright* (1936), a case involving a broad delegation of congressional power to the President to prohibit the shipment of arms to unstable foreign nations, the Court held that "the federal power over external affairs in origin and essential character [is] different from that over internal affairs" (319). The *Curtiss-Wright* Court made a clear distinction between the president acting in foreign affairs versus domestic matters. In *Curtiss-Wright* the Court went on to find that "the very delicate, plenary and exclusive power of the President as the sole organ of the federal government in the field of international relations . . . would not be admissible were domestic affairs alone involved" (319). In no uncertain terms, the Court made it clear that it is more deferential to presidential prerogatives in foreign, rather than domestic, affairs.

In other cases, especially those involving domestic policy or decisions, the president has not fared so well in court. In *Youngstown Sheet and Tube Co. v. Sawyer* (1952), for example, the Court ruled that President Harry S Truman had no power to seize the nation's privately owned steel mills. The Truman administration argued that national security concerns could be at issue if steel production stopped on account of a threatened strike by steel workers. The Court disagreed, finding nothing in the Constitution to grant that kind of encompassing power to the head of the executive branch.

The kind of distinction that the Court has drawn in the foreign versus the domestic sphere mirrors the distinction the justices have drawn concerning presidential vulnerability to suit while in office. For example, *Nixon v. Fitzgerald* (1982) involved a discharged Air Force employee who lost his job after he testified before a congressional subcommittee about cost overruns and unexpected technical difficulties in the design of a particular aircraft. Fitzgerald then sued President Nixon, alleging that Nixon, while acting as commander-in-chief, improperly dismissed him. In *Fitzgerald,* the Supreme Court ruled that a president enjoys absolute immunity from civil damage suits in cases arising out of his *official duties or actions as president* (emphasis added). The dissenters in *Fitzgerald,* Justices Thurgood Marshall and Harry Blackmun, expressed their concerns that "attaching absolute immunity to the office of the President, rather than to the particular activities that the President might perform, places the President above the law and is a reversion to the old notion that the king can do no wrong" (766). And, in a closely related case also decided in 1982, the Court ruled that even White House aides enjoy what the Court termed a "qualified immunity" related to their knowledge of wrongful acts.

The most significant modern-era case on the scope of constitutional protection and privileges accorded the presidency is *United States v. Nixon* (1974), which arose after a federal grand jury returned indictments against seven close aides of President Nixon. These defendants and the special prosecutor appointed by the president to investigate the break-in at the Democratic National Committee's headquarters in the Watergate complex sought the audiotapes of conversations that had occurred in the Oval Office. President Nixon asserted that he was immune from subpoena because of executive privilege, a term used to characterize the right of the chief executive or his aides to withhold information from the other branches of government to preserve confidential communications or to secure the national interest.

As the nation waited with baited breath for the Court's decision, speculation ran wild over whether or not the Nixon appointees to the Supreme Court would remain loyal to the man to whom they owed their positions on the Court. President Nixon had appointed not only then Chief Justice Warren Burger but also Justices Harry Blackmun, Lewis Powell, and William Rehnquist (who recused himself because a close friend and former colleague at the U.S. Justice Department was one of those on trial). In the end, the answer was a resounding no: All eight justices participating in the case ruled against the president and his generalized claims of executive privilege.

The unanimous Supreme Court held that neither separation of powers principles nor a president's generalized need for confidentiality can sustain an absolute, unqualified presidential privilege. The justices, in deciding that the privilege cannot be used to avoid the disclosure of criminal misconduct, for the first time limited the doctrine of executive privilege. The Supreme Court's decision in the *Nixon* case, which in the short run forced the president to turn over tapes to a federal court for use in a criminal trial, also gave members of the House Judiciary

Committee the ammunition they needed to bring several articles of impeachment against President Nixon, leading him to resign before he could be impeached, tried, and removed from office.

Little did anyone envision how important these Supreme Court precedents would collectively prove to be for the course of the Clinton presidency. Watergate, which led to Nixon's resignation, involved allegations that a sitting president obstructed justice by covering up the details of a break-in to obtain confidential campaign information. It also produced a major case on the scope of executive privilege. Whitewater, which was at the heart of the initial investigation of Clinton, involved allegations of financial misconduct in a twenty-year-old failed land deal. That case, however, produced no actionable charges against a sitting president. In the course of the independent counsel's investigations of Whitewater, however, President Clinton's self-admitted weaknesses for women were to prove to be his downfall. Unlike President Nixon, Clinton's presidency ultimately survived the ordeal. It also produced a major Supreme Court decision—this time on the scope of executive immunity.

The Paula Jones Story: Or, Living and Loving in Little Rock, Arkansas

There is no doubting that President Clinton has had several indiscrete relationships since marrying Hillary Rodham Clinton. According to former presidential advisor George Stephanopoulos (1999), the 1992 Clinton campaign managers lived in constant fear of what they called "bimbo eruptions." Whether the situation centered around a "love child" in Arkansas or a twelve-year affair with Gennifer Flowers, Clinton had some loyal staffer willing to deny the charges. When Flowers actually produced tapes of seemingly intimate conversations with the governor, however, the resulting coverage began to derail the Clinton campaign.[2] To stop the political hemorrhaging, both Clintons appeared before a huge television audience on Super Bowl Sunday: he to admit to problems in their relationship, she to protest that she was no Tammy Wynette standing by her man. It was a first-rate performance. Clinton's popularity shot up in the polls, and he went on to win the Democratic nomination for president and ultimately was elected in 1992, becoming the first Democrat to win since 1976.

Many Republicans, especially those on the right, were outraged by the election of the self-styled "Comeback Kid" from Arkansas. They feared that Clinton was a liberal in a moderate's clothing, and they were appalled by his apparent efforts to dodge the draft, avoid Gennifer Flowers's accusations, and deny any youthful experimentation with marijuana. Clinton's penchant for splitting proverbial hairs galled them in particular. And, once Clinton was in office, they were appalled when several members of the White House Travel Office were fired and then even more angered when it appeared the White House had targeted several influential Republicans for FBI investigation.

On the afternoon of May 8, 1991, more than a year and a half before Clinton's election, Paula Jones, a low-ranking state employee at the Arkansas Industrial Development Commission, was working at the registration desk of the Governor's Quality Management Conference at the Excelsior Hotel in Little Rock, Arkansas. As Governor William Jefferson Clinton addressed the meeting, a state trooper escorting him stopped by Jones's desk, where they engaged in a short conversation. Later the same officer told her, "You make the Governor's knees knock," and told her that the Governor wanted to see her (*The Economist* 1997). The trooper then gave her the number of Clinton's hotel suite and she went up to the room.

What subsequently happened in that hotel room is a classic "he said, she said." *She said* that he exposed himself and asked for oral sex. *He said* that he had no recollection of the event or of even meeting Ms. Jones. *She said* that as she fled the room, he said, "You are smart. Let's keep this between ourselves" (*The Economist* 1997, 21). He does not remember it. Jones, however, immediately related her version of what happened to her coworker when she returned to her post. She also called a friend and then her sister later that night.

Jones's story first surfaced publicly beyond her circle of family and friends in the January 1994 issue of the conservative *American Spectator* magazine. It published an article written by David Brock (author of a controversial book on Anita Hill), which referred to a "Paula" who was supposed to have had sex with Governor Clinton at the Excelsior Hotel. A state trooper recollected that he had arranged a sexual encounter with a woman named "Paula" and that on the way out she had agreed to be Clinton's girlfriend.

Jones was outraged by Brock's account and went to an attorney in Little Rock for help. He contacted friends and had Jones present her story at a February 1994 news conference held in conjunction with a Conservative Political Action Committee meeting in Washington, D.C. This association with a conservative group immediately hurt her credibility. The question raised by her association with rabid Clinton haters was easy to articulate: Was there a political motivation behind her charges? No matter how sincere Jones seemed, she could not deny the ideological symbolism of where she chose to make her announcement or her later selection of a conservative legal foundation to represent her.[3]

Undaunted by the questions surrounding her charges, on May 6, 1994, Jones filed a civil suit against Clinton in U.S. District Court. She sought $75,000 in actual damages and punitive damages in the amount of $100,000 from Clinton for his "willful, outrageous and malicious conduct" at the hotel three years earlier.[4] She accused Clinton of "sexually harassing and assaulting" her in violation of state and federal civil rights and sexual harassment statutes and then with defaming her with his denials that nothing ever happened. Jones further claimed that her career stagnated after she rejected him.

When Jones filed her lawsuit, the National Organization for Women (NOW) issued a statement saying that "(b)oth Paula Jones and President Clinton deserve their day in court." NOW President Patricia Ireland went on to say that NOW would continue to monitor this case but that the organization would "not be the right wing's bait . . ." Thus, NOW would not "herald" or "attack" either party (NOW 1994).

This was to be the beginning of a tortuous legal journey for both Jones and Clinton. Clinton could have simply decided to pay Jones's claim (or even negotiate a lower amount) to get rid of the suit and avoid the impeachment that he was to face later. Instead, from the start, Clinton advisors adopted a two-pronged strategy. First, Clinton denied any wrongdoing, and he and his inner circle launched a sustained media attack against Jones's credibility. Second, they simultaneously tried to delay the course of litigation by invoking the idea of presidential immunity.

Clinton lawyer Robert Bennett led the public relations charge against Jones, characterizing her lawsuit as "tabloid trash." White House strategest James Carville chimed in: "Drag $100 through a trailer park and there's no telling what you'll find" (*The Economist* 1997). Even her own sister questioned Paula Jones's motives (Rivera 1998).

On the legal front, Clinton followed a strategy of delay. He and his lawyers moved for permission to file a motion to dismiss the case on the grounds of presidential immunity. They also asked the court to defer the filings of any other motions until the immunity issue was considered.

Initially, this two-pronged strategy worked well. Public opinion polls taken at the time found that only 12 percent believed that Paula Jones was sexually harassed by Clinton.[5] A different poll found that only 3 percent of those polled believed her account was "completely true."[6] Then, in late December 1994, Judge Susan Webber Wright, a former law student of Clinton's, ruled on his legal motion to stop Jones's suit. Webber Wright concluded that although the president did not enjoy absolute immunity from the legal process, he was entitled to a temporary stay of the actual trial. She based her ruling on *Nixon v. Fitzgerald*. But, although Webber Wright stayed the actual trial, her order also allowed fact-finding procedures to proceed so that witnesses and their recollections would not be lost. Her ruling meant that discovery proceedings involving the president could go forward, while the actual trial could not. Jones then appealed that adverse decision to the 8th Circuit Court of Appeals in St. Louis, and Webber Wright delayed the rest of the proceedings pending the outcome of the appeal.

In September 1995, a three-judge panel of circuit court judges heard Clinton's lawyers' arguments that allowing the trial to proceed would distract the president from far more critical matters. In January 1996, that appeals court ruled two to one against Clinton, thus paving the way for the trial to proceed. The majority found that a judge could be sensitive to the demands on the president and his time to avoid any separation of powers problems (Weeden 1999).

Writing in dissent, and relying heavily on Chief Justice Warren Burger's concurring opinion in *Fitzgerald*, Circuit Court Judge Donald Ross argued for a total stay until after the President left office. He argued that the President's "unique position in our constitutional scheme"[7] made him an easy target of civil suits. Ross was especially concerned that regardless of how these cases arose, mandating a president to answer any and all civil charges levied against him would impair the president's ability to govern effectively. Said Judge Ross, "[W]here there is no urgency to pursue a suit for civil damages, the proper course is to avoid opportunities for breaching separation of powers altogether by holding the litigation in abeyance until a President leaves office."[8]

Four months later, on May 15, 1996, after the circuit court denied President Clinton's request that the entire circuit rehear the case, Clinton's lawyers appealed his case to the Supreme Court, asking the justices to delay the litigation until he left office. In June, the Court agreed to review the lower court's decision, thus delaying arguments until after the November elections, just as Clinton lawyers had hoped.

Clinton v. Jones

The enduring nature of the U.S. political system is undoubtedly due in large part to the delicate balance the Constitution accords to individual rights and the authority of the federal government. The success of the system is largely because of the checks and balances that flow from how power was separated among the three branches of government. "This prohibition against encroachment and aggrandizement of powers has prevented tyranny while preserving the integrity of legitimate authority" (Kasten 1998, 551). The U.S. Supreme Court has played a pivotal role in ensuring that this delicate balance created by the separation of powers doctrine never falters.

The fragility of this balance is never more tested than when the president claims a privilege not constitutionally bestowed on ordinary citizens. In *Clinton v. Jones,* the president sought immunity from the judicial process, a right unknown to others. Although the president enjoys a wide array of privileges and rights not accorded to most Americans, when he claims immunity from suit or the judicial process, he asks the courts to betray one of the most fundamental principles of the legal system: No one person is above the reach of the law.

When *Clinton v. Jones* reached the Supreme Court for oral argument, the central constitutional issue was whether "the Constitution affords a President temporary immunity from civil damages litigation arising out of events that occurred before he took office."[9] The *Jones* case also brought together an unusual array of parties on both sides. Paula Jones was represented before the Supreme Court by attorneys from the Rutherford Institute, a conservative public interest law firm that is, in its own words, "[d]edicated to the defense of civil liberties and human rights." This was, however, the institute's first appearance before the Court arguing on behalf of a woman claimant alleging sexual harassment. It more frequently appears as amicus in cases involving reproductive rights issues in support of abortion restrictions or in religious freedom cases on the side of those who advocate school prayer.

Conspicuously absent was the National Organization for Women (NOW) or any other traditionally liberal women's rights organizations. NOW, a leader in the fight to stop Clarence Thomas's appointment to the Supreme Court and a major defender of Anita Hill, failed to participate in the case in any way. Other nonparticipants included the Women's Legal Defense Fund, the Fund for a Feminist Majority, and the National Women's Political Caucus, all of which have participated in almost all other cases heard by the Court on the side of the party alleging gender discrimination.

Law professors on both sides of the ideological spectrum filed *amicus curiae* briefs in the case.[10] Several professors, including five who had testified against the confirmation of Judge Robert H. Bork to the Supreme Court, urged the Court to delay the Jones proceedings.[11] On the other side, several law professors, led by Ronald Rotunda, who had testified on behalf of Robert Bork, filed in support of Jones.

When the Court heard oral argument in *Clinton v. Jones,* court watchers thought that they heard some sympathy for Clinton in the justices' questions (Biskupic 1997). They were therefore surprised by the Court's opinion in which Justice Stevens, writing for the unanimous Court, first declined to decide two issues: (1) whether a comparable claim could be brought by Jones in state court and (2) whether a judge could force a president to appear at any specific time in a particular place. "We assume that the testimony of the President, both for discovery and for use at trial, may be taken at the White House at a time that will accommodate his busy schedule," wrote Stevens. Then Justice Stevens, considered by some to be the most liberal justice on the Court, delivered the remainder of the opinion. Court watchers noted that he appeared unfazed that the president was the petitioner. As he read his opinion aloud, he "flatly referred to William Jefferson Clinton . . . [and] could have been talking about any litigant in the United States," noted *the Washington Post*'s Court reporter (Biskupic 1997).

In turning to the merits of the case, the Court first rejected Clinton's claim that as president he enjoyed temporary immunity from civil litigation in "all but the most exceptional cases." In holding that Jones did not have to wait until President Clinton's term in office had expired before advancing her civil lawsuit, the Court concluded that the separation of powers doctrine did not require the federal courts to stay proceedings against a president until he completed his term.

The Court acknowledged that three former presidents were defendants in civil litigation before taking office. "Complaints against Theodore Roosevelt and Harry Truman had been dismissed before they took office; the dismissals were affirmed after their respective inaugurations." And John F. Kennedy was sued by delegates to the 1960

Democratic National Convention when they were injured by a car leased by his campaign. Kennedy settled his lawsuit out of court during his tenure as president. In rejecting those cases as a guide, the Court noted that "none of those cases shed(s) any light on the constitutional issue before us" because none of them involved a request for a trial during a president's term of office.

The Court was also unpersuaded by the historical arguments offered by Clinton's lawyers. Although Presidents Adams and Jefferson and Supreme Court Justice Story had called for absolute immunity for presidents while in office, others including James Wilson and Justice Jackson argued to the contrary. Thus, the historical evidence on this point was inconclusive and could not support Clinton's claim, said the Court.

The Court then analyzed what most believed was the president's strongest argument—the separation of powers doctrine. The Court accepted Clinton's premise that the president, as sole head of the executive branch, holds an office that demands his around-the-clock attention. But, said the Court, the separation of powers doctrine only prevents one branch from exercising authority over another. The Court also went on to reference six presidents who had interactions with the judicial branch while president and noted that those interactions did not substantially impair any of those presidents' abilities to perform their official duties.[12]

The Court, moreover, distinguished *Nixon v. Fitzgerald* (1982) from Jones's lawsuit because the "principal rationale for affording certain public servants immunity from suits for money damages arising out of their *official* acts is inapplicable to (claims involving) *unofficial* conduct" (emphasis added). According to the Court, President Nixon could dismiss Fitzgerald (a federal employee) for negative comments that he made regarding the Defense Department to a congressional committee with immunity from civil liability because his actions were part of his official responsibilities. In sharp contrast, the allegations of improper conduct contained in Jones's lawsuit were not related in any way to President Clinton's official actions. The Court made it clear that immunity from civil liability is "grounded in 'the nature of the function performed, not the identity of the actor who performed it.'" Thus, the distinction between official and unofficial acts made by the Court in *Fitzgerald* was at the heart of the Court's opinion in *Jones.* Once an unofficial act is alleged, there can be no protection from civil prosecution.

But, what of the president's claims that an adverse decision would not only require him to expend valuable time and effort to defend the lawsuit at hand but also result in a plethora of petty but potentially time-consuming lawsuits against him, diverting his attention from national security concerns? In the final section of its opinion, even the specter of interference with the chief executive's performance in foreign affairs was not enough to move the justices. Justice Stevens reasoned that history has shown these concerns to have little basis. If national security matters should arise, he went on to say, the Court has "confidence in the ability of our federal judges to deal with . . . these concerns." The Court also reasoned that the Federal Rules of Civil Procedure provided safeguards that federal judges could use to prevent any frivolous lawsuits.

The Rehnquist Court's decision in *Clinton v. Jones* (1997) provided a solid foundation for the Clinton-Lewinsky scandal to surface. The decision also opened the floodgates for other important constitutional issues to emerge, namely those involving the scope of an independent counsel's jurisdiction and the extent to which a president, his aides, and secret service agents enjoy executive privilege. (See Mark Rozell, "Executive Privilege in the Clinton Scandal," pp. 81–99, this volume.) Few at the time, however, predicted that the decision would lead to the impeachment of the president. They underestimated the independent counsel and the powers he enjoyed and how those powers would be used to derail a president and his presidency.

The Independent Counsel

The original special prosecutor was Robert B. Fiske, Jr., a moderate Republican appointed by Attorney General Janet Reno to the position in January 1994. Reno had that authority because the Independent Counsel statute was allowed to expire by Congress. Congress renewed the statute in August 1994. The three-judge panel it created to appoint independent counsels then removed Fiske after conservative Republicans charged that he was being "insufficiently aggressive in pursuit of the President"[13] (Marcus 1998). The panel also cited a possible conflict of interest because Fiske was named by Clinton's own attorney general. In Fiske's place, Kenneth J. Starr, a former U.S. solicitor general under President Bush, was appointed.

The new independent counsel's appointment was not greeted with any enthusiasm by the Clinton administration. Starr was a well-known conservative and a former federal appeals court judge. Starr, who continued to work as a partner at a large D.C. law firm, immediately proceeded to convene two grand juries, one in Little Rock, Arkansas, and one in D.C., to investigate the president and his allies.

When Kenneth Starr was initially appointed, his central mission was to investigate potential financial improprieties by President Clinton and the first lady involving the failed Arkansas Whitewater real estate deal that occurred in the late 1970s, long before Clinton became president. Over time, however, the scope of his investigation expanded tremendously to include "a bewildering range of accusations of fraud, obstruction of justice and abuse of power," allegedly involving both Clintons and many of their closest friends and advisors. The laundry list of topics under investigation included

- a $300,000 loan to Susan McDougal, some of which went to fund the Whitewater development
- the disappearance and reappearance of Hillary Clinton's Rose Law Firm billing records to determine how much time she spent on the land deal
- the dismissal of seven members of the White House Travel Office, who were replaced by Clinton friends (to become known as Travelgate)
- the 1993 suicide of Vincent Foster, White House lawyer and long-time friend and colleague of the first lady
- the collection of hundreds of FBI files of prominent Republicans by low-level White House aides (to become known as Filegate)
- the $700,000 plus paid to former Associate U.S. Attorney General Webster Hubbell by prominent Democrats just as he came under Starr's scrutiny.[14]

None of these investigations bore any fruit but, in the end, cost over $40 million. But, in the course of his protracted inquiries, Starr unearthed rumors of an alleged sexual affair involving President Clinton and a former White House intern, Monica Lewinsky. How did this happen? Because the Supreme Court's ruling allowed the *Jones* case to proceed, and President Clinton ultimately was deposed in the *Jones* matter on January 17, 1998.

To understand the importance of this deposition on the course of his presidency, however, one must go back in time. In July 1997, *Newsweek* published an explosive article about the president and the *Jones* case. In it, a story about Kathleen Willey, a part-time White

House volunteer, appeared. Linda Tripp, a former White House staffer, is quoted as the source for the story that recounts an incident in which Willey says the president made a crude pass at her in the Oval Office (Schmidt 1998).

Jones's lawyers immediately contacted Tripp; her allegations could help them establish a pattern of sexually predatory behavior by Clinton. At the same time, the president's lawyers, just as they had done after Jones went public, immediately began to impugn Tripp's behavior, credibility, and motives. Robert Bennett, the president's lawyer, "all but called Tripp a liar" (Schmidt 1998). Tripp, fearing for her job, contacted a friend, Lucianne Goldberg, a New York literary agent with close ties to the right. Goldberg advised Tripp to tape phone conversations with her friend Monica Lewinsky, whom Tripp knew to be having an affair with the president. Goldberg and Tripp figured that the tapes would protect Tripp from Bennett and provide her with real proof of Clinton's indiscretions. She might not have proof of the Willey incident, but she would be armed and prepared for further attacks on her credibility by Clinton strategists.

On October 3, 1997, Linda Tripp began to tape her conversations with Lewinsky. Three days later, Tripp and Goldberg met with *Newsweek* reporter Michael Isikoff.

In November, after meeting with Isikoff, who appeared to be doing nothing with the information that they had given him about Lewinsky, Goldberg contacted Jones's lawyers and Richard W. Porter, a lawyer at Kirkland & Ellis, where Kenneth Starr continued to practice while investigating the Clintons as independent counsel. On November 21, 1997, Jones's lawyers called Tripp directly to ask about Clinton's rumored affair with a White House intern. Tripp agreed to testify for Jones concerning Willey but told Jones's lawyers that she did not want Bennett to know that she had tapes of her conversations with Lewinsky because she feared for her government job at the Pentagon. According to the *Washington Post*, Tripp and Jones's lawyers then worked out language to be incorporated into their subpoena to testify (copies of which go to opposing counsel) that called on her to appear and produce "testimony" and "writings," deliberately omitting any mention of tapes that might tip off the Clinton legal team (Schmidt 1998).

As Tripp prepared for her deposition, Goldberg contacted her friend at Kirkland & Ellis to get a high-level contact for Tripp to call in the independent counsel's office. On January 12, 1998, late in the day, Tripp finally called Jackie Bennett (no relationship to Robert) in the independent counsel's office.

Starr's office then went into high gear. Lawyers from the office went to Tripp's home that night for their first talks with her. The next day, Tripp attended a planned lunch with Lewinsky at the Ritz-Carlton Hotel. All was not normal, however; unbeknownst to Lewinsky, her "friend" Linda was wearing an FBI wire.

The next day, Wednesday, January 14, Tripp received a call from the FBI demanding to know if she had talked to *Newsweek*'s Isikoff. There were rumors circulating that Isikoff was readying a bombshell story on Clinton. Goldberg had told Isikoff about the tapings at the Ritz-Carlton, and Starr's office feared that Clinton would get wind of the tapes before his upcoming deposition. Knowledge that Tripp had taped Lewinsky would undoubtedly alter the testimony he was preparing to give in the *Jones* matter. Jones's lawyers knew about Lewinsky and planned to ask an unprepared Clinton about it. The independent counsel's office especially wanted Clinton to answer questions *under oath* and *on the record* about Lewinsky—if he lied, he would be lying under oath, a potentially actionable offense.

On Friday, January 16, the day before Clinton was to testify, Kenneth Starr obtained permission to expand his mandate to investigate Clinton's alleged relationship with Lewinsky. He believed that Clinton already had tampered with the judicial process and was in the process of getting his good friend, Vernon Jordan, to help Monica Lewinsky secure a job in New York to make sure she would never admit to their affair. That same afternoon, FBI agents working with Starr's office (and knowing via Tripp where Lewinsky would be), confronted Monica Lewinsky at the Pentagon City Mall and took her into custody, questioning her about Clinton off and on all day and well into the night.

The next day, not knowing that Starr knew about his relationship with Lewinsky, Clinton was questioned under oath for six hours by Jones's attorneys in Robert Bennett's office. In many ways, it was like leading a lamb to the slaughter.

During his deposition, Clinton denied that he had had an affair with a former White House intern, Monica Lewinsky. He repeated that denial to the national public on January 21 and again on January 28, 1998.

The independent counsel then used the *Jones* deposition as the basis for further questioning of Clinton about Lewinsky, a course that ultimately led to another change in focus of the Starr inquiry. After Clinton's deposition in the Jones case, Starr subpoenaed scores of

White House aides and Clinton associates in an effort to prove that the president had lied under oath, obstructed justice, and suborned perjury.

The Clinton White House immediately went to court to block his closest aides, lawyers and secret service agents from testifying before the grand jury. Ultimately, the U.S. Supreme Court again ruled against Clinton in every case.

These victories emboldened the independent counsel, who then subpoenaed the president. On August 17, 1998, President Clinton appeared before the grand jury via videotape from the White House. That evening, he appeared before the American people to admit that he had had an inappropriate relationship with Lewinsky.

Following months of investigation and expenses of over $40 million, the independent counsel sent his report to Congress on September 9, 1998, alleging information that Starr believed constituted grounds for impeachment including perjury, subornation of perjury, and obstruction of justice stemming from Clinton's attempts to hide his relationship with Lewinsky. Had Clinton settled the *Jones* case, he never would have had to give the Jones deposition. Had he not been deposed in *Jones*, the independent counsel never could have investigated his relationship with Lewinsky. True, the relationship might have been made public, but because both parties initially denied it, it would have likely been assigned to the long list of rumors concerning Clinton and a host of other women.

The Implications of *Clinton v. Jones*

The Supreme Court's decision in *Clinton v. Jones* had myriad legal, political, and practical ramifications that went far beyond the immediate controversy before the Court. Although the Court allowed Jones to go forward, Judge Susan Webber Wright dismissed the lawsuit. Later, when Jones sought to reopen her suit in light of the Starr report, President Clinton finally agreed to pay Jones $850,000 to settle the suit. In his four-page agreement filed with Webber Wright's court, Clinton acknowledged no wrongdoing and offered no apology (Baker 1998). Although many speculated at the time that this action would prevent his impeachment and trial, they were wrong.

Even after the president's acquittal, the *Jones* case continued to haunt the president. On April 12, 1999, Judge Susan Webber Wright found the president in civil contempt of court for giving what she called intentionally false testimony about his relationship with Lewinsky. While Webber Wright reemphasized that even if Clinton had been truthful about his relationship with the former intern, she still would have dismissed the suit. She went on the say that it was unacceptable to employ deceptions and lies in an effort to obstruct the judicial process. Judge Webber Wright ordered Clinton to pay Jones's legal fees and sent her finding to the Arkansas bar, which could disbar Clinton.

The Legal Ramifications
In *Clinton v. Jones,* in dismissing the notion that the president might be inundated with civil lawsuits or be forced to spend significant amounts of time on civil litigation, the Supreme Court was clearly off the mark. Although the president has not yet been the target of a flurry of frivolous lawsuits, the Court opened up the doors to nuisance suits. One commentator notes that growth of the Internet, increased media attention to presidential actions, and interestingly, the lucrative nature of book deals about presidential scandals are potential catalysts for more lawsuits (Kasten 1998). Says Martin Kasten, these "kind of multi-million dollar contracts that the entertainment industry encourages only feed the frenzy of high profile lawsuits" (Kasten 1998). Even if sanctions are imposed by federal courts, those making charges against the president gain immediate celebrity status. Kathleen Willey appeared on the cover of *Newsweek* and in a "60 Minutes" segment; and Anita Broderick, who alleged that over twenty years ago Clinton raped her in an Arkansas motel, made front-page news all over the United States.

In the wake of *Clinton v. Jones,* litigation for political advantage could become another weapon in challengers' political artillery. Many liberals questioned the involvement of the conservative Rutherford Institute in Paula Jones's case. Others voiced concern about the role of conservative lawyers in feeding information to the independent counsel's office as well as Kenneth Starr's personal connections with those on the political right. Janet Reno even began an investigation of Starr's contacts with Jones's lawyers prior to his appointment as independent counsel, believing that some misconduct may have occurred. The president is a big target, and *Clinton v. Jones* made him an even easier target for random frivolous lawsuits as well as politically motivated ones (Seper 1998).

But the threat of potential lawsuits is not the only negative outcome of the *Jones* case. *Clinton v. Jones* produced the opportunity for Jones's lawyers to go forward and depose the president for six hours on January

17, 1998. No one knows how many hours the president spent preparing for his deposition or simply worrying about it, distracting him from arguably more important issues facing the nation. Just imagine the consequences of forcing a president to testify during the time of a national crisis. The *Jones* court had little problem with that specter.

Clinton v. Jones may also make it more difficult to attract men and women into the service of their government. Not only did the president's legal fees run into millions of dollars, many of his closest advisors and staffers also were left with hundreds of thousands of dollars in personal attorney's fees. They not only had to pay for lawyers to assist them with their grand jury appearances, but also, like the president, must have been distracted from the job at hand. When called to testify before the grand jury, knowing that their boss was the target of a high-stakes investigation, they were undoubtedly more concerned with their testimony and potential vulnerability to legal charges than they were with their jobs or policy.

The Political and Social Ramifications

While Clinton, his aides, and the entire White House were caught up in the media frenzy surrounding his relationship with Lewinsky, the government seemed to come to a grinding halt. Even after the president admitted to an inappropriate relationship with Lewinsky in August 1998, the media frenzy did not dissipate. In fact, in the midst of a military action in the Sudan and meetings with heads of state, the media remained focused on sexual shenanigans in the Oval Office and speculated more on a "Wag the Dog" effect (i.e., did the president do X, Y, or Z to distract the American public) than it did on reporting international crises. This kind of neglect of big issues desensitizes the American public and potentially lessens American prestige abroad.

Perhaps the most important legacy of *Clinton v. Jones* has little to do with the actual Court opinion or with opening the president up to lawsuits, discouraging federal employment, or hurting national prestige abroad. Rather, because the Supreme Court's decision paved the way, Kenneth Starr turned a costly, largely unproductive investigation of the president into one that ultimately led Starr to issue a report to Congress that became the basis for Clinton's impeachment and trial in the Senate. The Starr report was X-rated and contained intimate details of Clinton's sexual escapades in the Oval Office. These details produced a new flurry of outrage at the president's often juvenile and frequently distasteful encounters with Lewinsky. The report held up to public ridicule both the president and his office. While Clinton continued to enjoy the public's support for his leadership of the nation, most Americans voiced little trust in him or in politicians. Congress took a beating, and so did the executive branch.

Notes

1. Cases cited throughout this chapter:
   Jones v. Clinton, 858 F. Supp. 902 (E.D. Ark. 1994).
   Jones v. Clinton, 72 F.3d 1354 (8th Cir. 1996).
   Clinton v. Jones, 520 U.S. 681 (1997).
   Nixon v. Fitzgerald, 457 U.S. 731 (1982).
   United States v. Curtiss-Wright Corp., 299 U.S. 304 (1936).
   United States v. Nixon, 418 U.S. 683 (1974).

2. One poll, for example, showed that 16 percent of likely voters were less willing to vote for Clinton—a key number, given that five candidates sought the Democratic nomination. CC/USA/Gallup Poll, January 31, 1992.

3. Events surrounding Jones were made worse when several newspapers reported that ultraconservative Richard Mellon Scaife channeled as much as $600,000 a year to keep afloat the *American Spectator*'s secretive Arkansas Project, the purpose of which was to investigate both Clintons.

4. This account draws from "Jones v. Clinton Special Report—Time Line," *Washington Post.* <http://www.washingtonpost.com/wp-srv/politics/special/pjones/timeline.htm>

5. ABC News/Nightline poll of 520 adults conducted in May 1994. Question: "Was Paula Jones sexually harassed by Gov. Clinton?"

6. Gallup/CNN/*USA TODAY* poll conducted in May 1994. Question: "Paula Jones' Story is completely true, mostly true, mostly false, completely false?"

7. *Jones v. Clinton*, 72 F.3d 1354 (8th Cir. 1996) at 1369–70.

8. See *Jones v. Clinton*, 72 F.3d 1354 at 1369.

9. All direct quotes are to *Clinton v. Jones*, 520 U.S. 681 (1997).

10. Other groups filing in the case were a Coalition of American Veterans and the American Civil Liberties Union, both in support of Jones.

11. These professors included Paul Gewirtz, Burke Marshall, Judith Resnick, Kathleen Sullivan, and Lawrence Tribe.

12. Those presidents referred to were Monroe (written interrogatories), Nixon (audiotapes during the Watergate scandal), Ford and Grant (depositions in criminal trials), Carter (videotaped testimony in a criminal trial), and Clinton (videotaped testimony in two criminal cases).

13. Two of the three judges who rejected Fiske were Republican appointees, and one was considered very conservative.

14. See Dan Froomkin, "Untangling Whitewater," *The Washington Post Special Report* <http://www.washingtonpost.com/wp-srv/politics/special/whitewater/whitewater.htm>

References

Baker, Peter. 1999. "Clinton Settles Paula Jones Lawsuit for $850,000," *Washington Post*, 14 November, A1.

Biskupic, Joan. 1997. "Lawsuit against Clinton Can Proceed, Court Says," *Washington Post*, 28 May, A1.

————. 1998. "Jones Case Ruling Complicates Independent Counsel's Task," *Washington Post*, 31 January, A14.

Brock, David. 1994. "Living with the Clintons: Bill's Arkansas Bodyguards Tell the Story the Press Missed," *American Spectator*, January (NEXUS).

The Economist. 1997. "Monkey Business?" *The Economist*, 18 January, 21.

Kasten, Martin. 1998. "Summons at 1600: Clinton v. Jones' Impact on the American Presidency." *Arkansas Law Review* 51: 511–87.

Marcus, Ruth. 1998. "The Prosecutor: Following Leads or Digging Dirt?" *Washington Post*, 30 January, A1.

National Organization for Women (NOW). 1994. "Statement of NOW President Patricia Ireland Calling for Fair Treatment of Jones' Suit, Questioning Right Wing Disingenuous Fervor," 4 May.

————. 1997. "NOW President Patricia Ireland's Statement on Clinton v. Jones Supreme Court Decision." 27 May.

Puro, Steven. 1971. "The Role of the Amicus Curiae in the United States Supreme Court," PhD dissertation, State University of New York at Buffalo.

Rivera, Geraldo. 1998. "Looking Back on 11 Great Years," *The Geraldo Rivera Show*, 28 July.

Rotunda, Ronald D. 1997. "Can a President Plumbing the Constitutional Depths of Clinton v. Jones Be Imprisoned?" *Legal Times*, 21 July, 22.

Salokar, Rebecca Mae. 1992. *The Solicitor General: The Politics of Law*. Philadelphia: Temple University Press.

Scigliano, Robert. 1971. *The Supreme Court and the Presidency*. New York: Free Press.

Schmidt, Susan. 1998. "Tripp's Tapes: How They Got to Starr is a Complex Tale," *Washington Post*, 11 October, A1.

Seper, Jerry. 1998. "Starr's Contacts in Jones Case Eyed: Justice Examines Ethics Implications," *The Washington Times*, 17 October, A1.

Stephanopoulos, George. 1999. *All Too Human: A Political Education*. Boston: Little, Brown.

Weeden, L. Darnell. 1999. "The President and Mrs. Jones Were in Federal Court: The Litigation Established No Constitutional Immunity for President Clinton," *George Mason Law Review* 7 (winter): 361–89.

Wildavsky, Aaron, ed. 1975. *Perspectives on the Presidency*. Boston: Little, Brown.

F O U R

The Independent Counsel Statute

Louis Fisher

President Clinton was investigated by two outside counsels. After the Independent Counsel statute expired in 1992, Attorney General Janet Reno invoked her own authority a year later to appoint Robert Fiske as special prosecutor to investigate several issues, including the Clintons' involvement in what became known as Whitewater and the death of White House aide Vincent Foster. When Congress reauthorized the Independent Counsel statute in 1994, Reno asked the special panel of three federal judges to appoint an independent counsel. They could have reappointed Fiske but instead selected Kenneth Starr. Starr's tenure as independent counsel from 1994 to 1999 was marked—or marred—by ceaseless, scathing attacks on his performance. That is nothing new for this position, in fact, it is standard operating procedure. From the appointment of Archibald Cox in 1973 to investigate Watergate to the appointment of Lawrence Walsh in 1987 to investigate Iran-Contra to the appointment of Starr, outside counsels attract devastating criticism. Anyone who investigates the president and draws blood can expect the president and his friends to use every available means to destroy that individual. Any hope of taking these investigations "out of politics" is pure fantasy.

Although Cox, Walsh, and Starr conducted their investigations with vigor and diligence, their efforts to reach a full understanding of presidential conduct were stymied by a variety of roadblocks, ranging from invocations of executive privilege to presidential pardons. The lesson to be drawn from Watergate, Iran-Contra, and the Starr investigations is this: Even the ample resources available to an independent counsel are unlikely to penetrate the hardy defenses erected within the executive branch, especially when it threatens top public officials.[1]

The Experience of Archibald Cox

On May 16, 1973, Archibald Cox received a call from Elliot Richardson, who served in several cabinet positions with the Nixon administration and who was now nominated to replace Richard Kleindeinst as attorney general. As part of an agreement with the Senate Judiciary Committee, Richardson had agreed to name a special prosecutor to investigate the Watergate scandal and to give that person extraordinary independence. He offered Cox the position.

Given the barbs thrown at Starr for his "tin ear" for politics, it is instructive to examine Cox's record. Cox immediately ran into trouble because of the way he arranged his swearing-in ceremony. At least ten members of the Kennedy family were present, including Senator Ted Kennedy and Ethel Kennedy, the widow of Robert Kennedy. Cox had worked for John F. Kennedy during his years in the Senate, helped Kennedy's presidential campaign, and served as solicitor general under Attorney General Robert Kennedy. The animosity between the Kennedys and Nixon was of legendary proportions. Erwin Griswold, former dean at Harvard Law School and solicitor general under Nixon, said the swearing-in ceremony "was a terrible mistake. But I kept my mouth shut."[2] Cox conceded "he still had plenty to learn about politics."[3] His biographer, Ken Gormley, remarked that political acumen "was never Cox's strong suit."[4]

Cox's insensitivity to political considerations is stunning. Given his previous identification with the Kennedys and the imperative to maintain the appearance of neutrality and independence, it is almost inconceivable that he would have allowed the swearing-in ceremony to be handled this way. President Nixon did not need additional reasons to believe that Cox was "out to get him."[5]

On June 6, 1973, Cox met with the attorneys who were representing President Nixon: White House counsel Leonard Garment, special counsel J. Fred Buzhardt, and outside counsel Charles Alan Wright. At every turn they blocked access to requested documents.[6] When he pushed for tapes that might incriminate Nixon and his aides, the days of Cox were numbered.

The "Saturday Night Massacre" sent Cox, Elliot Richardson, and Deputy Attorney General William Ruckelshaus out of government.

Nevertheless, heavy public pressure forced the White House to select Cox's successor, Leon Jaworski. His investigation led to jail sentences for former attorney general John Mitchell and top officials in the administration, the Committee to Re-Elect the President, and private citizens who had assisted the administration. In addition to sentences imposed on the seven men who participated in the burglary, jail sentences were meted out to Dwight Chapin, Charles Colson, John Dean, John Ehrlichman, Bob Haldeman, Herbert Kalmbach, Egil Krogh, Frederick LaRue, Jeb Magruder, Herbert Porter, and Donald Segretti. Others went to prison for related activities, such as illegal campaign contributions. These actions culminated in the resignation of President Nixon.

The details on Watergate are important to recall because future probes of the White House would pale by comparison. In later investigations, punishment was confined to lower-level and mid-level executive employees, not top officials. Watergate did not cleanse the political system by teaching executive officials to avoid criminal activity. The lesson, instead, is to avoid being caught. Conversations are less likely to be taped. The paper trail is kept to a minimum. As few fingerprints as possible are left behind. If some executive employees must be sacrificed, the brunt falls not on major figures, as it did with Watergate, but on those in the middle. Top elected officials remain unaccountable.

The Independent Counsel Statute

The special prosecutor (later called independent counsel) emerged from the politics of Watergate. Congress considered legislation to establish a permanent office of special prosecutor to investigate allegations against top executive officials. The special prosecutor would be appointed by a panel of federal judges and could be removed, for cause, by the attorney general. The Ethics in Government Act of 1978 created the office of special prosecutor and the act was reauthorized in 1983, 1987, and 1994.

The Carter administration supported this reform as a necessary step in restoring the reputation of the Justice Department. The enabling statute of 1978 created the office of special prosecutor for a period of five years to investigate charges against the president, the vice president, heads of executive departments, and other high-ranking executive officials specified in the law. The attorney general, on receiving specific information about these individuals, would perform a preliminary investigation during a ninety-day period. If the attorney general found that the matter was so unsubstantiated that no further investigation was warranted, the attorney general would notify the panel of federal judges established to appoint special prosecutors. If the attorney general found that the matter warranted further investigation or if the ninety-day period elapsed, the attorney general would apply to the court for the appointment of a special prosecutor. The judges would select the person and define the scope of jurisdiction.

Checks were placed on the special prosecutor. The attorney general could remove the person, but "only for extraordinary impropriety, physical disability, mental incapacity, or any other condition that substantially impairs the performance of such special prosecutor's duties." The office of special prosecutor terminated when he or she notified the attorney general that the investigation was complete and filed a report. The panel of three judges, either on its own motion or on the suggestion of the attorney general, could also terminate an office of special prosecutor at any time if the panel determined that the work of the special prosecutor had been completed.[7]

Experience with the 1978 statute revealed a number of deficiencies and weaknesses that were addressed in subsequent reauthorizations. One issue was the information needed to trigger the appointment of a special prosecutor (renamed independent counsel in the reauthorization statute of 1983). The attorney general, on receiving allegations about an executive official, would consider the degree of specificity of the information received and the credibility of the source of the information. Instead of finding that a matter is "so unsubstantiated that no further investigation or prosecution is warranted," the attorney general would find that "there are no reasonable grounds to believe that further investigation or prosecution is warranted." The revised statute allowed individuals investigated by an independent counsel to recover attorney's fees if they had not been indicted. The removal provision was changed by striking "extraordinary impropriety" and inserting "good cause."[8]

Reauthorization in 1987 changed the procedures for the initial determination by the attorney general. Not later than fifteen days after receiving information, the attorney general would determine whether grounds to investigate existed. If within that period the attorney general determined that the information was not specific or was not from a credible source, the attorney general shall close the matter. Otherwise, the attorney general shall commence a preliminary investigation and determine, over the next ninety days, whether to ask the panel of judges to appoint an independent counsel. The attorney general was entitled to request from the court a single extension of not more than sixty days. If the attorney general determined that there were no reasonable grounds to warrant further investigation, the attorney general would notify the court.[9]

The Independent Counsel statute was challenged in court as unconstitutional on the ground that it vested part of law enforcement in an officer not appointed by the president. Moreover, the removal feature was considered an impermissible restriction on presidential power. In 1988 the Supreme Court, by a 7 to 1 majority, upheld the constitutionality of the independent counsel.[10] Justice Scalia penned an elegant dissent, warning about the dangers of placing such power in a prosecutor with unlimited time and money. Although concern remained about the impact of the independent counsel on presidential power, no president vetoed any of the reauthorization bills.

When the 1987 reauthorization terminated on December 15, 1992, Congress did not immediately reinstate the Independent Counsel statute. Republicans, angry about the manner in which Independent Counsel Lawrence Walsh investigated the Iran-Contra affair, blocked the reauthorization. However, with the election of Bill Clinton in 1992, Republicans looked at the legal baggage he brought to the White House and thought the independent counsel statute was not such a bad idea. Republicans were particularly intrigued with Clinton's investments in an Arkansas land development venture called Whitewater Development Company. Because the law had lapsed, Attorney General Reno had to rely on her own authority on January 20, 1994, to name a special prosecutor, Robert B. Fiske, Jr., to investigate Whitewater.

On June 30, 1994, Congress reauthorized the independent counsel law for another five years. It placed new restrictions on expenditures by independent counsels and clarified the attorney general's authority to use independent counsels in cases involving members of Congress. The statute left to the discretion of the federal court the reappointment of Fiske or the selection of someone else. The panel selected a replacement, former Solicitor General Kenneth W. Starr.

Lawrence Walsh and Iran-Contra

Before turning to Starr, some lessons need to be drawn from the Iran-Contra affair. Beginning in 1982, Congress enacted a variety of statutory directives to restrict the Reagan administration's assistance to the Contra rebels in Nicaragua. Each year Congress learned of evasions and circumventions by the administration. Finally, on October 12, 1984, Congress adopted strict language in the Boland Amendment intended to prohibit all executive assistance of any kind to provide military support to the Contras. Administration witnesses assured Congress that the new statutory language was clear and there would be full compliance.[11] In other hearings, the administration pledged that it would not attempt to solicit funds from outside sources—foreign governments or private citizens—to assist the Contras.[12] Yet at the very moment the administration offered these assurances, executive branch officials were actively soliciting funds from private parties and foreign governments to assist the Contras. Moreover, American citizens learned in November 1986 that President Reagan had traded arms to Iran for the release of American hostages. This sale of weapons violated a number of policies that executive departments had been articulating: neutrality in the Iran–Iraq war, an embargo on arms sales to Iran, and the policy of not paying ransom to hostage takers.

President Reagan directed Attorney General Edwin Meese III to go to the special panel and request that they select an independent counsel. Walsh was appointed on December 19, 1986. His efforts to uncover the full scope of the scandal were regularly thwarted by the administration's strategy of withholding information, denying classified documents, and issuing presidential pardons.

As part of his investigation, Walsh looked into the activities of Joseph Fernandez, the CIA station chief in Costa Rica who helped Colonel Oliver North supply the Contras in violation of the Boland Amendment. On June 20, 1988, the grand jury indicted Fernandez for false statements and obstruction and for conspiring with North and others to carry out the covert action. The conspiracy count was later dropped. Nevertheless, the pursuit of Fernandez would illuminate the CIA's role and probably lead to others in the administration who worked with Fernandez. However, that line of inquiry was snuffed out when Attorney General Richard Thornburgh refused to release classified information needed for the trial.[13]

On June 16, 1992, a grand jury indicted Caspar Weinberger, former secretary of defense in the Reagan administration. He was charged with five felonies, including one count of obstructing a congressional investigation, two counts of making false statements, and two charges of perjury. Here was an opportunity to learn about the involvement of a cabinet official. Moreover, President George Bush was likely to be called to Weinberger's trial to testify. Although Bush had denied knowing that Weinberger and Secretary of State George Shultz had opposed the sale of arms to Iran, the indictment revealed that Bush, as vice president, had attended the White House meeting where Reagan overrode Weinberger and Shultz.[14]

Once again Walsh hit a stone wall. On December 24, 1992, President Bush pardoned six people involved in the Iran-Contra affair. Heading the list was Weinberger, but the pardon order also covered three members of the CIA involved: Duane Clarridge, Alans Fiers, and Clair George. Clarridge had been indicted on seven felony counts; Fiers, facing indictment for felony, had agreed to plead guilty to two misdemeanors and cooperate with Walsh; and George was charged with lying to three congressional panels and a federal judge. That case ended in a mistrial, but at retrial George was found guilty of two felony counts of lying to Congress.[15] The pardons wiped out the last chance to learn the extent of CIA involvement.

A number of executive officials and private citizens pleaded guilty to various offenses for their actions in Iran-Contra. The convictions of North and National Security Adviser John Poindexter were overturned on appeal because North's immunized testimony before Congress had "tainted" the jury verdicts. After it was all over, Walsh offered this assessment: "What set Iran-Contra apart from previous political scandals was the fact that a cover-up engineered in the White House of one president and completed by his successor prevented the rule of law from being applied to the perpetrators of criminal activity of constitutional dimension."[16]

Enter Kenneth Starr

Starr was appointed on August 5, 1994, to continue the investigation of Whitewater and Foster's death begun by Robert Fiske. There is good reason to believe that Starr should never have been selected. First, although he had a distinguished record as federal appellate judge and solicitor general, he had no experience as a prosecutor. Second, he had considered running for Republican U.S. senator from Virginia and had offered legal advice as to whether President Clinton should have immunity in the Paula Jones case. Given that background, it would be hard to argue strongly either for his competence or his objectivity. Reno and the panel of judges expanded Starr's jurisdiction on March 22, 1996, to look into the firing of staff from the White House Travel Office, and again on June 21, 1996, to investigate charges that the White House had misused confidential FBI files. On January 16, 1998, Reno again requested that Starr's jurisdiction be expanded to include allegations of subornation of perjury, obstruction of justice, and intimidation of witnesses surrounding the affair between President Clinton and White House aide Monica Lewinsky.

These repeated expansions of jurisdiction were a mistake by Reno, the federal judges, and Starr. Clearly, Starr was having trouble finishing his initial assignments. He issued one report to the court in July 1997 (released October 11, 1997), reaffirming the findings of earlier investigations that Vincent Foster's death was a suicide. On September 11, 1998, Starr forwarded to the House of Representatives a report on the Lewinsky matter, concluding that President Clinton may have committed impeachable offenses.

Otherwise, Starr was not concluding his investigations and reporting the results. As of November 1999, Starr had never reported on the White House Travel Office or the dispute over the FBI files. Only after the 1998 elections were over did Starr announce that Clinton had committed no legal offenses in those two matters. Did Starr reach that conclusion before the elections? If so, why had he not made the announcement then? What of others involved in Travelgate and Filegate, including First Lady Hillary Clinton and former White House aides David Watkins, Craig Livingstone, and Anthony Marceca? Three years had elapsed after the assignment of these duties to Starr, and he had yet to release a report to the public and to Congress.

Part of Starr's problem was his decision to juggle a number of activities beyond his independent counsel duties. A story in September 1997 reported that in 1996 he had been paid $87,385 for his work as independent counsel and $1.12 million from Kirkland & Ellis, the law firm where he continued his private practice. In addition, he received $25,000 for teaching a course at New York University's School of Law. He spent much of his time traveling around the country giving speeches, often to conservative groups, which again raised questions about his detachment and objectivity. He continued to serve on outside groups including the Council for Court Excellence, the Institute of Judicial Administration, and a Duke Law School alumni association. He sat on the boards of seven other organizations including American University, Shenandoah University, Wesley Theological Seminary, the Supreme Court Historical Society, and the American Judicature Society.[17]

His outside clients remained extensive. During 1996, fourteen clients, including GTE, the Chicago Board of Trade, Ronald Haft, General Motors, Brown & Williamson, Amoco, Suzuki Motor Corporation, Hughes Aircraft, and the National Football League Players Association each paid him more than $5,000. His personal attorney said that none of the new clients required court appearances by Starr.[18] However, Starr would soon appear in court in high-profile cases. He represented the Bradley Foundation in an effort to uphold Wisconsin's experimental school-choice program, taking a position contrary to that advanced by the Clinton administration. The Bradley Foundation was identified as supporting a number of organizations and publications that were highly critical of President Clinton.[19] Right in the middle of the Lewinsky investigation, Starr defended Meineke Discount Muffler in a class action suit. He argued the case before the Fourth Circuit on May 5, 1998.[20]

On his probes into Whitewater and the Rose law firm in Little Rock, Starr obtained guilty pleas from many individuals: David L. Hale, Charles Matthews, Eugene Fitzhugh, Robert W. Palmer, Christopher Wade, Neal T. Ainley, Stephen A. Smith, Larry Kuca, William J. Marks Sr., former Arkansas governor Jim Guy Tucker, and John Haley. Former associate attorney general Webster Hubbell spent fifteen months in prison for mail fraud and tax evasion. James McDougal and Susan McDougal, the Clintons' former business partners in the Whitewater investment, were convicted on fraud and conspiracy charges. Jim Guy Tucker was convicted on separate charges. Some individuals were acquitted, including Arkansas bankers Herbert Brancum and Robert Hill.

On April 30, 1998, Starr won an indictment of Webster Hubbell, his wife, and two other individuals regarding charges that Hubbell had failed to pay federal income taxes. Although a district court dismissed the case as exceeding Starr's jurisdiction, it was reinstated by the D.C. circuit court on January 26, 1999. Moreover, on November 13, 1998, Starr obtained an additional fifteen-count indictment against Hubbell alleging concealment and false statements made about the Rose law firm's involvement in land deals in the 1980s. On June 30, 1999, Hubbell pleaded guilty to one misdemeanor charge of tax evasion and to one felony charge of false statements. Charges against the other three individuals were dropped. An indictment was also returned against Julie Hyatt Steele, on January 7, 1999, for alleged perjury and obstruction of justice in the Monica Lewinsky investigation. After a mistrial was declared on May 7, 1999, Starr issued a statement that Steele would not be retried.

This impressive record was offset by what the public saw as heavy-handed prosecution, such as photos of Susan McDougal being led away in manacles and leg braces, although such treatment is standard court procedure. Part of her incarceration resulted from refusing to answer questions about President Clinton's videotaped statement to grand jurors on Whitewater matters. She had a choice: To her knowledge, was he telling the truth or not telling the truth? She chose not to respond, landing her in jail for civil contempt.

It is difficult to understand McDougal's strategy. She argued that had she testified that Clinton was, to her knowledge, telling the truth, Starr would have sought an indictment for perjury. He might have. Would he have won that case? Maybe so. Why was that prospect worse than staying in jail for eighteen months for civil contempt and facing criminal contempt charges after that? Was she so determined to discredit Starr that she willingly served jail time? It is hard to understand.

McDougal refused to answer any questions put by Starr's office because they were "conflicted." She told the grand jurors: "Get another independent counsel, and I'll answer every question."[21] This position is clearly untenable. May any other witness refuse to answer questions put by prosecutors, insisting that they be replaced by others more acceptable and agreeable to the witness?

After Susan McDougal was released from jail, Starr indicted her again on May 4, 1998, this time for criminal contempt. On April 12, 1999, a jury acquitted her of the charge of obstruction of justice and failed to reach a verdict on other counts.

Monica Lewinsky and Impeachment

Starr's reputation had been battered by the end of 1997. His probe of Whitewater had been successful, resulting in many guilty pleas and convictions, but other investigations (Travelgate and Filegate) seemed to languish. He astonished the country on February 17, 1997, by announcing that he was stepping down as independent counsel to accept a position with Pepperdine University in California. Widely attacked for walking away from a public duty, he four days later reversed course and stayed on. People again questioned his judgment and resolve.

Then came the Reno decision, on January 16, 1998, to assign the Lewinsky matter to Starr. Given Starr's earlier probes into Whitewater, Travelgate, and Filegate, this added jurisdiction helped create the impression that Starr was on a one-man mission to nail Clinton. If earlier investigations failed to reveal incriminating evidence against Clinton, maybe this new assignment would bear fruit, or so it could be argued by partisans. The Lewinsky investigation should have been assigned to someone else.

Having been handed a hot potato, what did Starr do right and where did he go wrong?

First, he deserves credit for eventually prevailing on legal disputes after the White House placed one hurdle after another in his path. Presidential aides insisted that they could not be compelled to testify at the grand jury. Hillary Clinton believed that her discussions with a government attorney were privileged. The secret service argued that the agents responsible for protecting the President should not be forced to testify about matters of Clinton's conduct. On all those matters and others, Starr won at every level: from the district court through appellate courts. Efforts by the administration to take the matter to the Supreme Court were unsuccessful. These victories for Starr came at substantial cost, however, for the investigation dragged on and seemed to reinforce the view that Starr was out to "get the president"—the same issue that had bedeviled Cox and Walsh.

Starr took flak for calling Monica Lewinsky's mother to the grand jury. Her mother seemed relaxed and poised after the first appearance, but on the return trip to the grand jury the television camera showed her crushed and distraught. Starr had a right to call Monica's mother to determine if she had evidence relevant to the criminal probe. Certainly Justice Department attorneys do not recognize a mother-daughter privilege. But they do not work in the fishbowl the way Starr did. The pain in the face and body of Monica's mother contributed to the impression that Starr was conducting a cruel, vindictive, and heavy-handed probe, even if it was entirely appropriate to call her to the grand jury.

Also criticized was Starr's effort to obtain from a bookstore the purchases made by Monica. At that stage of the game, neither Monica nor her attorney, William Ginsburg, had cooperated with Starr. If anything, Monica and Ginsburg seemed intent on shielding Clinton. Under these conditions, Starr had every right to get whatever documentary information he needed to check and corroborate Monica's statements. Was she someone who lied all her life (as she once put it)? The more Starr could buttress her comments, the stronger her credibility. Eventually he reached a settlement with the bookstore and got what was necessary. The investigative technique was appropriate, but Starr paid a price, as he did by calling Monica's mother. These incidents were overplayed by the media.

William Ginsburg was a walking calamity. Will Rogers said he never met a man he didn't like. The same could be said of Ginsburg and TV monitors. Dazzled by media opportunities, he rarely lost the chance to opine on television. Ginsburg constantly promoted his interests (whatever they were) at the expense of his client. Federal Judge Norma Holloway Johnson chastised him for his frequent public comments about the case and voiced concern about the inconsistency of his statements, pointing out that they were not serving his client.[22] After Monica replaced him with two seasoned attorneys, Plato Cacheris and Jacob Stein, Starr made quick progress.

As an independent counsel, Starr was never in a position to counter the charges streaming from the White House. Presidential aides and Clinton's private counsel were at liberty every hour to hurl new accusations at Starr, whether false or not. After one of his grand jury appearances, Sidney Blumenthal of the White House walked out of the courthouse, stepped in front of the microphones, and proceeded to ridicule the questions put to him.[23] A grand jury witness is entitled to say what goes on in the grand jury room but has no license to mischaracterize and misrepresent. Blumenthal violated that rule. On his return to the grand jury he was admonished by the foreperson:

> The work that we are doing here is very serious, and the integrity to our work as representatives of the United States of America is very important to us.
>
> We are very concerned about the fact that during your last visit that an inaccurate representation of the events that happened here were retold on the steps of the courthouse.
>
> We would hope that you will understand the seriousness of our work, and not in any way use it for any purpose other than the purpose that is intended, and that you would really represent us the way that events happened in this room.[24]

Starr was regularly accused by the White House and Clinton supporters of leaking grand jury testimony. Anthony Lewis of the *New York Times* asked: "Is his office leaking to the press? Does the sun rise in the east?[25] But Starr was not the only one with access to grand jury testimony. The White House and Clinton's private attorneys were able to debrief any friendly witness who appeared before Starr's prosecutors and could have easily leaked material and put the blame on Starr, forcing him to defend himself and conduct time-consuming reviews of his internal operations.

In the midst of the Senate's impeachment trial, it was charged that someone in Starr's office had leaked to the *New York Times* that Starr was considering indicting Clinton after he left office. Was this a leak from Starr's office or another White House effort to discredit him? The charge was strange. First, this was not news. Anyone following the investigation knew that Starr and his assistants were debating that option. Second, why would someone in Starr's office leak such a story? To hurt Clinton? But the availability of an indictment after Clinton left office could be used by Clinton's supporters as a reason to acquit him of the articles of impeachment. How convenient to argue that if something has to be done because of Clinton's conduct, let Starr do it later.

What of Monica's blue dress and DNA evidence? Starr was again rebuked for disreputable tactics and being obsessed about sex, but without irrefutable evidence—provided by the dress and the FBI analysis—there is no reason to think that Clinton would have ever inched toward the truth. Only by putting him in a corner with no escape route would some of the truth come out.

Finally, what of Starr's report to the House of Representatives concluding that Clinton may have committed impeachable offenses? Was Starr acting like an overzealous prosecutor? First, the statute placed that responsibility on him. An independent counsel "shall" advise the House of any "substantial and credible information which such independent counsel receives . . . that may constitute grounds for an impeachment."[26] The only way to satisfy that duty is to develop in your mind what an impeachable offense is, and whether the information in your possession qualifies. It was appropriate for Starr to compile the report, identify what he thought were impeachable offenses and why, and then submit the report to Congress. Starr, having done that to discharge a statutory duty, was mistaken in personally appearing before the House Judiciary Committee; submitting the report was all that was required. Anything beyond that invited charges of overzealousness and political, partisan advocacy.

The Senate's Vote on Impeachment

Starr had done his homework well, providing detailed evidence of Clinton's perjury and obstruction of justice. Nevertheless, Clinton was "acquitted" on both articles of impeachment. On the issue of perjury, forty-five Senators voted "guilty" and fifty-five voted "not guilty." The vote on obstruction of justice was only fifty to fifty, far short of the two-thirds needed for removal. However, the actual judgment in the Senate was distorted by the procedure it followed. As a result, many senators voted "not guilty" even when they knew Clinton was guilty as charged.

From 1789 to 1936, the Senate followed a two-step process: first a vote to determine guilt and then a vote on removal. A senator could vote for guilt and decide for other reasons not to remove. The judgment on guilt stood alone, unaffected by the decision on removal.

Matters changed in 1936 during the Senate's consideration of seven articles of impeachment against Judge Halsted Ritter. The vote on the first six articles was "not guilty." When the Senate reached the two-thirds margin for guilty on the seventh article, it started to take up the second step: removal. At that point a senator raised a point of order, arguing that the Constitution expressly states that any civil officer found guilty of an impeachable offense "shall be removed." Thus, there was no need for a separate vote on removal. It was automatic. The chair agreed with that reasoning and no one challenged the chair's ruling.[27] Ever since 1936, the two decisions on guilt and removal have been collapsed in a single vote. If a senator decides that an impeached official should not be removed, even if guilty as charged, there is only one option: to vote "not guilty."

Consider how senators handled this dilemma with Clinton. Senator Robert C. Byrd (D-WVa.) voted "not guilty" on both articles even though he said that Clinton's behavior constituted "an impeachable offense, a political high crime or high misdemeanor against the state." Yet Byrd recognized that a vote to convict "carries with it an automatic removal of the President from office. It is not a two-step process." Senators were forced to cast a vote either "to convict and remove or a vote to acquit." Not wanting to remove, Byrd voted "not guilty" after judging Clinton guilty on both counts.[28]

Senator Susan Collins (R-Maine) voted not guilty on the two articles, yet explained that the House managers had proved to her satisfaction that Clinton "did, in fact, obstruct justice."[29] Another Maine Republican senator, Olympia Snowe, joined Collins in voting not guilty on the articles, but that decision did not accurately reflect Snowe's position. She concluded that Clinton had "unlawfully" influenced a potential witness, Betty Currie. Snowe said that if she were a juror in a standard criminal case, she would have convicted Clinton of "attempting to unlawfully influence a potential witness."[30] Senator James Jeffords (R-Vt.) voted not guilty on both articles. Still, he agreed that the House managers had proven one of their allegations that Clinton had obstructed justice.[31] In short, the 50-50 vote misses the real judgment on Clinton's obstruction.

The vote on perjury is also confused. Senator Fred Thompson (R-Tenn.) voted against this article after concluding that Clinton had perjured himself a number of times, such as in his statements "concerning Betty Currie, and the statements concerning what he told his aides." Rather than Clinton speaking to Currie to "refresh" his recollection, Thompson thought it was more likely that Clinton was "coaching a witness about the nature of a sexual relationship." For a variety of reasons, Thompson voted "not guilty" on the perjury article. Even if Clinton's statements were wrong and "perhaps indictable after the President leaves office," he found that they did not justify removal.[32]

Senator Ted Stevens (R-Alaska) voted against the perjury article, although he said that if he were sitting as a juror in a criminal case he would find Clinton "guilty of perjury as charged." According to Stevens, Clinton's "criminal activity" under the perjury article did not merit removal.[33] Another "not guilty" vote on perjury, from Senator Slade Gorton (R-Wash.) fails to capture his position. He said that Clinton's "representations about the nature and details of his relationship with Miss Lewinsky are literally beyond belief." Gordon had "no reasonable doubt" that Clinton committed perjury when he told the grand jury that the purpose of his five statements to Currie was to refresh his memory. In the end, Gorton voted "not guilty" on perjury because he thought removal was unwarranted.[34]

Some senators, like Bob Graham (R-Fla.), never explained in detail what they thought of the perjury and obstruction charges, other than to say that the charges, if true, did not merit removal.[35] For all we know, Graham and some other senators may have concluded that Clinton did commit perjury and obstruction but should not be removed because his actions, as Graham said, "did not cause permanent injury to the proper functioning of our government. He did not upset the constitutional balance of powers."[36]

For these reasons, newspaper headlines trumpeting "Clinton acquitted" gave a misleading impression of what senators thought of his guilt. With only one vote to cast, a senator could easily conclude that Clinton was guilty as charged but that the charges did not justify removal. John Chafee (R-R.I.) voted against both articles but also said that he had no doubt "that if I served in the House, I would have voted to impeach" Clinton and that he was convinced that Clinton "acted to circumvent the law."[37]

Senator Snowe put it this way: "Acquittal is not exoneration."[38] John Breaux (D-La.) voted against the articles but cautioned that his vote "is not a vote on the innocence of this President. He is not innocent."[39] Bob Kerrey (D-Nebr.) added: "While there is plenty of blame to go around in this case, the person responsible for it going this far is the President of the United States."[40]

Other Investigations

The multiple investigations of President Clinton were matched by a remarkable number of probes of his cabinet officials. On September 9, 1994, Donald C. Smaltz was appointed independent counsel to investigate charges that Secretary of Agriculture Mike Espy had received various gifts and entertainment from companies he regulated. Smaltz was able to obtain eight guilty pleas and one "no contest" plea from individuals and companies. There were two settlements of civil suits, resulting in fines. Smaltz also won six jury convictions against other parties. After this string of successes, he failed to sustain the charges against Espy, who had been indicted on thirty-five counts. The jury acquitted Epsy on all counts.

On May 24, 1995, David M. Barrett was appointed independent counsel to investigate charges against Henry Cisneros, secretary of the Department of Housing and Urban Development (HUD). On December 11, 1997, Cisneros was indicted for making false statements to the FBI during a background check. Included in this indictment were his former mistress, Linda Medlar Jones, and two former aides at HUD. Charges against the other two aides were later dropped. In a separate indictment, Jones was charged along with her sister and brother-in-law for fraud, false statements, money laundering, and conspiracy regarding the purchase of a house. They pleaded guilty to a number of felony counts, some of them related to funds received from Cisneros. On September 7, 1999, Cisneros agreed to plead guilty to a single misdemeanor count and pay a $10,000 fine.

On July 6, 1995, Daniel Pearson was appointed independent counsel to look into allegations against Secretary of Commerce Ronald Brown. This investigation ended with Brown's death in Croatia. The remainder of the case, however, involving Brown's former business partner Nolanda Hill, was transferred to the Justice Department for further action. On March 13, 1998, she was indicted for diverting more than $200,000 from companies she controlled to buy clothes and jewelry for herself and for failing to report it as income on her tax returns. She was also charged with diverting more than $557,000 from one of her companies to Brown.[41]

Two other independent counsels were appointed to examine charges against members of the Clinton cabinet. On May 19, 1998, Carol

Elder Bruce was appointed to investigate allegations of false statements to Congress by Bruce Babbitt, secretary of the Interior Department. Bruce announced on October 13, 1999, that no criminal indictments would be brought. On May 26, 1998, Ralph I. Lancaster was appointed independent counsel to review allegations of unlawful solicitation of campaign contributions by Alexis Herman, secretary of Labor.

Should We Continue the Independent Counsel?

An independent counsel—whether statutory or not—is necessary because the Justice Department cannot investigate some matters without creating an unacceptable conflict of interest. That is why Archibald Cox investigated Watergate, and that is why Reno, without an Independent Counsel statute, appointed Fiske special prosecutor to investigate Whitewater. The Justice Department could not conduct a credible probe in either case.

Critics of the independent counsel law urge its repeal because of the risk of overzealous prosecution. The statute supposedly enables an independent counsel to target an individual and use unlimited funds and time to indict. No doubt the potential for abuse is great for any prosecutor, including those in the Justice Department. Improvements can be considered every time the statute is reauthorized. The emotional and financial cost of defending oneself is huge, even when there is no indictment.

But the record of the statute does not support the claim of extravagant prosecution. From 1978 to the present, independent counsels have investigated about twenty controversies. No indictments were brought in twelve of them. The investigation of Commerce Secretary Brown was closed after his death in a plane crash in Croatia. In most cases, no charges are brought by independent counsels.

The first two investigations involved allegations of cocaine use by Hamilton Jordan and Tim Kraft, aides in Jimmy Carter's White House. There were no indictments. Independent counsels investigated Labor Secretary Raymond Donovan and Attorney General Edwin M. Meese III and two former assistant attorneys general, Theodore Olson and W. Lawrence Wallace. Meese was investigated a second time. None of those cases resulted in indictments. In 1986, an independent counsel won a perjury conviction against Michael Deaver, former White House deputy chief of staff under President Reagan. A year later, Lyn Nofziger's conviction for violating a lobbying law was overturned on appeal, and the case was not retried. This first decade of the Independent

Counsel statute contains no evidence of rampant, bare-knuckled prosecution.

The major investigation of the 1980s was by Lawrence Walsh into the Iran-Contra affair. There should be no question about the seriousness of the crimes committed and the scope of the scandal, reaching high into the intelligence community, the Defense Department, the State Department, and the White House.

In the 1990s, no indictments resulted from an investigation into possible abuse of passport files by Bush administration officials. In two other investigations, sealed by court order, there was no indictment. No indictment was brought against Eli Segal, former head of Clinton's national service organization.

So where is the evidence of heavy-handed prosecution? An independent counsel won several convictions in the widespread scandals affecting HUD. There should be little doubt about the need for that investigation. The probe by Independent Counsel Donald Smaltz into allegations of criminal activity in the Agriculture Department resulted in many guilty pleas. Corruption within executive departments must be fully investigated to serve as a deterrent to other agencies and regulatory bodies.

What is left? The investigation of Henry Cisneros, secretary of the Department of Housing and Urban Development, ended with a guilty plea, no charges were brought against Babbitt, and the Herman investigation continues.

Regarding Starr, it is true that his jurisdiction was repeatedly expanded, but each time it was necessary for Reno to go to the special panel of federal judges and receive their approval to widen Starr's field of inquiry. Like Walsh pursuing Iran-Contra, Starr found that a great deal of the expense, delay, and burdens of his investigation came from factors beyond his control, including obstruction from his targets and their friends.

Even if one could say that Starr overstepped at times, why should the record of a single prosecutor undermine the value of the independent counsel statute? Two decades of experience provide no pattern of reckless and insensitive prosecution.

Complaints about independent counsel expenditures are almost totally partisan. Democrats did not care how much Lawrence Walsh spent on Iran-Contra; Republicans were livid at the cost. Party positions reversed entirely once it came to Kenneth Starr's budget. No one asks the Justice Department how much it spent for prosecutions related to the World Trade Center, the Oklahoma City bombings, or the current campaign-finance probe. Investigations are expensive, but much of the Walsh and Starr costs came from responses to White House and Justice Department obstruction.

Clearly the Independent Counsel statute needs major changes. If an independent counsel like Starr cannot complete initial assignments (Travelgate and Filegate), the attorney general should not add other duties (Monica Lewinsky). Also, Starr pursued too many side activities: private litigation, teaching, and speeches to organizations hostile to President Clinton. Independent counsels need to complete their work expeditiously and professionally. Even when their work is exemplary, however, once the investigation uncovers illegal or embarrassing conduct by the president and White House aides, there will be unceasing and often irresponsible attacks on the independent counsel.

Conclusion

Much of what happened in Starr's investigation could not have been anticipated. The lockstep loyalty of Democrats was extraordinary. Only five Democrats in the House voted for impeachment. After the House impeachment, many Democrats traipsed over to the White House for a Clinton "pep rally." This public show of solidarity occurred after House Democrats had drafted a scathing censure resolution accusing Clinton of "egregiously" failing in his constitutional obligations, violating the trust of the American people, lessening their esteem for the presidency, dishonoring the office, making false statements about "his reprehensible conduct with a subordinate," and "wrongly" taking steps "to delay discovery of the truth."[42] Not a single Democratic senator voted guilty on the two articles, notwithstanding statements for the record that many of them thought that Starr had made his case on Clinton's perjury and obstruction of justice.

Public opinion and interest group positions undercut Starr. Public support remained high for Clinton's performance in office and his policies. Many of these arguments were silly: the stock market is up, unemployment and inflation are down. Had economic indicators turned sour, would that have justified Clinton's impeachment and removal from office? Impeachment cannot make headway in this climate.

Had women's groups remained faithful to their principles (that a supervisor abuses power when engaging in sex with a subordinate and that sex under these conditions is not consensual), the result might have been different. Here we had a president involved sexually with

THE INDEPENDENT COUNSEL STATUTE

a White House intern. Even more graphic, the Commander in Chief had sex with an employee who worked in the Pentagon. But these groups decided that loyalty to Clinton's policies was more important than their often-stated values. These factors, among others, enabled Clinton to escape removal. Judgments about his character will not be as kind.

Notes

1. For a detailed study of techniques used by the White House in responding to independent counsel investigations, see Charles Tiefer, "The Specially Investigated President," University of Chicago Law School Roundtable, 5, p. 143 (1998).

2. Ken Gormley, *Archibald Cox: Conscience of a Nation* (Reading, Mass.: Addison-Wesley, 1997), 246.

3. Ibid.

4. Ibid., p. 250.

5. In his memoirs, Nixon wrote: "No White House in history could have survived the kind of operation Cox was planning. If he were determined to get me, as I was certain that he and his staff were, then given the terms of their charter it would only be a matter of time until they had bored like termites through the whole executive branch." Richard M. Nixon, *The Memoirs of Richard Nixon* (New York: Simon & Schuster, 1978), 912.

6. Gormley, *Archibald Cox: Conscience,* 274–77.

7. 92 Stat. 1867–75 (1978).

8. 96 Stat. 2039 (1983).

9. 101 Stat. 1293 (1987).

10. *Morrison v. Olson,* 487 U.S. 654 (1988).

11. Senate Committee on Foreign Relations, *Security and Development Assistance,* hearings on S. 660, 99th Cong., 1st sess., 1995, 910.

12. House Committee on Appropriations, *Department of Defense Appropriations for 1986,* part 2, 99th Cong., 1st sess., 1985, 1092.

13. Lawrence E. Walsh, *Firewall: The Iran-Contra Conspiracy and Cover-Up* (New York: Norton, 1997), 210–11, 218–19.

14. Ibid., 415, 419.

15. Ibid., 285–86, 313, 423, 446.

16. Ibid., 531.

17. "Law Firm Gave Starr a $163,000 Raise," *Washington Post,* 14 September 1997, A8.

18. Ibid.

19. Statement by Senator Robert Torricelli, 144 *Cong. Rec.* S626 (daily ed. February 11, 1998).

20. *Broussard v. Meineke Discount Muffler Shops, Inc.,* 155 F.3d 331 (4th Cir 1998).

21. "Excerpts from Session that Led to the Indictment of Susan McDougal," *New York Times,* 5 May 1998, A26.

22. "Lott Urges Starr to End Probe Soon," *Washington Post,* 7 March 1998, A7.

23. "Blumenthal Recounts His Media Contacts," *Washington Post,* 27 February 1998, A1; "A Clinton Adviser Details Testimony," *New York Times,* 27 February 1998, A1.

24. H. Doc. No. 105-316 (Part 1), 105th Cong., 2d Sess. (1998), 206.

25. Anthony Lewis, "Decency and Liberty," *New York Times,* 9 February 1998, A23.

26. 28 U.S.C. §595(c) (1994).

27. 80 Cong. Rec. 5607 (1936).

28. 145 Cong. Rec. S1636 (daily ed. February 12, 1999).

29. Ibid., S1568.

30. Ibid., S1546–47, S1669–1671.

31. Ibid., S1595.

32. Ibid., S1554–55.

33. Ibid., S1599.

34. Ibid., S1462–64.

35. Ibid., S1560–61.

36. Ibid., S1561.

37. Ibid., S1639.

38. Ibid., S1546.

39. Ibid., S1501.

40. Ibid., S1505.

41. "Brown Business Partner Indicted," *Washington Post,* 14 March 1998, A1.

42. *Congressional Quarterly Weekly Report,* 12 December 1998, 3294.

F I V E

Executive Privilege in the Clinton Scandal

Mark J. Rozell

$\mathbf{D}$uring the Lewinsky scandal, the president and several of his advisers made extensive use of the presidential power of executive privilege. Although it is nowhere mentioned in the Constitution, executive privilege is an implied power that enables presidents and high-level executive branch officers to withhold information from Congress, the courts, and ultimately the public.

In most cases, executive privilege controversies are legislative-executive disputes. Congress requests a document or testimony from an executive branch official, the White House refuses, citing the doctrine of executive privilege. In the Lewinsky scandal, the president and some of his advisers (including the first lady) asserted executive privilege to thwart the investigation of the Office of Independent Counsel (OIC).

Executive privilege is a controversial power. Some scholars suggest that it is not a legitimate presidential power at all (Berger 1974; Prakash 1999). According to their interpretation, because executive privilege is not mentioned in the Constitution, it lacks legal standing. Raoul Berger goes so far as to call executive privilege "a constitutional myth," and Saikrishna Prakash agrees that just because presidential secrecy has utility, that does not make it legal.

Those arguments indeed are truly academic at this point. Extensive presidential use of executive privilege and court decisions validated that power. The more common debate today is whether particular uses of executive privilege have merit. Precedents and case law have established certain standards for the proper use of executive privilege. In general, executive privilege has legitimacy when it is applied to certain national security needs and to protect the privacy of White House deliberations when it is in the public interest to do so.

The Clinton administration made extensive and improper use of executive privilege in the Lewinsky scandal. Although the president's attorneys asserted some valid arguments in defense of executive privilege, their position ultimately failed because the debate with the OIC was not over the basic legitimacy of that power but, rather, over the application of it in the context of a presidential sex scandal.

One of the original proposed articles of impeachment against President Clinton concerned abuse of powers, in particular executive privilege. Many of the advocates of Clinton's impeachment argued reasonably that the use of executive privilege to conceal wrongdoing and to frustrate and thwart the legitimate inquiries of the OIC constituted an abuse of presidential powers. Yet the executive privilege language did not stay in the article eventually voted out by the House Judiciary Committee (and later rejected by the full House). The authors of this article of impeachment either lacked sufficient confidence in their own constitutional argument or they simply believed that the chances of House approval were too slim.

The confusion over whether to proceed with the charge of abuse of executive privilege evidenced the fact that for many the proper parameters of this constitutional doctrine remain unclear. During much of 1998 Clinton's lawyers argued that the president has a broad-based right to assert executive privilege and that to deny that claim is to do nothing less than to strip away the legal protections for confidential White House deliberations. The OIC countered that the Clinton scandal involved personal rather than official government matters and therefore the White House's various claims of executive privilege could not stand. Each side cited substantial constitutional law, scholarly opinion, and historic precedents in defense of its case ("Ruff's Argument," 1998; "White House Motion Seeking Privilege," 1998).

Judge Norma Holloway Johnson ultimately sided with the OIC—not because she believed that Clinton's arguments in defense of executive privilege were weak but, rather, because Independent Counsel Kenneth Starr had made a compelling showing of need for access to the information shielded by executive privilege. Judge Johnson applied the classic constitutional balancing test, similar to that of the unanimous decision in *United States v. Nixon* (418 U.S. 683, 1974): in a criminal investigation the need for evidence outweighs any presidential claim to secrecy ("Judge Johnson's Order," 1998).

Judge Johnson's decision resolved the immediate controversy but it did little to clarify the proper parameters of executive privilege. As a consequence, the OIC declared victory because it achieved access to testimony crucial to the investigation. The White House declared victory because the judge had upheld the principle of executive privilege. After then dropping its claim of executive privilege, the White House later asserted additional claims as the investigation moved forward (see "Referral to the U.S. House of Representatives," 1998).

To better understand Clinton's use of executive privilege in the context of the Lewinsky scandal, it is necessary first to examine the earlier presidential exercises of that power; second, to also describe the evolution of that power in light of the events of the Watergate scandal; and, third, to describe and assess Clinton's use of executive privilege both prior to and during the Lewinsky scandal.

Executive Privilege in History

Executive privilege is an implied power derived from Article II. It is most easily defined as the right of the president and high-level executive branch officers to withhold information from those who have compulsory power—Congress and the courts (and, therefore, ultimately the public). This right is not absolute. The modern understanding of executive privilege has evolved over a long period—the result of presidential actions, official administration policies, and court decisions.

As in so many areas, President Washington had a profound influence on the development of executive privilege because of the precedents he established. In the first controversy over executive withholding of information from Congress, the president decided that he indeed possessed such a power, but only if his actions were in the service of the public interest. Washington determined that he could not withhold information merely for the purpose of concealing politically damaging or embarrassing information.

The particular circumstance involved the disastrous November 1791 St. Clair military expedition against Native Americans in which General St. Clair lost many of his troops and supplies. The loss being a huge embarrassment to the administration, Congress convened an investigation and directed the president to turn over any documents or information germane to the decision to initiate the expedition. The political temptation for the president not to cooperate was clear.

With the unanimous advice of his cabinet, the president determined that he had the right under the Constitution to withhold the information, as long as it was in the public interest to do so. Thomas Jefferson attended the cabinet discussion and later recorded in his notes that the cabinet members had all determined "that the executive ought to communicate such papers as the public good would permit, and ought to refuse those, the disclosure of which would injure the public" (Ford 1892, 189–90). In the end Washington determined that there were no potentially serious public consequences to divulging the information, and he cooperated with the congressional investigation.

That Washington turned over all information requested by Congress in this controversy leads some to assert that this incident actually argues against the constitutional legitimacy of executive privilege (Berger 1974; Prakash 1999). The key point is that Washington first addressed the issue of the legitimacy of presidential withholding of information from Congress and concluded that the Constitution allows such an action. And of equal importance is that Washington set the precedent for use of executive privilege to protect the public interest, not the president's own political interests. On other occasions Washington asserted a right to withhold information, and he followed through on those claims.

In 1794 the U.S. Senate requested copies of diplomatic correspondence between U.S. officials and officials of the Republic of France. Washington believed that full disclosure of such correspondences was inappropriate. Again the president convened his cabinet, who all agreed that he had the right to withhold the information from Congress. Washington replied to the Senate that he would direct copies and translations of the correspondences be made available, "except in those particulars, in my judgment, for public considerations, ought not to be communicated" (Sofaer 1975, 1319). The Senate never challenged the president's right to withhold portions of the correspondences.

In 1796 the House requested from the administration information concerning the president's instructions to John Jay regarding treaty negotiations with Great Britain. Washington refused the House request and replied that "the nature of foreign negotiations requires caution, and their success must often depend on secrecy" (Richardson 1897, vol. 1, 186). The House reacted by passing a nonbinding resolution stating that Congress had a right to the information. During debate over the resolution, the principle author of the Constitution, Representative James Madison, spoke on the floor of the House and declared "that the executive had a right, under a due responsibility, also, to withhold information, when of a nature that did not permit a disclosure of it at the time" (5 *Annals of Congress* 1796, 773).[1] During the ratification stage, the Senate voted to keep the treaty secret, as Alexander Hamilton wrote, "because they thought it [the secrecy] the affair of the president to do as he thought fit" (Lodge 1903).

The secrecy decisions of other presidents from the constitutional period are germane to the debate over the origins and legitimacy of executive privilege. President John Adams withheld from Congress information germane to the 1798 "XYZ Affair." In response to a House request that the president make public certain diplomatic correspondences from the French government, the president mostly complied, although he omitted information that he deemed necessary to be kept secret (Chambers 1963, 134–35).

During his presidency Thomas Jefferson classified his correspondence as either public or secret. He withheld from Congress correspondence he deemed secret (Sofaer 1977, 16–17). In 1807 Jefferson denied a congressional request for information about the Aaron Burr conspiracy. A House resolution requested that the president "lay before this House any information in the possession of the Executive, except such as he may deem the public welfare to require not to be disclosed" (16 *Annals of Congress* 1806–1807, 336). It is significant that the House recognized the legitimacy of presidential withholding of information, when in furtherance of the public good. Jefferson responded that although Burr obviously was guilty of treason, it would be improper to divulge materials that would reveal the names of other alleged conspirators. The president wrote to the prosecutor in the case that it was "the necessary right of the President of the United States to decide, independently, what papers coming to him as President, the public interest permit to be communicated, and to whom" (Ford 1892, 55).

James Madison withheld information from Congress during his presidency. For example, he withheld information about French trade restrictions against the United States, which eventually led to widespread support for war against Great Britain (Sofaer 1977, 19–24). Madison, and then later President James Monroe, withheld information from Congress regarding the U.S. takeover of the Florida territory (Sofaer 1977, 28–45). In 1825 the House requested from Monroe information about the "Steward incident," except, most importantly, any details that the president determined it was not in the public interest to disclose (*House Journal* 1825, 102). Monroe refused to provide the information and replied that doing so "would not comport with the public interest" (Richardson 1897, vol. 2, 847).

These examples of presidential secrecy established precedents for the exercise of what we today call executive privilege. A common thread emerges in these early uses of executive privilege: these presidents and members of Congress accepted the legitimacy of such a power *when exercised in the service of the public interest.*

It is not possible here to recount all of the instances of presidential withholding of information. Several prominent examples will suffice. In 1848, in response to a House request for documents pertaining to the return of President General Lopez de Santa Anna to Mexico, President James Polk released only those deemed "compatible with the public interest to communicate" (Richardson 1897, vol. 5, 2415). Polk cited the precedent of Washington's 1796 message to Congress that a president had the authority to refuse to release documents "improper to be disclosed" (Richardson 1897, vol. 5, 2416–17). Later that year Polk acceded to a separate House request for documents but made it clear that he retained the power to withhold information when in "the public interest" to do so (Richardson 1897, vol. 6, 2529–37).

After President Theodore Roosevelt refused a Senate resolution requesting information from the attorney general, a Senate committee requested the same materials in the possession of the Bureau of Corporations. The president personally seized the documents and dared Congress to impeach him (Corwin 1957, 429–30). Roosevelt's objective, he said, was to ensure that the government's promise of secrecy to certain parties was upheld.

Executive Privilege and the Modern Presidency

Presidents Franklin Roosevelt, Harry Truman, and Dwight Eisenhower all refused on certain occasions to permit cabinet officers to testify before Congress about confidential matters (Rozell 1994, 43–44). Eisenhower holds the presidential record for assertions of executive privilege at more than forty. Many of those assertions amounted to refusals to comply with congressional requests for testimony from White House officials. Eisenhower felt so strongly about the principle that at one point he stated, "[A]ny man who testifies as to the advice he gave me won't be working for me that night" (Greenstein 1982, 205). A key event in the development of executive privilege was Eisenhower's letter of May 17, 1954, to the secretary of defense, instructing department employees not to comply with a congressional request to testify about confidential matters in the army-McCarthy hearings.

Eisenhower articulated the principle that candid advice was essential to the proper functioning of the executive branch and that limiting candor would ultimately harm "the public interest" (*Public Papers of Presidents* 1954, 483–84).

Although many of Eisenhower's uses of executive privilege were clearly justified, the breadth of his understanding of that power disturbed many. At one point he effectively declared that executive privilege belonged to the entire executive branch, when in fact over the course of history the practice had been to confine its use to the president and high-level White House officials when directed by the president. He declared all advice to the president not subject to the compulsory powers of the other branches, although the development of executive privilege law more recently has resulted in a key distinction between discussions about official governmental matters and those about private matters.

Eisenhower's administration originated the use of the phrase executive privilege and expanded the actual practice of that power. Members of Congress rightfully concerned about the expanded practice sought to rein in Eisenhower's successors through the articulation of standards for the use of executive privilege. Representative John Moss (D-Calif.), the chairman of the House Subcommittee on Government Information, led the effort. Beginning with the Kennedy administration, Moss sent letters to successive presidents, requesting written clarification of policy toward the use of executive privilege. President John Kennedy replied that executive privilege "can be invoked only by the president and will not be used without specific presidential approval" (Mollenhoff 1962, 239). President Lyndon Johnson similarly responded to a letter from Moss: "the claim of 'executive privilege' will continue to be made only by the president" (*Executive Privilege* 1971, 35).

Ironically, President Richard Nixon responded most forthrightly to Moss's inquiry when he wrote: "the scope of executive privilege must be very narrowly construed. Under this Administration, executive privilege will not be asserted without specific presidential approval. . . . I want open government to be a reality in every way possible" (Nixon to Moss, 1969). Nixon issued the first detailed presidential memorandum specifically on the proper use of executive privilege.

> The policy of this Administration is to comply to the fullest extent possible with Congressional requests for information. While the Executive branch has the responsibility of

withholding certain information the disclosure of which would be incompatible with the public interest, this Administration will invoke this authority only in the most compelling circumstances and after a rigorous inquiry into the actual need for its exercise. For those reasons Executive privilege will not be used without specific Presidential approval (Nixon to Executive Department Heads, 1982).

The memorandum outlined the procedure to be used whenever a question of executive privilege was raised. If a department head believed that a congressional request for information might concern privileged information, he would consult with the attorney general. The two of them would then decide whether to release the information to Congress or to submit the matter to the president through the counsel to the president. At that stage, the president either would instruct the department head to claim executive privilege with presidential approval or request that Congress give some time to the president to make a decision.

The story of Nixon's vast abuse of executive privilege is well known and analyzed in detail elsewhere (Rozell 1994, chap. 3). Nonetheless, Nixon's response to Moss and the executive privilege memorandum were important to the development of standard procedures on the scope and application of that doctrine.

Unfortunately, Nixon's practices gave executive privilege a bad name and had a profoundly chilling effect on the ability of his immediate successors either to clarify procedures or properly exercise that power. President Gerald Ford began what became a common post-Watergate practice of avoiding executive privilege inquiries and using other constitutional or statutory powers to justify withholding information. Within a week of Ford's inauguration, Representative Moss sent his usual inquiry to the president requesting a statement on executive privilege policy (Moss to Ford, 1974). Unlike Presidents Kennedy, Johnson, and Nixon, Ford ignored the letter. Other members of Congress weighed in with their own requests and Ford ignored their letters too. Numerous discussions took place within the White House over the need for the president to either reaffirm or modify Nixon's official executive privilege procedures. Ford took no action on the recommendations.

The associate counsel to the president summed up the dilemma nicely when he suggested three options: (1) cite exemptions from the

Freedom of Information Act "rather than executive privilege" as the basis for withholding information; (2) use executive privilege only as a last resort—even avoid the use of the phrase in favor of "presidential" or "constitutional privilege"; or (3) issue formal guidelines on executive privilege (Chapman to Buchen, 1974). Ford chose to handle executive privilege controversies on a case-by-case basis rather than to issue general guidelines. He understood that for many people "executive privilege" and "Watergate" had become joined.

President Jimmy Carter similarly did not respond to congressional requests for clarification of administration policy on executive privilege. It was not until the week before the 1980 election that the Carter administration established some official executive privilege procedures. On October 31, 1980, White House Counsel Lloyd Cutler issued an executive privilege memorandum to White House staff and heads of units within the executive office of the president. The memorandum established that those considering the use of executive privilege must first seek the concurrence of the office of counsel to the president. The memorandum also emphasized that only the president had the authority to waive executive privilege (Lloyd Cutler to Heads of All Units, 1980). Cutler later would become counsel to the president in the Clinton administration and in 1994 would write new procedures on the use of executive privilege.

On November 4, 1982, President Ronald Reagan issued an executive privilege memorandum to heads of executive departments and agencies. The Reagan procedures dovetailed closely with the 1969 Nixon memorandum. For example, Reagan's guidelines affirmed the administration policy "to comply with congressional requests for information to the fullest extent consistent with the constitutional and statutory obligations of the executive branch." The memorandum reaffirmed the need for "confidentiality of some communications" and added that executive privilege would be used "only in the most compelling circumstances, and only after careful review demonstrates that assertion of the privilege is necessary." Finally, "executive privilege shall not be invoked without specific presidential authorization."

The Reagan memorandum developed greater clarity of procedures than before. All congressional requests must be accommodated unless "compliance raises a substantial question of executive privilege." Such a question arises if the information "might significantly impair the national security (including the conduct of foreign relations), the deliberative process of the executive branch or other aspects of the performance of the executive branch's constitutional duties." Under these procedures, if a department head believed that a congressional request for information might concern privileged information, he or she would notify and consult with both the attorney general and the counsel to the president. Those three individuals would then decide to release the information to Congress, or have the matter submitted to the president for a decision if any one of them believed that it was necessary to invoke executive privilege. At that point, the department head would ask Congress to await a presidential decision. If the president chose executive privilege, he instructed the department head to inform Congress "that the claim of executive privilege is being made with the specific approval of the president." The Reagan memorandum allowed for the use of executive privilege, even if the information originated from staff levels far removed from the Oval Office (Reagan to Heads of Executive Departments, 1982).

By avoiding executive privilege, Presidents Ford and Carter actually succeeded more than Reagan did at protecting secrecy. Ford and Carter understood in the post-Watergate era the negative connotations of executive privilege. President Reagan tried to reestablish the legitimacy of executive privilege, only to be harshly criticized and fought against every step of the way by the opposition party–led Congress. Reagan ultimately backed down from his several claims of executive privilege and did more to weaken the doctrine as a result (Rozell 1994, chap. 4 and 5).

President George Bush did not initiate any new executive privilege procedures. The 1982 Reagan memorandum remained in effect as official executive privilege policy during the Bush years. Bush frequently withheld information without invoking executive privilege. Like Ford and Carter, he avoided the negative taint of executive privilege and generally used other bases of authority for withholding information. When the Bush administration wanted to withhold information from Congress, it used a variety of terms other than executive privilege to justify that action. Among them were "internal departmental deliberations," "deliberations of another agency," and the "secret opinions policy" (Rozell 1994, chap. 5). The chief investigator to the House Committee on the Judiciary during the Bush years said that Bush "avoided formally claiming executive privilege and instead called it other things. In reality, executive privilege was in full force and effect during the Bush years, probably more so than under Reagan" (Lewin interview).

Executive Privilege in the Clinton Administration

President Clinton used executive privilege elaborately. Unlike Bush, he did not conceal executive privilege. Like Nixon, he concealed wrongdoing—or tried to—by resorting to executive privilege. Like Nixon, Clinton gave executive privilege a bad name and made it difficult once again for a future president to reestablish the legitimacy of this constitutional doctrine.

In 1994, the Clinton administration issued its own executive privilege procedures. In the memorandum from the special counsel to the president Lloyd Cutler stated: "The policy of this Administration is to comply with congressional requests for information to the fullest extent consistent with the constitutional and statutory obligations of the Executive Branch. . . . [E]xecutive privilege will be asserted only after careful review demonstrates that assertion of the privilege is necessary to protect Executive Branch prerogatives." The memorandum further stated, "Executive privilege belongs to the President, not individual departments or agencies."

The Cutler memorandum described formal procedures for the use of executive privilege, and these were not significantly different from those outlined in the Reagan memorandum. In light of Clinton's aggressive use of executive privilege in the presidential scandal of 1998–1999, one sentence stands out: "In circumstances involving communications relating to investigations of personal wrongdoing by government officials, it is our practice not to assert executive privilege, either in judicial proceedings or in congressional investigations and hearings" (Lloyd Cutler to All Executive Departments, 1994).

The Clinton administration also adopts the very broad view that all White House communications are presumptively privileged and that Congress has a less valid claim to executive branch information when conducting oversight than when considering legislation (Reno to Clinton, 20 September, 30 September, 1996).[2] On several occasions the administration has used executive privilege to thwart congressional investigations of alleged White House wrongdoing.

The Clinton administration did not limit its use of executive privilege to matters pertaining to the Lewinsky scandal. In fact, the administration made extensive and controversial use of that power prior to the scandal. Because executive privilege is a secrecy power, it is often challenging to obtain a complete record of actual presidential claims for recent administrations. Evidence to date suggests that the Clinton administration claimed executive privilege perhaps as many as six times prior to the Lewinsky scandal. Several of those cases are revealing of Clinton's broad use of executive privilege.

The most prominent case was the administration's refusal to turn over documents from its 1994 ethics review of Secretary of Agriculture Mike Espy. An independent counsel accused Espy of bribery and of accepting various illegal gifts including one worth approximately $34,000 from a company regulated by the Agriculture Department. In June 1997 the independent counsel requested eighty-four documents concerning the Espy investigation. Later that year an appeals court declared that the claim of executive privilege in this case had been overcome by the OIC's need for the documents in a criminal investigation. Judge Patricia Wald nonetheless issued a sweeping opinion in which she ruled that executive privilege generally protects communications among White House advisers as well as discussions and written correspondences with the president (*In Re: Sealed Case,* 121 F.3d 729, 1997).

Another controversial use of executive privilege involved an internal administration memorandum that was critical of U.S. antidrug policy. At the request of the Pentagon, FBI Director Louis Freeh wrote a memorandum on administration antidrug efforts. Freeh's wording was critical of the president's leadership. A House subcommittee requested a copy of the memorandum. Clinton refused, claiming executive privilege. In part, this claim rested on the valid position that there is a strong governmental interest in protecting the privacy of internal administration correspondences. Yet Republican leaders of the subcommittee maintained that the president was merely covering up information that was embarrassing rather than crucial to protecting the public interest. The fact that this dispute occurred in the midst of an election year furthered suspicions on both sides of political motivations.

Even if the Republicans truly did have partisan motives and wanted to embarrass the president in an election year, that does not make the claim of executive privilege valid. If revealing internal deliberations posed no real threat to the national security or to the public interest, Congress's request for the information must override the privilege unless it can be demonstrated that Congress's actions were outside the scope of any legitimate investigation. The burden is on the president to prove a compelling need to withhold information and not on Congress to prove that it has the right to investigate. Clinton never made a case that releasing the memorandum would cause undue harm. It appeared that he stood to harm only his own political standing by releasing a document that contained embarrassing information. The president never proved that Congress's inquiry lacked any legitimate basis under the normal legislative power of investigation.

In this particular case the president requested the opinion of his attorney general on the use of executive privilege. Attorney General Janet Reno backed the president's claim. Yet Reno's argument in defense of the president's action rested on the dubious assumption that in cases of investigations rather than legislation, Congress has a much weaker claim to executive branch information.

In January 1996 the administration claimed executive privilege to protect some three thousand White House Travel Office documents from congressional investigators. The administration had earlier fired several Travel Office employees and ordered FBI investigations of possible criminal activity by the officials. The firings were highly controversial, and critics suggested that the president and first lady had embarked on the firings in order to reward cronies with the jobs. In May 1996 a House subcommittee held White House counsel Jack Quinn and aides David Watkins and Michael Moore in contempt of Congress for refusing to comply with the congressional requests for documents. The White House eventually released the documents, and the evidence clearly shows that the use of executive privilege in this case lacked merit. Documents for which the president claimed executive privilege included those involving discussions between the first lady and White House staff, and White House talking points for sympathetic Democratic committee members, among other materials not traditionally covered by executive privilege.

In one case the evidence to date seems to support the president's claim of executive privilege. In 1996 the House Committee on International Relations subpoenaed 47 White House and State Department documents concerning U.S. policy toward Haiti. The House requested these materials in light of accusations that U.S.-trained security forces of the Haitian regime were involved in political assassinations and that efforts to stop drug trafficking from Haiti to the U.S. were a failure. White House counsel Jack Quinn notified the committee that the president claimed executive privilege over the documents. Republican committee leaders again alleged coverup, and the White House claimed that the documents protected sensitive national security information. In this case the House committee had pushed for memoranda from the national security adviser to the president, lending credibility to Clinton's position that releasing the documents might harm national security. The House committee ultimately did not fight the president's claim of privilege, making it impossible to fully judge the president's action.

Executive Privilege in the Lewinsky Scandal

How does Clinton's use of executive privilege in the Lewinsky investigation measure up to the legal standards that have been developed to control its applications? There was obviously no national security justification to withholding information about presidential and staff discussions over how to handle that episode, although Clinton's White House counsel tried to make the argument that by harming "the president's ability to 'influence' the public," the investigation undermined his ability to lead foreign policy ("Ruff's Argument" 1998). The White House case for executive privilege ultimately hinged on the claim that the president had the right to protect the privacy of internal deliberations.

As correctly decided in the Mike Espy case (*In Re: Sealed Case*, 1997), presidents are entitled to candid, confidential advice. The executive privilege extends to presidential advisers because they must be able to deliberate and discuss policy options without fear of public disclosure of their every utterance. Without that protection, the candor and quality of presidential advice would clearly suffer.

The Clinton administration maintained that this decision justified any claims of privilege on behalf of discussions between the president and his aides, between and among aides, and even between the first lady and an aide. As a general principle, it is correct that such discussions can be covered by the privilege, although extending such protection to the first lady is very controversial.

Executive privilege for the first lady is unprecedented and, regarding her deliberations during the Lewinsky investigation, quite likely a real stretch of the doctrine. To properly cover the first lady with a claim of executive privilege, it would have to be established that (1) she has an official position in her husband's administration; (2) in such a capacity, she has played an active role in those matters and participated in some of those official discussions that led to a claim of executive privilege; and (3) such discussions concern matters that actually deserve the protection of the privilege.

The key issue is whether the White House discussions indeed had anything to do with official governmental business as opposed to being merely deliberations over how to handle political strategy during a scandal. Judge Norma Holloway Johnson ultimately ruled against

Clinton's use of executive privilege in the Lewinsky investigation. Although much of her reasoning gave credibility to some debatable White House arguments, she correctly determined that the balancing test weighed in favor of Independent Counsel Kenneth Starr's need for access to information that was crucial to a criminal investigation.

For the White House position to have prevailed, Clinton needed to make a compelling argument that the public interest would somehow suffer from the release of information about White House discussions over the Lewinsky investigation. Not only had he failed to do so, but for months he even refused to answer basic questions as to whether he had formally invoked the privilege.

Once Judge Johnson ruled against Clinton, the White House dropped its flawed claim of executive privilege. In an obvious face-saving gesture, White House counsel Charles Ruff declared victory because Judge Johnson, in ruling against the president, had nonetheless upheld the legitimacy of the principle of executive privilege and therefore had preserved this presidential power for Clinton's successors.

The doctrine of executive privilege certainly did not need this kind of help. That doctrine already stood as an unarguably legitimate presidential power, although one clearly tainted in the public mind by the Watergate episode. Reestablishing the good reputation of executive privilege required a much more compelling circumstance for its exercise than a personal scandal—a military action, for example.

Further, there is little evidence from this episode to suggest that the Clinton White House undertook this drawn-out battle merely to make a principled stand on executive privilege. All evidence to date suggests that Clinton used executive privilege to frustrate and delay the investigation—all the while successfully convincing most of the public that the blame for the inquiry taking so long and costing so much belonged to the OIC.

Although the White House publicly claimed victory in protecting the principle of executive privilege and led everyone to believe that the issue was no longer germane to the investigation, additional claims of the privilege followed. In August 1998 a White House attorney and deputy White House counsel claimed executive privilege in testimony before the grand jury. Clinton told the grand jury that he merely wanted to protect the constitutional principle and did not want to further challenge the independent counsel's victory; yet the president several days later challenged one unfavorable court ruling and directed another aide to assert executive privilege.

For months, the Clinton White House clearly did a masterful job of presenting its case before the court of public opinion. The president's approval ratings remained strong, and most of the public had tired of the scandal and had become convinced that Starr lacked the objectivity necessary to conduct a fair investigation.

Many observers may ask why this dispute—and the politically motivated effort to delay its obvious resolution—mattered. Because executive privilege embodies the principle that no one is above the law—not even a president and not even when that president might otherwise be seen as a great foreign policy leader (Nixon) or as contributing to a thriving economy (Clinton). White House efforts to obstruct and delay for the sake of some perceived political advantage cynically undermined both the privilege and the principle. Regarding executive privilege, Clinton's legacy appears to be not that of a president who reestablished this necessary power but, rather, like Nixon before him, that of one who gave executive privilege a bad name (Rozell 1999).

Conclusion

Executive privilege clearly is a constitutional power. Since the Nixon years, presidents have not made effective use of that power. Some have devised means of concealing executive privilege, and some have used that power improperly. Congress has shown little deference toward presidential secrecy. The reality is that presidents have secrecy needs and Congress has investigative powers. Executive privilege inevitably leads to interbranch clashes—usually between the president and Congress, but most recently and prominently between the president and the OIC.

President Clinton benefited from his use of executive privilege in the Lewinsky scandal. By claiming that power, the president time and again thwarted the efforts of the OIC to conduct a full and timely investigation. Although the president lost the key legal battles and ultimately weakened executive privilege for his successors, he succeeded in delaying the OIC investigation and bought his administration crucial time to wage a public relations campaign against the investigation. Over time the White House indeed succeeded in convincing much of the public that the OIC investigation was a partisan-motivated travesty. Regrettably, critics of executive privilege for years to come may point to President Clinton's misdeeds as evidence that the doctrine of executive privilege, not the administration that misused it, was the problem. It will take a long time indeed for executive privilege to overcome this stigma and become a generally accepted presidential power.

Notes

1. There are two different readings of the House action. When I previously discussed this case of executive privilege, Professor Saikrishna Prakash argued that he was more persuaded by the fact that a majority of the House rejected Washington's claim, whereas Judge Kenneth Starr retorted, "I'll go with Madison" ("Executive Privilege," 1998).

2. The administration draws its view that Congress lacks a compelling need for executive branch information in cases of oversight from a dubious interpretation of the D.C. circuit court's 1974 ruling in *Senate Select Committee on Presidential Campaign Activities v. Nixon* (498 F.2d 725). Although the court did not explicitly acknowledge Congress's need for information in cases of oversight, that is not the same as saying that the court overruled the well-established investigative powers of legislative committees. The Reagan and Bush administrations similarly made too broad claims in this regard.

References

Annals of Congress, 5:1791.

Annals of Congress, 16:1806–07.

Berger, Raoul. 1974. *Executive Privilege: A Constitutional Myth.* Cambridge, Mass.: Harvard University Press.

Chambers, William Nisbet. 1963. *Political Parties in a New Nation: The American Experience, 1776–1809.* London: Oxford University Press.

Chapman, Dudley to Philip W. Buchen et al. 5 November 1974. Memorandum. Folder: "Executive Privilege—General (1)," Box 13. Edward Schmults Files, Gerald R. Ford Library, Ann Arbor, Mich.

Corwin, Edward S. 1957. *The President: Office and Powers, 1787–1957,* 4th ed. New York: New York University Press.

Cutler, Lloyd to All Executive Department and Agency General Councils. 28 September 1994. Memorandum. Copy obtained by author.

Cutler, Lloyd N. to Heads of All Units within the Executive Office of the President and Senior White House Staff. 31 October 1980. Memorandum. File: "Executive Privilege, 6/77–11/80." Box 74, Lloyd Cutler Files, Jimmy Carter Library, Atlanta, Ga.

Executive Privilege. 1971. U.S. Senate, 92nd Congress, 1st sess. Hearings Before the Subcommittee on Separation of Powers of the Committee on the Judiciary.

"Executive Privilege: 25 Years after *Nixon.*" 1998. University of Minnesota Law School Forum, 24 October, Minneapolis, Minn.

Ford, Paul. 1892. *The Writings of Thomas Jefferson.* New York: Putnam.

Greenstein, Fred I. 1982. *The Hidden-Hand Presidency: Eisenhower as Leader.* (New York: Basic Books).

House Journal. 1825. 18th Congress, 2d Session.

In Re: Sealed Case, (121 F.3d 729, 1997).

"Judge Johnson's Order on Executive Privilege," issued 26 May 1998. <www.washingtonpost.com/wp-srv/politics/special/clinton/stories/order 052898.htm>

Lewin, James. 1992. Author interview. 19 November.

Lodge, Henry C., ed. 1903. *The Collected Works of Alexander Hamilton.* New York: Putnam, 10: 107.

Mollenhoff, Clark. 1962. *Washington Cover-Up.* Garden City, N.Y.: Doubleday.

Moss, Rep. John E. to President Gerald R. Ford. 15 August 1974. Folder: "Executive Privilege (2)," Box 13, Philip W. Buchen Files, Gerald R. Ford Library, Ann Arbor, Mich.

Nixon, President Richard M. to Executive Department Heads. 24 March 1969. Memorandum. Folder: "Executive Privilege [1973]," White House Staff Files, Ronald Ziegler Files, Nixon Presidential Materials Project, Alexandria, Va.

Nixon, President Richard M. to Rep. John E. Moss. 7 April 1969. Folder: "Executive Privilege (2)," Box 13, Edward Schmults Files, Gerald R. Ford Library, Ann Arbor, Mich.

Prakash, Saikrishna Bangalore. 1999. "A Comment on the Constitutionality of Executive Privilege." *Minnesota Law Review,* May: 1143–90.

The Public Papers of Presidents: Dwight D. Eisenhower, 1954. Washington, D.C.: Government Printing Office.

Reagan, President, to Heads of Executive Departments and Agencies. "Procedures Governing Responses to Congressional Requests for Information," 4 November 1982. Memorandum.

"Referral to the U.S. House of Representatives Pursuant to Title 28, U.S. Code 595C," Submitted by the Office of the Independent Counsel, 9 September 1998.

Reno, Attorney General Janet to President Clinton. 20 September 1996. Copy obtained by author.

Reno, Attorney General Janet to President Clinton. 30 September 1996. Copy obtained by author.

Richardson, James. 1897. *A Compilation of the Messages and Papers of the Presidents.* New York: Bureau of National Literature.

Rozell, Mark J. 1994. *Executive Privilege: The Dilemma of Secrecy and Democratic Accountability.* Baltimore: The Johns Hopkins University Press.

Rozell, Mark J. 1999. "Executive Privilege and the Modern Presidents: In Nixon's Shadow." *Minnesota Law Review,* May: 1069–1126.

"Ruff's Argument for Executive Privilege," unsealed 27 May 1998. <www.washingtonpost.com/wp-srv/politics/special/clinton/stories/ ruff052898.htm>

Schmitt, Gary J. 1981. "Executive Privilege: Presidential Power to Withhold Information from Congress," in Joseph Bessette and Jeffrey Tulis, eds. *The Presidency in the Constitutional Order.* (Baton Rouge: Louisiana State University Press), 154–94.

Sofaer, Abraham. 1977. "Executive Power and Control over Information: The Practice under the Framers," *Duke Law Journal 1977* (March): 1–48.

Sofaer, Abraham. 1975. "Executive Privilege: An Historical Note," *Columbia Law Review* 75:1319–24.

"White House Motion Seeking Privilege," filed 17 March 1998. <www.washingtonpost.com/wp-srv/politics/special/clinton/stories/whitehouse052898.htm>

SIX

"Below the Law"?

David A. Yalof and Joel B. Grossman

T he political and legal events surrounding the formal impeachment of President Bill Clinton by the House of Representatives
in December 1998 have raised, once again, the issue of whether the
president is, or should be, "above the law." This has been an enduring
concern of the American polity, debated at length in the context of
President Nixon's actions during the Watergate crisis. Assessing the
legitimacy of presidential actions, and his accountability for them,
however, is not furthered by catchy slogans or mere rhetoric that
obscure rather than illuminate important constitutional governance
issues. To contend that the president cannot be "above the law,"
without regard to context, the nature of the political system, the
president's role within it, and other circumstances reveals a serious
case of constitutional myopia. It is a fateful misreading of the purposes
and benefits of the doctrine of separation of powers. And such a
contention ignores the offsetting reality that by virtue of the position
he holds, a president may just as often be "below the law" for purposes
of civil litigation or other criminal matters.

The controversial issue we address here, whether the president
should in fact be placed above the law in certain contexts, has been
complicated by emerging questions of how to deal with his so-called
"unofficial" or "private" behavior. "Even presidents," Bill Clinton
told a national audience, "have private lives." But a president's private
life does not exist in a vacuum outside of his public life, and the law

100

must reflect this reality. The Supreme Court's many efforts to establish a rigid demarcation between a president's public and private behavior have thus been misguided. The Senate impeachment trial of Bill Clinton made clear just how difficult it is to apply this so-called "bright-line" distinction: House impeachment managers seeking more time to present their case before the Senate argued that it was necessary to have Monica Lewinsky testify live about the nature of her relationship with the president. By confirming the most "private" of details about an adulterous affair, they hoped to buttress their case that "public" crimes (perjury and obstruction of justice) may have been committed.

Given the realities of divided party government, the Independent Counsel statute, in effect since 1978, and ever more aggressive media coverage of the president, even a president's most private behavior (and reactions to it) will escalate quickly into matters of political, legal, and even constitutional significance. This chapter represents an effort to conceptualize the presidency holistically and to explore how the law and the Constitution should deal with "private" presidential actions that appear to lie outside the line of acceptable behavior. While this chapter flows from the Clinton impeachment controversy, its analysis and recommendations are not dependent on those particular events. Those events are used here to illustrate a problem of much broader import and applicability.

The nub of the dilemma, as suggested above, is the problematic private-public distinction formulated by the Supreme Court. The legal precedents established in *Nixon v. Fitzgerald*[1] and, more recently in *Clinton v. Jones*,[2] have contributed significantly to the current legal and political disarray. The former case concerned what could unarguably be considered "public" or "official" misbehavior: a retaliatory discharge by the president against an executive branch whistleblower. By contrast, the latter case lies at the opposite end of the public-private continuum: an alleged incident of sexual harassment by the president that occurred *prior* to his term in office.[3] Of course whether even the latter case is, for constitutional purposes, purely a "private" matter is complicated by assertions that, while president, Clinton (1) committed perjury in denying the allegations in a trial deposition, (2) committed perjury again when testifying about related matters before a grand jury, and (3) attempted to obstruct justice and suborn perjury to cover up his behavior. The Nixon administration's cover-up of a clearly public matter (the burglary of the opposing political party's national headquarters by individuals connected to the president) obviously fell within the "public sphere" of Nixon's presidency. By contrast, if the cover-up of private misdeeds that are nevertheless not illegal (such as an extramarital affair) will necessarily evolve into public matters, then *all* private actions by a president risk being brought under the guise of "official" or "public" matters. Consider the ultimate irony of the president's situation: only by preemptively airing his private matters to the public (and thus avoiding the cover-up) can the president keep such matters "private" in the eyes of the law. Not even President Clinton's most bitter enemies would contend that a president is obligated, upon demand, to reveal every single detail of his private life.

Thus, neither of the two precedents created in *Fitzgerald* and *Jones* helps to resolve the dilemma of how to draw effective public-private boundaries. Where does one place the myriad of cases that sit somewhere between these two ends of the spectrum? The Lewinsky affair illustrates most effectively why a president's "public" and "private" actions are nearly impossible to distinguish in theory or discern in practice. A sitting president is expected to publicly defend nonpresidential (or "prepresidential") actions (or inactions) but can only do so in a presidential context. Which controls the definition—the original acts (occurring either before becoming president or while president in a private capacity) or the president's response to them and the constitutional implications thereof? Viewed in this way, *no* act of a president can ever be considered purely private.

The President in Court: Defining the Chief Executive's Privileges and Immunities

Article II, Section 4 of the Constitution provides that the "President . . . Shall be removed from Office on impeachment for, and Conviction of, Treason, Bribery, or other high crimes and misdemeanors." Other than impeachment (or for disability under the 25th Amendment), the Constitution specifies no alternative way of removing a president before the expiration of the term. Nor does Article III (or for that matter, any federal statutory authority) vest the judiciary with the power to compel a president in office to answer in court for crimes or other wrongdoing that may have been committed. As far as the Constitution is concerned, primary oversight of presidential conduct is vested in Congress and the political system.

Notwithstanding this original understanding, both public and private presidential actions have been reviewed by the Courts. In foreign affairs, presidential power has rarely been constrained by constitutional pronouncements. Indeed, the Supreme Court has been exceptionally deferential to claims of executive power. For example, the Court approved the use of executive agreements to sidestep the need for Senate ratification of treaties under the Constitution.[4] More recently, the Court refused even to address the merits of the Senate's suit against President Carter to block his unilateral termination of the Taiwan Defense Treaty without congressional approval.[5] In military affairs the president has also received considerable deference from the courts. While Congress maintains the theoretical power to limit presidential war powers claims, as it attempted to do in the 1973 War Powers Act,[6] realistically it enjoys only restricted influence over the commander-in-chief.[7] Even when the Supreme Court has uncharacteristically criticized presidential actions, its admonitions have had little effect.[8]

By contrast, in domestic affairs the Supreme Court has done something of a "two-step" during the past fifty years, adopting language of deference to the institution of the *presidency* on the one hand, while still managing to impose prohibitions on *presidents* making specific claims. In *Youngstown Sheet & Tube Co. v. Sawyer,*[9] the White House (albeit in a losing effort) learned that it possessed an unenumerated right to act in emergencies in the absence of express congressional authorization or disapproval. In *United States v. Nixon,*[10] the Court, for the first time, formally articulated a doctrine of "executive privilege," although it held that President Nixon himself could not hide behind the privilege in refusing to turn over the Watergate tapes in response to a subpoena in a criminal prosecution. Eight years later, in *Nixon v. Fitzgerald,* five justices bestowed on the president an absolute immunity from private lawsuits concerning acts within the outer perimeter of his "*official*" (or "public") duties, arguing that, despite constitutional silence on the matter, such immunity was a "functionally mandated incident of his unique office."[11] Each of the above decisions concerned potentially illegal or unconstitutional presidential acts that occurred clearly within the public sphere of the president's responsibilities. Although one could argue that Nixon's actions to "obstruct justice" had private behavior implications, his original misbehavior was primarily a misuse of his constitutional authority rather than any wrongful private acts. Thus these same doctrines may or may not apply to mixed public-private behavior such as President Clinton's alleged actions in the Monica Lewinsky affair.

Discerning when and how the separation of powers doctrine, which was designed to deal with the allocation and division of public responsibilities and not private behavior, applies in "nonofficial" (or "semi-official") contexts thus presents a vexing problem. There is little precedent since, in the past, the improper private acts of most presidents were either shielded by the media and/or assumed to be nonactionable. Presidents could be confident that, while the electorate might judge them on any basis, legally (and practically) they retained some privacy in, and protection for, their personal behavior.

However, a number of recent political and legal developments (e.g., the litigation revolution, increased media scrutiny following Watergate, and the institution of the independent counsel) have further clouded this unofficial but long-standing public-private distinction.

Speaking for the majority in *Clinton v. Jones,* Justice Stevens wrote:

> Frequently our decisions have held that an official's absolute immunity should extend to actions in performance of particular functions of his office . . . immunities are grounded in "the nature of the function performed, not the identity of the actor who performed it."[12]

Unfortunately, Stevens's opinion glossed over the difficulty of actually drawing an effective line between a president's official and unofficial actions. It would have been better to recognize that the presidency is a unique office that may require at least some partial immunity merely by virtue of that office. Not only must a president forced into self-defense against specific charges while still in office expend ample financial resources on his own behalf, but also the White House bureaucracy must dedicate considerable time and energy waging a public relations war to defend its leader. Even before any formal accusations or allegations have been made public, the president will consider ways to prevent those allegations from being revealed. And as President Clinton himself can attest, the White House must concern itself not only with fending off impeachment charges (or the potential that they might eventually be brought) while he is still in office, but also with keeping the president out of legal jeopardy during and after he leaves office.

In sum, a president's response to allegations of purely private misbehavior may—surely will—have public implications. Dicta from past Supreme Court decisions addressing the president's relationship to the legal process may have offered Stevens some guidance in the *Jones* case, but those past decisions offer little help in resolving the public-private issue. They fail to define the appropriate constitutional methods for dealing with alleged private misbehavior, including when and how such behavior may be addressed by an independent counsel.

To be sure, many of the allegations that have been leveled at President Clinton throughout his nearly two terms in office fall somewhere on the spectrum between the *Fitzgerald* and *Jones* cases. But where? Allegations regarding the Whitewater business transactions, as well as Paula Jones's accusations of sexual harassment and the veracity of Clinton's testimony in that case, concerned prepresidential behavior. Yet what about allegations of a cover-up concerning the Vince Foster suicide and its relationship to Whitewater? Allegations regarding the firing of employees in the White House Travel Office? The controversy surrounding the Democratic Party's alleged violations of campaign finance laws in the 1996 presidential election? The line between official and unofficial behavior becomes ever more hazy as the jurisdiction of independent counsels escalates in accordance with partisan political demands and as civil lawsuits against the president multiply.

Presidential Responsibilities and Immunities: A More Effective Balance

Out of this doctrinal and conceptual confusion, three overriding questions emerge:

When, How, and Why Should the President Be "Above the Law"?

As Justice Scalia so eloquently stated in his dissenting opinion in *Morrison v. Olson*, ". . . when crimes are not investigated and prosecuted fairly, non-selectively, with a reasonable sense of proportion, the president pays the cost in political damage to his administration." [13] Failed reelection and impeachment are not merely the last resorts by which we check the executive under the Constitution; they are, with the exception of the Independent Counsel statute, the *only* such resorts.

Certainly it remains an open question whether a sitting president can even be criminally indicted in the first place. [14] With a president at least theoretically able to "pardon himself" from any federal indictment or conviction while still in office, [15] it would seem counterintuitive to permit criminal indictments of the president in the first place. But regardless of how that constitutional question is ultimately answered, at least two constitutional checks on the president still remain. First, criminal charges may be brought against the president (whether under federal law, state law, or both) upon the conclusion of his term in office. Once the president is treatable as a private citizen, there would be no restriction as to how such charges might be brought, save all the normal political pressures and legal privileges prosecutors across the country must routinely address. Concerns that the statute of limitations for such charges might lapse while waiting for the president's term to finish could be alleviated by congressional action to extend the statute in advance. Naturally, the political aspects of such a "postterm" indictment would be inescapable. A federal prosecutor entrusted with the discretion to bring such charges against a former president will no doubt feel pressure from both sides of the political spectrum: Political allies of the president will demand that charges not be brought so that the proverbial "healing process" may begin, while the president's enemies will no doubt press that "justice be done."[16] Many of those same arguments have already been raised in the context of Independent Counsel Kenneth Starr's astoundingly public consideration of whether to indict Clinton while he is still in office. Of course those same "political" factors enter the consideration of whether to indict any other suspect; all prosecutors must routinely balance the costs and benefits of each individual prosecution. To downplay the threat that future indictments might pose for a president would unnecessarily treat the president as "above" (i.e., not subject to) the criminal and civil codes other citizens must obey.

Second, given the events of late 1998, it now seems beyond argument that for all practical purposes the House of Representatives enjoys nearly unlimited discretion in determining the effective boundaries of "high crimes and misdemeanors."[17] Much scholarly debate has been waged in the past (and we expect it to continue) concerning the theoretical limits of the constitutionally authorized impeachment of a president. Given the fervent disagreement between the president's counsel and the House managers concerning whether the president's misdeeds constituted "public" or "private" misdeeds, it is impossible to know what precedent (if any) was established by the House of Representatives' decision to vote two articles of impeachment against President Clinton. Although the president's defenders might argue that the episode broke entirely new constitutional ground, others would disagree. This much we did learn: if those in the House of Representatives pressing for impeachment can gather a working majority to vote against the president, all of the president's references to history, logic, and the purpose of impeachment are rendered irrelevant. President Clinton fell victim in the House despite well above average levels of public support for his presidency and an intervening congressional election that sent five additional members of his own party to

Congress. The Senate also enjoys its own absolute discretion to vote "up" or "down" on any such articles. The constitutional reality of impeachment at the turn of the century is thus crystal clear: notwithstanding evidence that the Founders did indeed seek to limit the proper scope of impeachment to high crimes and misdemeanors, there exists no practical limit as to how the House of Representatives (and by implication the Senate) can interpret that phrase. President Clinton's acquittal by the Senate in no way negates the awesome power Congress seemingly enjoys when attempting to reel in unruly executives.

Both of the above-described checks (the threats of post-term indictment and impeachment) counsel against additional, extra-constitutional sanctions, such as forcing a sitting president to defend actions in a court of law. The time and energy expended by a president who must engage in self-defense against either a criminal prosecution or a myriad of civil lawsuits adds further weight to the argument that in a well-functioning constitutional democracy, we must accept some instances in which a president is above (or outside) the law. The purpose of shielding the president from legal action is not to create presidential license but, rather, to ensure that the system can function. At the core of the decision in *Clinton v. Jones* lay the assertion that "if the past is any indicator, it seems unlikely that a deluge of litigation will ever engulf the presidency." Justice Stevens's opinion relied on the factual premise that in the entire history of the Republic only three sitting presidents had ever been subject to civil lawsuits and that each of those cases had been quietly resolved.[18] Unfortunately, Stevens's reliance on history has proved to be a poor predictor of a modern president's legal vulnerability.

In modern times even one lawsuit may become unduly burdensome. Following the *Jones* decision, a virtual circus atmosphere erupted, drawing on much of the president's time and resources even after the trial judge dismissed the case.[19] From the Jones litigation rose the Lewinsky matter, which eventually cornered the market on media coverage. Cable news stations soon blanketed the airwaves with daily news of "the White House in crisis," and MSNBC became the network laughingly referred to as "all-Monica, all-the-time." Just as opponents of Clinton benefited from these numerous new opportunities to mobilize support for their case against the president, the White House responded in kind, unleashing its own talking heads onto those same news shows as part of an elaborate public relations strategy. The rise of the Internet as a means of mass news distribution allowed columnist

Matt Drudge and others to fan the flames on a nearly hourly basis with new information about the president's legal troubles. Thus, in the two years since *Clinton v. Jones* was handed down, the Court's various assumptions about the expenditures of presidential resources already seem wholly unrealistic. Justice Stevens's opinion failed to pick up on the greater difficulty that is endemic in any so-called private litigation against a sitting president. As Professor David Strauss summed it up, "Any private lawsuit against the president is bound to become much more than a private case."[20]

When Is the President "Below the Law"?

By virtue of his status as head of the executive branch, a president must be prepared to sacrifice certain privacy rights that most ordinary citizens take for granted. As with all public officials, the burden is considerably greater for a president trying to prove a case of libel.[21] As a consequence, every detail of the president's life risks coming under the public's microscope. The president may also enjoy less constitutional protection of privacy because, as Jeffrey Rosen points out, the president necessarily lives and works in the same place and thus is constantly scrutinized even in the presidential private quarters.[22] Thus the virtual fishbowl that presidents must live in renders them more vulnerable than most to the threat of routine legal process. This loss of personal privacy may be a necessary (and constitutionally acceptable) burden of the office, but should it also become the basis for exposing the president to legal actions that citizens outside the public glare are unlikely to face?

As part of the fallout from Watergate, presidents also have been forced to labor under additional and unique legal burdens. Most notably, the advent of the independent counsel, a product of the Ethics in Government Act of 1978,[23] has subjected four presidents (and to a lesser degree other high-level executive branch officials) to a uniquely invasive brand of prosecutorial discretion and invasive inquiry. An independent counsel enjoys statutory authority to "fully investigate and prosecute" the subject matter under his jurisdiction, as well as "all matters related to that subject matter."[24] Originally the independent counsel law was created to deal with the public wrongs of certain public officials, but in 1998 it was de facto expanded by the combined actions of Kenneth Starr and Attorney General Janet Reno (who authorized Starr's jurisdiction over the Lewinsky affair) to include the essentially private behavior of a president that might have public implications. As we noted above, such an enlargement of independent counsel authority seems all but inevitable given the nature of the president's office and attendant responsibilities; whenever the president acts, it is nearly impossible to separate public behavior from private behavior. Yet while a prosecutor who is accountable directly to the public (or whose superiors are accountable to the public) may be forced to defend his decision to investigate the private lives of his targets, the same cannot be said of an independent counsel, whose job does not depend on continued public confidence.

Additionally, normal prosecutorial concerns of resource allocation (i.e., the decision to aggressively prosecute one person reduces the overall funds available to aggressively prosecute others) also do not apply in this context. Indeed, according to the statute, it is the Department of Justice that is charged with paying all costs relating to the operation of the independent counsel's office.[25] Unfortunately, the attorney general—whose admitted conflict of interest led to the appointment of an independent counsel in the first place—seems especially poorly suited for aggressive oversight of the independent prosecutor's policies and resource decisions. Thus, unlike the prosecutors of ordinary citizens (under real-life economic and time constraints), a special prosecutor may always feel that it seems "worth it" to forge ahead with an investigation whose costs he or she does not have to pay, and which may vastly outweigh possible benefits.

Nor can a president targeted by a special prosecutor realistically assert his Fifth Amendment rights against self-incrimination before a grand jury. Thus, what for ordinary citizens represents a standard (and seemingly logical) strategy to make life more difficult for prosecutors targeting them, is not realistically available to a chief executive. Invoking the Fifth Amendment privilege would in most cases, rightly or wrongly, be interpreted as an admission of guilt in the court of public opinion and by the Congress in an impeachment inquiry. Indeed, one of the two articles of impeachment voted against President Clinton charged him with lying before a federal grand jury in response to questions about the extent of his relationship with Monica Lewinsky. If President Clinton had acted as any ordinary grand jury target would have under the circumstances, he would have invoked his privilege against self-incrimination instead. Thus, that entire article of impeachment was made possible only because the independent counsel knew that this particular target could not invoke the Fifth Amendment without such an invocation itself being seen as an impeachable act.

The Clinton controversy also led courts to begin considering the imposition of further legal handicaps on the president as he attempted to mount a legal defense. Ruling on an issue in the Whitewater executive privilege case, the United States Court of Appeals for the Eighth Circuit in April 1997 held that even the attorney-client privilege may be waived whenever the president's private lawyers are meeting in the same room as his official lawyers.[26] In July 1998 a federal appeals court in Washington, D.C., further constricted the circle of people in whom a president can confide. Presented with White House attorney Bruce Lindsey's refusal to testify, the court of appeals ruled that White House counsel may *not* invoke the attorney-client privilege in response to grand jury questions, as "there is no basis for treating legal advice differently from any other advice the Office of the President receives."[27] Thus, unlike the CEO of a large corporation, whose conversations with any member of the general counsel's office are presumptively privileged, or Supreme Court justices or members of Congress, whose conversations with their assistants appear to be presumptively (or at least effectively) privileged, the president must work in an environment surrounded by lawyers in whom he or she cannot absolutely confide. As Jeffrey Rosen has noted, this subjects the president to a unique form of purgatory and subjects the nation to the risk of presidential paralysis.[28] Dissenting in the Bruce Lindsey case, federal appellate judge David Tatel warned of the dangers of this burdensome legal framework:

> No President can navigate the treacherous waters of post-Watergate government, make controversial official legal decisions, decide whether to invoke official privileges, or even know when he might need private counsel, without confidential legal advice.[29]

The D.C. circuit court's recent rejection of a "secret service privilege" is perhaps less remarkable but no less significant when considered in light of all the other legal disabilities a president already faces.[30] Lacking a "protective function immunity," agents protecting the president may now be forced to bear witness to the president's words and actions, public or private.[31] Finally, only President Clinton's agreement to provide a taped deposition to a grand jury (an agreement rooted no doubt in fear of public reprisals) made it unnecessary to litigate whether a president was even subject to, or constitutionally protected from, such a subpoena. (No president has ever been required to answer a grand jury subpoena in a case in which he was a target of the investigation.) Taken as a whole, these decisions go a long way toward compromising the separation of powers principle, which surely includes some protection for the internal deliberations of each branch.

At the time this book went to press, future presidents are already slated to receive at least one political benefit. On June 30, 1999, the Independent Counsel Reauthorization Act of 1994 (28 U.S.C. Sec. 599) lapsed in accordance with the provisions of its original enactment. Congress, after a series of hearings in February 1999 in which it considered whether to pass a modified version of the legislation, ultimately took no action to renew the law in any form. Certainly the demise of the Independent Counsel statute should reduce considerably the nature of the threat posed by the variety of unfavorable legal precedents described above. Still, Congress cannot so easily avoid the consequences of the Supreme Court's decision in *Clinton v. Jones* and other binding legal precedents that either encourage lawsuits filed by civil plaintiffs against the president, or aid the indictment and conviction of a sitting president by state and local prosecutors. While either of those two sources of litigation would at least be subject to practical economic considerations, one should not underestimate the passions and staying power of those who seek to topple a president. For example, the Rutherford Institute and other Republican contributors assumed a significant role in organizing and financing Paula Jones's lawsuit in the period leading up to the dismissal of her sexual harassment lawsuit against the president. Thus, while eliminating the Independent Counsel statute seems a logical enough response in the short run, the current legal framework that poses so many problems for sitting presidents remains intact.

How Should the Legal Process Distinguish between the President's Public and Private Acts?

Is such a distinction (in any form) even workable in the current political environment? The short answer is "No." One need only consider the impact that the bizarre, circus-like drama the Lewinsky affair had on President's Clinton's ability to perform his constitutional duties. As Clinton's lawyers persuasively argued, the premise that a single human being—who legally acts in both official and individual capacities—shares no common interest with himself stretches the laws of metaphysics.[32]

The vague Supreme Court decisions discussed above can be briefly contrasted to the Court's handling of the broader issue of presidential inherent/emergency powers. Other than the constitutional anomaly of *United States v. Curtiss-Wright Corporation*, the Supreme Court (as we have seen) has rarely endorsed extralegal actions of the president outright.[33] When faced with challenges to presidential action in a crisis, it has employed doctrinally flexible and nonconfining means to support emergency actions; and when the Court's intervention seems inadvisable or constitutionally ambiguous, it has deferred to one of the other branches, sometimes citing the "political questions" doctrine, other times finding technical threshold issues to rationalize its deference.

That same deferential attitude would seem appropriate here as well. Clearly uncomfortable micromanaging executive behavior, the Court has managed to grant the president sufficient authority to fulfill constitutional responsibilities in particular instances while at the same time not creating permanently harmful constitutional doctrine. Those earlier Courts recognized implicitly that to unduly restrict and hamper the president would not benefit the nation. Whether or not the president acted wisely or properly was a judgment primarily committed to Congress and the electorate. The wisdom of that Janus-like response has long been recognized.

The wise course of action in situations such as the one that played itself out during Clinton's second term would be to give the president considerable leeway in fending off both civil lawsuits and criminal prosecutions—something akin to the "functionally mandated immunity" created in the *Fitzgerald* case. Accordingly, we argue that even a private lawsuit against the president should be treated legally as public (and thus functionally immune) regardless of the underlying subject matter at issue or the time when the events occurred. *Clinton v. Jones* is both bad history and bad law; it fails to consider adequately the distracting impact and intimidating costs of multiple and high-profile lawsuits on the office of the presidency. Such lawsuits will now almost certainly escalate in number, limited only by the resources of those who wish to use them to harass or undermine a disfavored incumbent. *Clinton v. Jones* is based on very unrealistic and naive assumptions; it should be modified or, better, overruled. Granting this kind of immunity to the president is not to confer a personal privilege so much as it is to recognize his temporary unique status and the importance of warding off unnecessary impediments to carrying out duties that no one else can perform.

Likewise, the constitutional presumption that a sitting president is not subject to criminal indictment should be, once and for all, judicially affirmed. It is, in fact, the most plausible interpretation of the impeachment clauses, which state clearly that a president is subject to criminal process *after* having been impeached and removed from office (thus implying that the president is not subject prior to impeachment). This issue was brought to the Supreme Court by President Nixon's lawyers in 1974, but the Court declined to decide it. One argument against this interpretation is that some federal judges have been indicted and convicted before they were impeached. But the proper response is that federal judges do not bear the unique responsibilities of the president: There are hundreds of them, but only one president. We would thus not extend this temporary immunity to federal judges or to the vice president, whose distraction or absence would not seriously affect the conduct of government.

Another argument against this interpretation is that it might permit a president to escape responsibility for a criminal act if the statute of limitations has run before he leaves office. But as we argued above, Congress can enact laws that suspend the statute of limitations and thus postpone civil and criminal litigation against the president, in either federal or state courts, until he has left office. This kind of temporary immunity, which the Supreme Court rejected in the *Jones* case, would ensure that victims not be deprived of their day in court, and the president, once out of office, would have to acknowledge responsibility for personal actions.

Recognition of the need for this temporary immunity would violate no constitutional prohibition or principle. If the Congress is unwilling to act, then the Court should assume responsibility. It should recognize that all personal or unofficial behavior of the president becomes a matter of public concern for the very reason that it involves a sitting president in the first place. The Court must recognize the futility of demarcating public and private presidential behavior; the broad immunities from civil suit granted to the president under *Nixon v. Fitzgerald* should be extended to all matters, public or private, while the president holds office. (This immunity would preclude lawsuits against the executive branch in its institutional capacity, such as the recent successful constitutional challenge to the line item veto law.)[34]

Finally, even if the independent counsel law is allowed to lapse, the constitutional power vested in Congress to impeach the president will remain a continuing problem. An unfortunate precedent was established in the Lewinsky matter: an elected president was impeached despite widespread (and often fervent) disagreement over whether the articles of impeachment themselves even alleged high crimes and misdemeanors on their face. The threat of impeachment must remain a bulwark of our constitutional system—presidents must know that corruption or abuse of public office will not go ignored. But false or frivolous exercises of that impeachment power create the risk that the constitutional check itself will be undermined; members of the president's party will come to see it as just another act of extreme political partisanship with no real value to the maintenance of our constitutional system.

Accordingly, we also propose amending the Constitution to restore the impeachment power to its rightful place in our polity. The president should be removed from office only on impeachment for and conviction of serious abuses of official power that undermine his or her conduct of office and threaten the integrity and legitimacy of the government. (Consistent with the view of the Founders, such abuses may include treason, bribery, and other serious crimes, as well as serious public misdeeds that are not technically criminal in nature.) To maintain a sense of *continued* accountability to the public, no impeachment of a president should be able to survive the biennial adjournment of Congress, as it did between the 105th and 106th Congresses in Clinton's case. The Supreme Court should be empowered under its original jurisdiction to review (in an expedited fashion), prior to trial by the Senate, the *procedures* employed in and the *constitutional basis* of any articles of impeachment voted against a president by the House of Representatives. (By contrast, the Court should not enjoy the power to review impeachments against other officers and it should not have the power to substitute its judgment on the *merits* of the conviction of any person by the Senate.) Finally, the Constitution should make clear that Congress may devise alternative means to criticize the president, short of impeachment, such as the power to censure, rebuke, or otherwise publicly condemn misconduct.[35]

The day after he took office on August 9, 1974, President Gerald Ford sought to reassure the nation by declaring that "the Constitution works." No similar assurances were warranted following the Clinton impeachment affair, even after a majority of the Senate voted down both articles of impeachment against the president. In our judgment, the bitter and often rancorous fight that was waged in the Congress, in courts, and on the airwaves demonstrates instead that the current system of checking potential executive branch corruption and abuse no longer "works." Only by narrowing the reach of Congress's impeachment power will this core constitutional check remain legitimate and strong; this, along with the other reforms listed above, may strike a better long-term balance between presidential responsibilities and immunities.

Conclusion

By the reforms suggested above, we do not mean to advocate that the president be transformed into an imperial monarch, free to ignore all legal proceedings in his or her wake. A president is neither free from media scrutiny of actions, nor from the numerous incidental burdens that the legal process may impose on the president and the office, nor from accountability for actions when no longer president. As noted above, the modern president (unlike most predecessors) already forfeits a number of legal privileges that most ordinary citizens take for granted. On balance, the president is not only occasionally "above the law" but also often "below the law" in the sense that he or she may be held to higher standards of personal behavior by the press and the public and be accorded fewer constitutional and legal protections than the ordinary citizen, by virtue of the fact of the office. Contrary to the implications of *Clinton v. Jones,* the president cannot temporarily step into a private citizen's shoes for purposes of one narrowly defined legal matter. We should not deprive the president of various privileges and rights in the name of a free and open post-Watergate government and then at the same time treat him or her as less than an ordinary citizen, subject to a myriad of lawsuits and criminal prosecutions.

Our proposals are not Faustian bargains that the nation should strike with the devil. Nor would they lead to a diminution of the rule of law. Rather, they follow from an increased recognition of the complexities of modern governance and political leadership, and the indispensable need to have a president who is able to function effectively despite personal predilections that trouble or offend some people. Lacking the parliamentary option of a vote of "no confidence" and a change of governments in midstream, it is nonetheless sufficient to deal in one of two ways with a president whose public or private behavior is deemed unacceptable: by not reelecting that president (for any reason) or by impeachment for commission of a serious crime or for constitutional wrongs or even when an essentially private act of misbehavior may have important constitutional or political ramifications that seriously impede the conduct of government. When the president is again a private citizen, the law can resume its course. The current conundrum, which sets the nation on a dangerous course, is brought on in large part by the institutionalization of attack politics in the office of the special prosecutor, polarization caused by semi-permanent divided government, and dissolution of the separation of powers based practical immunities enjoyed by most pre-Watergate presidents.

It is unrealistic and self-defeating for the republic to accept the premise that anything the president does may be subject to ordinary legal processes because, at least for such purposes, the president is just an ordinary citizen. That approach should be discarded. All acts of the president should be deemed potentially public or official for legal and constitutional purposes and thus subject to the same exclusive sanctions: electoral rejection and/or legitimate impeachment. The legal fiction of the president as a private citizen for a day should be rejected as unworkable.

This does, however, create a paradox: in order to protect a president's private life, we must presume that it is public and entitled, while he or she is president, to the same constitutional immunities as official acts (which remain immune after the president has left office). This would still permit the president to be impeached for high crimes and misdemeanors or for serious personal misconduct that amounts to an abuse of constitutional authority or that results in an inability to carry out important presidential duties necessary to the operation of government. High crimes and misdemeanors, a term of art which replaced maladministration in the constitutional text, need not be criminal acts (although they may be), but they should rise above the level of personal distaste or mere political advantage. With this caveat, the paradox is one that we cannot afford to deny, or live without.

Notes

1. *Nixon v. Fitzgerald,* 457 U.S. 731 (1982).
2. *Clinton v. Jones,* 520 U.S. 681, 117 S. Ct. 1636 (1997).
3. What privileges and responsibilities a former governor of Arkansas should possess vis-a-vis the state justice system lies outside the scope of this chapter. We thus treat the actions of a president prior to his assuming office the same, whether they were actions taken by a governor of a state or by a private citizen.
4. *United States v. Belmont,* 301 U.S. 324 (1937); *United States v. Pink,* 315 U.S. 203 (1942).
5. See *Goldwater v. Carter,* 444 U.S. 996 (1979). In *Goldwater,* six justices directed the lower court to dismiss the complaint, with four justices noting their reluctance to even rule because of the political questions doctrine.
6. The War Powers Resolution of 1973, which was enacted over President Nixon's veto, provided a framework for a "collective judgment" of Congress and the president regarding the introduction of American armed forces into combat or "imminent hostilities." Enforcement of the act, and compliance with it, have been

weak, as proponents of executive supremacy (including all subsequent presidents) claim that the act unconstitutionally limits the "president's war powers." The Supreme Court has never passed on its merits.

7. In *Dellums v. Bush*, 752 F. Supp. 1141 (D.D.C. 1990), a district court denied the request for an injunction against the president's proposed military actions in the Persian Gulf on the grounds that the lawsuit was brought by only a minority of Congress's members and thus was not yet "ripe."

8. See, for example, *Ex Parte Milligan*, 71 U.S. 2 (1866), which strongly criticized Lincoln's martial law policy during the Civil War and, more generally, his disregard of constitutional limits in the crisis. The decision has had little practical effect on the emergency actions of subsequent presidents.

9. *Youngstown Sheet & Tube Co. v. Sawyer*, 343 U.S. 579 (1952).

10. *United States v. Nixon*, 418 U.S. 683 (1974).

11. *Nixon v. Fitzgerald*, 457 U.S. at 749.

12. *Clinton v. Jones*, 520 U.S. 117 S. Ct. at 1644.

13. *Morrison v. Olson*, 487 U.S. 654, 728 (1988) (Scalia, J., dissenting).

14. See Harvey Berkman and Marcia Coyle, "Can a Sitting President Be Indicted? If Monica Lewinsky Talks, the Answer Becomes Critical," *National Law Journal*, 22 June 1998, A20.

15. Although nothing in the text of the Constitution theoretically would prevent a president from "pardoning himself," a cogent argument could be made that such an exercise of presidential power would violate the spirit of the constitutional structure. No court has ever addressed this issue. See Brian Kalt, "Pardon Me? The Constitutional Case against Presidential Self-Pardons," 106 *Yale Law Journal* 799 (1996). It appears, however, that President Nixon's lawyers advised him that he could pardon himself, which he did not. See Bob Woodward and Carl Bernstein, *The Final Days*, 325–26 (1976). A president who pardoned himself would almost certainly encounter harsh political sanctions, probably immediate impeachment, if he did not resign or leave office immediately thereafter.

16. For purposes of this discussion, we assume that the prosecutor considering indictment of a former president would be one other than the independent counsel himself. Of course, nothing in the now-lapsed Ethics in Government Act prevented an independent counsel from seeking indictments against the president or other covered officials after the president's term has expired. See 28 U.S.C. § 595.

17. In *Nixon v. United States*, 506 U.S. 224 (1993), the Court signaled its willingness to oversee certain procedural aspects of the impeachment process when it addressed the merits of one judge's claim that under the Constitution the full Senate, and not merely a committee, must consider the impeachment charges against him. (The Court ultimately rejected Judge Nixon's claim, holding that the Senate's "sole power to try impeachments" gave it an unreviewable discretion to proceed in this manner so long as it was the full Senate that ultimately voted to convict him on impeachment charges.) Still, the Supreme Court has never shown a willingness to examine the "substance" of an impeachment and subsequent conviction (including determining the meaning of "high crimes and misde-

meanors"), and little in the *Nixon* case provides a precedent for its doing so in the future.

18. Complaints against Theodore Roosevelt and Harry Truman were dismissed before either took office, although the dismissals were not affirmed until after their respective inaugurations. Two companion cases arising out of an automobile accident were filed against John F. Kennedy, but they were settled out of court soon after he took office.

19. In light of the Supreme Court's decision in *Burlington Industries v. Ellerth* 524 U.S. 742 (1998), there had remained the slight possibility that the *Jones* case might eventually be reinstated, but Jones settled her case with the president out of court for $850,000 on November 13, 1998.

20. Cited in Joan Biskupic, "Consequences Unseen by the Court: In Allowing Jones Case, Justices Predicted Suits Wouldn't 'Engulf' Presidency," *Washington Post,* 29 January 1998, A12.

21. *New York Times v. Sullivan,* 376 U.S. 254 (1964); *Gertz v. Robert Welch, Inc.,* 418 U.S. 323 (1974).

22. Jeffrey Rosen, "The End of Privacy," *The New Republic,* 16 February 1998, 21.

23. 28 U.S.C. §§ 591 *et. seq.* The independent counsel (or special prosecutor) idea developed, of course, during Watergate. The first two special prosecutors, Archibald Cox (dismissed by President Nixon in the famous "Saturday Night Massacre" in 1973) and Leon Jaworski, were appointed by the attorney general with congressional approval. The office of independent counsel was later formally created by the 1978 statute.

24. 28 U.S.C. § 593(b)(3). The independent counsel may also prosecute federal crimes arising out of that matter, including perjury, obstruction of justice, destruction of evidence, and intimidation of witnesses. *Ibid.* His or her jurisdiction may be expanded further only at the attorney general's request; 28 U.S.C. § 593(c)(1).

25. 28 U.S.C. § 594(d)(2).

26. See *In Re Grand Jury Subpoena Duces Tecum,* 112 F.3d 910 (8th Cir. 1997).

27. *In Re Bruce R. Lindsey (Grand Jury Testimony),* 148 F.3d 1100, 1102 (D.C. Cir. 1998).

28. Jeffrey Rosen, "How to Isolate a President," *New York Times,* 30 July 1998, A-21.

29. 148 F.3d at 1122 (Tatel, J., concurring in part, dissenting in part).

30. See *In Re Sealed Case,* 148 F.3d 1073 (D.C. Cir. 1998).

31. Congress could provide such immunity by statute but has not done so.

32. Brief of the Office of the President, June 15, 1998, filed in *In Re: Sealed Case* (D.C. Cir., 98-95).

33. 299 U.S. 304 (1936).

34. See *Clinton v. City of New York,* 524 U.S. 417 (1998).

35. See Joel B. Grossman and David A. Yalof, "The Day After: Do We Need a '28th Amendment?' " *Constitutional Commentary,* in press.

SEVEN

Scandal Time: The Clinton Impeachment and the Distraction of American Politics

Paul J. Quirk

The impeachment of President Bill Clinton is in many ways a reflection of a much broader and critically important phenomenon in contemporary American politics: the remarkable prominence of the politics of scandal. American politicians, journalists, and citizens devote extraordinary time and energy to controversies about matters of moral and legal propriety. Instead of debating good and bad policy or effective and ineffective leadership, Americans very often debate about righteousness and wrongdoing.

To some degree, these controversies are the inevitable result of trying to enforce serious standards of proper conduct. But the preoccupation with discovering, proving, and rooting out wrongdoing often reaches a point of pathological excess. Striking at Democrats and Republicans, liberals and conservatives, and elected officials and appointed ones, scandals destroy or damage useful political careers. Scandals distract attention and disrupt the processes of government and thus may distort public policy or undermine the ability to deal with crises. Apart from these immediate effects, scandals are likely to cause cynicism and alienation among the citizenry.

It is highly doubtful that the improved compliance with various legal and ethical requirements that presumably results from the heightened threat of scandal and punishment is enough to justify all the disruption. Moreover, the flood of scandals shows no sign of abating. The title of this chapter, "Scandal Time," therefore highlights two points: that

American politics in this era is dominated by scandal, and that the major cost (although not the only one) of scandals is simply their enormous amount of wasted time and attention.[1] Whatever else the Clinton impeachment stood for, it was symptomatic of a chronic and frequently debilitating condition of the political system. In its aftermath, we need to consider how to cope better with the politics of scandal.

The Clinton–Lewinsky Episode and the Politics of Scandal

The fourteen-month episode of investigation by Independent Counsel Kenneth Starr, impeachment by the House of Representatives, and trial by the Senate—arising from President Clinton's relationship with Monica Lewinsky and his testimony about it in the Paula Jones lawsuit—were the reduction to absurdity of the politics of scandal. This is not because Clinton was unfairly maligned, innocent of any serious wrongdoing. To the contrary, there were few defenders of Clinton's behavior in the Lewinsky matter, one of most unedifying episodes in the history of the presidency. Clinton was admittedly guilty of having a sexual affair with a White House intern and of lying about it for several months to all of Washington and the American public, as well as his family. But it was primarily his false and misleading testimony under oath that transformed an embarrassing bimbo eruption (the Clinton staff's sardonic term for revelations of his womanizing) into a constitutional crisis that threatened his presidency—the mother of all bimbo eruptions. By most accounts he gave perjurious testimony on several points in his deposition in the Jones case. More important, he largely repeated the same false and misleading testimony in his August 1998 grand jury testimony. There was also circumstantial evidence of his having suborned perjury and obstructed justice in the same proceedings.

Moreover, although Kenneth Starr's investigations of other matters—Whitewater, the Travel Office, the FBI files, and the death of Vincent Foster—apparently will not lead to formal charges against the president or Hillary Clinton, they uncovered various grounds for serious suspicion, such as the business assistance rendered to potential witness Webster Hubbell by friends of the president. Despite Starr's unstinting efforts, it is possible that Clinton has gotten away with crimes in one or more of these matters.

Nevertheless, the effort to investigate Clinton's conduct and ultimately to remove him from office was disproportionate and unwarranted by any standards that would win broad acceptance. As with other
overblown scandals, the Clinton-Lewinsky scandal was unnecessarily
prolonged, divisive, and distracting at each stage.

The Investigation

Starr's investigation showed an extraordinary lack of proportion between the resources it expended and the disruption of government it
caused, on the one hand, and the seriousness of the president's suspected misdeeds and their relevance to his official duties on the other.
The Whitewater case concerned business dealings that had occurred
a decade earlier. The Travel Office case concerned an isolated violation
of contracting and civil service regulations. Of the pre-Lewinsky matters, the FBI files case alone was both relevant to the president's
conduct in office and potentially serious. The case concerned the
possibility of White House misuse of confidential FBI files to do harm
to political enemies, but there was never substantial evidence that
the mishandling of the files actually represented anything more than
incompetence among low-level White House staff.

The Lewinsky inquiry initially concerned possible perjury, suborning of perjury, or obstruction of justice in a private lawsuit. Although
it soon expanded to include more serious offenses—obstruction and,
later, perjury in the ensuing criminal investigation—those initial offenses had a peculiar character for the starting point of a massive
investigation. They were offenses that almost certainly would never
have been investigated and prosecuted if the suspected offender had
been a private citizen.

During the House Judiciary Committee hearings on impeachment,
Republicans attempted to show that ordinary citizens were in fact
subject to criminal prosecution for similar offenses. Although the effort
may have looked reasonably successful in the media, examined closely
it was by no means convincing. Through a nationwide search, the
committee managed to find two individuals (both women, as it happened) who had been prosecuted, convicted, and punished for testifying falsely in civil proceedings about sexual activity. But in each case
the sexual activity they denied had been the central issue in the civil
proceeding. A medical doctor was being dismissed from employment
for having sex with a patient; a basketball coach was being dismissed
for having sex with a member of the team. Each woman falsely denied

the sexual relationship, was caught in the lie, and was prosecuted for it. In neither case had the offender lied about a sexual relationship that was (like Clinton's relationship with Lewinsky) wholly separate from the matter at issue in the civil proceeding.

The Republicans did not produce any cases in which ordinary citizens were prosecuted for false testimony in circumstances that actually resembled those of Clinton's civil deposition, that is, with false testimony about a peripheral issue. More generally, many commentators pointed out that prosecutions for perjury in civil cases are, under any circumstances, highly unusual. Pro-Clinton talk-show host Geraldo Rivera offered a $10,000 reward to anyone who could identify a single such case in the federal courts. It was widely noted that parties in divorce cases often lie about extramarital affairs and that such perjuries are essentially never prosecuted. The Republicans argued, in essence, that perjury was perjury and that any form of it undermines the legal system. But that same legal system had a firmly established practice of making distinctions about the nature and circumstances of perjury and, indeed, of ignoring the preponderance of it. (Of course, recognizing the generally lax treatment of civil perjury in the American legal system does not imply approval of it).[2]

During the impeachment debate there was little or no discussion about the frequency of prosecution for suborning of perjury or for obstruction of justice in civil cases. These charges are not likely to be much more common than prosecutions for perjury. In any case, the Starr investigation never produced compelling evidence on these charges. Clinton's later offenses—especially perjury in the grand jury—were more serious but derivative: induced by the prosecutor rather than merely discovered by him. Apart from the Filegate matter, there was never any apparent prospect that the Starr investigation would turn up misdeeds of direct importance for the conduct of government.

On the other hand, the cost of these investigations was stupendous. Starr assumed an attitude that getting at the truth about any criminal or potentially criminal allegation about Clinton was worth whatever time, money, intrusion, distraction, or other harm required—without limit. (Starr and his staff were also accused of illegally leaking grand jury information to the media, and a federal judge, finding prima facie evidence of such leaks, has ordered a further inquiry that could lead to the imposition of sanctions on Starr or members of his staff.)

It is useful to reflect on those costs as they stood even prior to any formal consideration of impeachment. Starr's critics often complained about his expenditures of more than $40 million over four years. But that was a minor part of the real cost. The spending amounted to less than twenty cents per citizen—a very affordable figure if the investigation were a constructive means to keep presidents on the straight and narrow.

The main cost of the investigation was the massive distractions it caused for the president, Congress, and the public. Those costs cannot be calculated with any precision, but a few speculative exercises suggest their order of magnitude. Consider what it would cost a commercial or political advertiser to purchase the same amount of public attention as was devoted to the Lewinsky affair from January to September 1998. Or consider the scope of the policy issues and the stakes in reaching good decisions—converted somehow into monetary terms—that would have been required to command comparable attention of the president and Congress. The astronomical figures that would result from these calculations—certainly hundreds of billions of dollars—indicate something of the value of the attention wasted.

In fact, from January to September 1998, Clinton undoubtedly spent a large amount of his time and mental energy dealing with the scandal and investigation. So did his staff. His policy initiatives were often ignored by the media, especially if they had the misfortune to coincide with news of the Lewinsky case. And Congress largely ignored his agenda. With some degree of exaggeration, one could say that the scandal squandered, before the impeachment, about one-sixth of Clinton's second term: All this to prosecute an alleged crime that the legal system habitually overlooks.

Starr's defenders have a point to make about all the disruption and other costs: By the simple expedient of admitting the truth himself in the Jones deposition or at least after the Tripp tapes were revealed, Clinton could have prevented most of the disruption of the Lewinsky inquiry. Instead, he lied, stonewalled, and fought Starr's investigation at every step. Quite so. Far more than anyone else, Clinton himself was responsible for the outlandish cost of the investigation. In my view, this was his most serious offense in the Lewinsky affair. And it vitiated his otherwise strong defense about the unimportance of his basic crime.

To borrow a term from tort law, Clinton and Starr were jointly liable for the vast waste and humiliation of the Lewinsky investigation. Each could foresee the other was not going to prevent it. Each had the opportunity to spare the country this experience. Neither Clinton nor Starr chose to serve the country's interest. Clinton's failure in this regard provided some basis for calls for his resignation: If a president puts the country through months of turmoil over an issue of his veracity and he turns out indeed to have been lying all along, perhaps he should have the decency to take his leave. In my view, the strongest objection to a Clinton resignation was that it would have rewarded the excessive prosecutorial zeal of Kenneth Starr. With public servants like Clinton and Starr, who needed enemies?

The Impeachment

If the initial civil perjury fell below any plausible threshold for an impeachable offense, Clinton obliged the impeachment advocates by upping the ante, extending his strategy of dissembling into the criminal investigation. By most readings, Clinton gave false or misleading testimony in his August appearance before the grand jury. On some points, assessing the truthfulness of his testimony turns on details about how he had understood certain questions in the civil deposition, whether he was paying attention to his attorney's incorrect statements, and what he had meant by certain replies. But if Lewinsky's account was substantially accurate, it was fairly clear that Clinton testified falsely in denying having had a sexual relationship with her, even under the peculiar definition used in the *Jones* deposition. According to Lewinsky, Clinton had fondled her breasts and genitals, actions that clearly fit the *Jones* definition of a sexual relationship. In his grand jury testimony, with the issue of fondling specifically posed, Clinton insisted that his deposition had been accurate.

The grand jury perjury was a significantly more serious offense than the civil perjury in two respects. First, a criminal investigation is in principle a more serious and important proceeding than a civil trial. Criminal prosecutions, unlike civil lawsuits, can deprive people of their freedom, so everything about them is weightier. Second, the matters about which Clinton gave false or misleading testimony were now central to the proceeding. In a criminal investigation, Clinton was lying directly about the suspected crime. Ordinary citizens are certainly prosecuted for similar offenses. To be sure, one could debate how much the seriousness of the grand jury perjury was mitigated by the fact that with an ordinary citizen as the suspect, the offense almost certainly would never have been investigated and no grand jury testimony would even have occurred. Put differently, the issue was whether the seriousness of the underlying, original offense governs the seriousness of grand jury perjury. But compared with the original civil perjury, the grounds for discounting the grand jury perjury were far weaker.

Most Republican members of the House Judiciary Committee did not make sharp distinctions about the seriousness of the various allegations against Clinton or the strength of the evidence concerning them (e.g., civil case versus grand jury, direct versus circumstantial evidence) and demanded impeachment on a grab bag of supposed high crimes.[3] With the grand jury perjury thrown into the mix, there was a serious and responsible argument that Clinton's offenses reached the constitutional standard for impeachment. One could plausibly argue that any felony is a high crime, regardless of circumstances, and show that ordinary citizens are regularly prosecuted for the sort of perjury Clinton committed. One could also argue that Clinton's concerted strategy of lying to the public, although not criminal, aggravated his offenses. Yet the argument for impeachment was also subject to very cogent, if not compelling, objections; in particular, that Clinton's offenses did not involve the powers of his office or directly affect the operation of government and that no precedent existed for considering impeachment of a president for remotely similar offenses. In fact, no serious consideration had been given to impeaching President Ronald Reagan for arguably more serious and constitutionally relevant offenses in the Iran-Contra affair.[4]

It is not necessary to rehash all of the arguments or reach a conclusion about the substantive merits of this debate, because one fact, sufficient for our purposes, is undeniable: There was nothing approaching a broad consensus that Clinton's offenses warranted impeachment and removal. To the contrary, the predominant view was just the opposite. Polls showed with remarkable consistency that the public opposed impeachment by an overwhelming margin of about two to one (Pious 1998). Most Republican voters favored impeachment, many of them strongly; but very few Democrats favored it. And most significant, few Independents did, either. Roughly speaking, those people who started out disliking Clinton—and almost no one else—favored impeachment. The public opposition held firm as events unfolded over many months.

An impeachment advocate could discount public opinion as uninformed—an eminently defensible position on a matter that required applying constitutional principles to complex facts. But well-informed opinion also was apparently largely opposed. Separate groups of American historians and professors of constitutional law, together comprising several hundred scholars, signed public letters strongly condemning the impeachment effort. There were many scholars who endorsed impeachment, but their numbers evidently did not come close to matching those of the group that opposed it. From what we know of the politics of academe, we can infer that the letter signers opposing impeachment were mostly liberal Democrats—most historians and constitutional law professors are. But they were not party hacks. Moreover, some informed Republicans shared their view. Charles Wiggins, a Republican federal judge who had served on the House Judiciary Committee during the Nixon impeachment proceedings, testified against impeaching Clinton. The public opposition to Clinton's impeachment was mirrored by widespread opposition among some highly informed commentators, including some Republicans.

In such circumstances, one might have expected the Republican congressional majority to avoid provoking a prolonged, divisive battle in an effort to force an outcome—impeachment and removal—whose merits were at best debatable and whose prospects were extremely remote. One might have expected that the Republican majority would seek a way to condemn Clinton's mendacity that would win broad bipartisan and public support, if not consensus. Arguably, a congressional resolution of censure had that potential. Various polls showed that a majority of the public favored censure, and most Democrats in Congress would probably have supported it. Even some leading Republicans embraced the logic. Former president Gerald Ford and former majority leader and presidential candidate Bob Dole both wrote newspaper articles advocating censure. The Republican congressional leadership, however, worked hard and successfully to foreclose the censure option, which they feared would undermine support for impeachment. Rather than seeking a consensus solution, they insisted on pushing the impeachment as far as it would go.

What accounted for the grim determination? In explaining their conduct, Republicans attempted to portray themselves as heroic figures, standing firm in the face of grave political risks to defend the principles of their party. There were of course various principles that provided rationales for the impeachment effort. But none of those principles were in fact Republican.

One pro-impeachment principle held that Clinton's extramarital affair with Lewinsky was itself enough to warrant removal from office. That view probably had support among the Christian Right, an important Republican constituency. But most Republicans explicitly disavowed it, insisting that the charges against Clinton were not about sex. If one credits this disclaimer, Republicans' commitment to family values was not the basis for their position on impeachment.

A second principled position occasionally put forth to support impeachment stressed the seriousness of any sexual harassment offense, emphasized the importance of the issues in the *Jones* case, and defined such harassment broadly to cover Clinton's affair with a 21-year-old intern. But it was implausible for Republicans to claim a hard line on sexual harassment as a party principle: The more aggressive policy initiatives on sexual harassment generally have been Democratic, and Republicans had been slow to condemn Senator Bob Packwood (R-Ore.) when a procession of women accused him of sexual harassment.

The main principled arguments for impeachment, however, were either to elevate the crimes of perjury and obstruction to a level of extreme seriousness, regardless of circumstances, or to argue for a very broad impeachment power—rejecting the view that high crimes had to threaten the constitutional system or be in other ways exceptionally grave. But here again, the Republican party had no particular history of championing these positions. There has not been a long-standing partisan debate about the crime of perjury. Former Republican defense secretary Caspar Weinberger, charged with perjury in the Iran-Contra investigation, was pardoned by Republican president George Bush, an action applauded by most Republicans. In general, neither party has been historically associated with a more expansive view of the impeachment power than the other's.

Republicans also claimed they had principled objections to censure; however, nothing in prior Republican or conservative doctrines would have predicted they would oppose it. In fact, they argued against censure in contradictory ways—holding at one moment that censure was virtually meaningless and at another that the precedent of censure would weaken the presidency. The implication was that Congress would intimidate future presidents by threatening a meaningless gesture. In short, the issues in the impeachment controversy had nothing to do with traditional morality, limited government, decentralization, or any other Republican notion. Although one could stand on various principles to demand Clinton's removal from office, those principles were not recognizably Republican.

The Republican effort was not merely a crass strategy to take advantage of a Democratic president's vulnerability for partisan electoral gain. The party as a whole would have been better off in the 2000 elections if Republicans had cashed in their chips while they were ahead and moved to censure Clinton at an early stage of the scandal. At no point did the impeachment proceedings look like a good bet to win public support or to succeed in removing the president. And even if the Republicans had managed to remove Clinton or induce him to resign, the result would have been to promote the probable Democratic presidential candidate, Al Gore, to the presidency: an incumbent president would have been much stronger competition than a vice president to a discredited Clinton.

The Republicans' commitment to impeachment was at bottom primarily psychological: As a result of battling against Clinton and his policies over the years, Republican officeholders, activists, and constituency groups had grown to dislike and distrust him. For a variety of reasons—from his draft avoidance and history of womanizing to the suspicious Filegate, Whitewater, and other matters—they disdained his character and deeply resented his political success. In that frame of mind, Republican members of Congress and their core constituencies were inclined to suspect the worst of Clinton, to perceive any offense as serious, and to want badly to see him punished. They wanted to impeach Clinton not because of any party principles or because it would help the party electorally, but because they felt viscerally that he deserved it. Because core constituencies felt this way, Republican representatives from conservative districts probably had electoral incentives to support impeachment, regardless of national polls or consequences for the national party.

Ultimately, the Republicans' monomaniacal pursuit of impeachment ended as a neutral observer would have predicted: badly. With a two-thirds vote required for conviction and removal in the Senate trial, no article of impeachment was approved by even a majority of senators. Several moderate Republicans declined to convict. And the public mostly disapproved the Republicans' handling of the impeachment issue. In the aftermath, House Judiciary Committee Republicans vented anger at the American public, and the chairman, Henry Hyde (R-Ill.), admitted feelings of defeat and rejection.

The lack of any bipartisan formal condemnation of Clinton's behavior left the national judgment of it, in some sense, unresolved. In a March 1999 television interview with CBS News anchor Dan Rather, Clinton took advantage of the ambiguity to claim, however preposterously, something akin to vindication. He denied feeling shame about the episode and expressed satisfaction that those who had used the impeachment process for purely partisan purposes were defeated.

Shortly afterward, the trial judge in the *Jones* case clarified matters to some degree by finding Clinton in civil contempt for giving false and misleading testimony in his deposition. Judge Susan Webber Wright imposed financial penalties on Clinton and referred her findings to the Arkansas Supreme Court, which had the authority to bar him from the practice of law in the state. It would be ironic if an offense that did not keep Clinton from serving out his term as president did prevent him from returning to the practice of law. But there would be no contradiction in that result: Clinton was not elected by the American people to practice law in the state of Arkansas and protecting the constitutional separation of powers does not require that he be permitted to do so.[5]

The Republicans' impeachment effort extended the period of national distraction another five months—to the Senate vote in February 1999—resulting in the loss of essentially a full year of the Clinton presidency. The major policy problems facing the country were largely put on hold. One of the most serious problems, the spring 1999 conflict with Serbia over Kosovo, may have been made worse by neglect. According to a *New York Times* account of the Clinton administration's decision making (Sciolino and Bronner 1999), impeachment politics narrowed the president's options and distracted White House attention in January, when decisive U.S. action might have prevented the Serbian assault on Kosovo.[6]

Both in the Starr investigation and the subsequent impeachment and trial, the effort to discover, prove, and punish Clinton's wrongdoing went well beyond what was likely to be useful or constructive in enforcing appropriate standards of official conduct. Instead of effectively condemning Clinton's conduct, the effort caused division and distraction on a grand scale. This turn of events was of course an extraordinary development in American history. Yet from another perspective, the whole episode was merely an extreme manifestation of normal occurrences in contemporary American politics: increasingly, politics are about scandal.

An Era of Scandals

The contemporary politics of scandal is associated with the post-Watergate era. In her compelling book, *Scandal*, Suzanne Garment (1992, 3) reported that in the first fifteen years after the Watergate scandal, "more than 400 relatively senior federal officials and candidates for federal office . . . [were] publicly accused in the national press of personal wrongdoing." The numbers had been far smaller in previous periods. It appears scandals will routinely threaten the positions of a large percentage of the nation's highest officials. Three of the last five presidents (Richard Nixon, Ronald Reagan, and Clinton) have undergone major investigations (Watergate, Iran–Contra, and Whitewater and Lewinsky) with talk of impeachment or criminal liability or both. Two of the last three Speakers of the House have had similar troubles—Jim Wright resigned from office and Newt Gingrich escaped with censure and a large fine. In addition, Speaker-elect Bob Livingston in 1998 resigned his seat rather than endure an apparently minor scandal about an extramarital affair.

The causes of the politics of scandal are not entirely clear. Although reliable measurements of corrupt behavior are impossible, the frequency of scandals certainly cannot reflect an increase in actual corruption. Regulation of campaign finance, restrictions on lobbying, other ethics restrictions, and scrutiny of political figures' private lives have all become stricter in the post-Watergate era. Many of the actions that get politicians in trouble were undoubtedly undertaken with impunity until recently.

One theory suggests that the prevalence of scandals and investigations in this era represents "politics by other means," a substitute for electoral conflict in a period when a stable division of party control of government made elections incapable of delivering a decisive victory (Ginsberg and Shefter 1990). That theory does not work, however, for the late 1990s. Since the 1994 election, the House, Senate, and presidency have all been genuinely in play in elections, and elections have powerfully affected the direction of policy. But scandal politics have not subsided. Scandals are politics by *additional* means, and their prominence in this era does not depend on a stable division of party control.

More plausibly, Garment (1992) attributes the proliferation of scandals to the rise of a "culture of mistrust," a widespread willingness to believe the worst about political leaders, in the aftermath of the Vietnam War and Watergate. But it is puzzling why events of twenty-five to thirty years ago would still dominate contemporary attitudes. Others have pointed to the Watergate episode as demonstrating opportunities for personal and corporate advancement through investigative journalism (Patterson 1994). But if this is the case, why weren't such opportunities discovered before Watergate?

Whatever produced the change, one aspect of the workings of scandals is clear. They thrive on wall-to-wall coverage in the media and, ultimately, on an insatiable public appetite for scandal-related news. As gripping newspaper or television fare, scandals have all the advantages over the politics of policy. Even when a scandal has worn out its welcome with the public, as the Clinton scandal clearly did, it still sells newspapers and attracts large audiences to television news broadcasts and talk shows. Widespread publicity usually permits the sponsors of scandal to profit handsomely in their careers. (Kenneth Starr is the partial exception that proves the rule. His reputation for probity severely damaged, Starr probably will never be a judge or the dean of a major law school, and even his corporate law practice may suffer. But he is assured of an exciting and remunerative career as a conservative hero, if that is his desire.) To the extent that the politics of scandal depend on the public's attention and general approval of the focus on wrongdoing, the prominence of scandal during the past twenty-five years may reflect an increasingly populist political system (Quirk and Hinchliffe 1998). That is, we have more scandals because politics are increasingly about the problems and solutions that ordinary citizens can most readily understand.

Finally, in the last decade or so, the propensity to seek scandals and push them to the limit has been exacerbated by the increasing partisan and ideological polarization of American politics. Congress is now populated overwhelmingly by liberal Democrats and conservative Republicans (McCarty, Poole, and Rosenthal 1997). Conservative or moderate Democrats and liberal or moderate Republicans have largely disappeared—mostly the result of the passing of traditional Democratic loyalties in the South and Republican ones in the Northeast. Moreover, even the public has become more polarized, with a higher percentage of ideologically aware and committed citizens at both ends of the political spectrum (King 1997).

This polarization has important effects on policy making, raising the barriers to centrist approaches and reducing efforts to find agreement (Jacobs and Shapiro 1998, chap. 1; Quirk and Nesmith 1998; Quirk and Cunion 1999). And it also intensifies the politics of scandal. Very conservative Republican members of Congress, for example, with highly ideological core constituencies, see no way to work constructively with a liberal or even moderate Democrat. They thus have little or no concern about maintaining mutual trust with Clinton and are likely to detest what they think he stands for. If a possible scandal seems to provide even a remote opportunity to punish such an opponent or, better yet, end his career, they will seize upon that strategy and give it up very reluctantly. This is indeed how polarization affected Republican strategy in the Clinton impeachment. And of course, the same dynamic affects the attitudes of very liberal Democratic members toward conservative or moderate Republicans. Ideologues of either liberal or conservative persuasion are prone to investigate, prosecute, or impeach their opponents even for matters that have nothing to do with ideology.

Managing Scandal

Americans should look for ways to reduce the role of scandal in the political process—to keep the fate of parties, candidates, and policies from turning on who gets caught in what (generally modest) offense and to recapture for elections and the policy process the public attention required to make such choices deliberately on their merits. The basic features of the political system that foster the politics of scandal cannot be changed. But some tinkering with the rules, practices, and institutions for enforcing standards of integrity in the political process could make a difference.

First, the general strategy for enforcing these standards should put more emphasis on detection and less on punishment. To the extent that politicians are rational, the effectiveness of deterrence is a function of both probability and severity of punishment (Cooter and Ulen 1997). It should be possible, therefore, to maintain about the same level of overall compliance with laws and regulations by increasing the frequency and thoroughness of monitoring, and thus the probability of punishment, while decreasing the severity of that punishment. More frequent detection of violations, with smaller penalties attached, should drive these matters off the front pages and dramatically reduce their disruptive effect.

Consider the offense that ended Speaker Wright's political career and the offense that almost ended Speaker Gingrich's. Wright used bulk sales of his book in an attempt to disguise large corporate contributions to his personal income. Gingrich raised money for a supposedly nonpolitical educational foundation that he actually used in violation of the federal tax code to promote Republican causes and his own political agenda. The temptations both men faced were obviously strong. Each must have believed he would avoid detection. Both got caught. But with more frequent and thorough auditing of their personal and professional finances, they might not have expected to get away with the chicanery. With a higher risk of getting caught, the threat of a political death penalty might not have been needed as a deterrent. Had they not been deterred, however, and got caught, much smaller penalties would have reduced public attention and allowed the Speakers to go about their business more or less normally while matters were resolved. In other words, instead of destroying an occasional Speaker, we should check all their receipts and mete out some fines.

An effective way to reduce punishments and the distraction caused by enforcement would be to decriminalize lesser violations of conflict-of-interest and campaign finance regulations, punishing violators with civil fines rather than criminal convictions and jail terms. Indeed, to do so would often serve our sense of just punishment. Former agriculture secretary Mike Espy, for example, was acquitted in 1999 of charges of accepting illegal gifts. The charges had been brought by an independent counsel after a multimillion-dollar investigation. In fact, Espy had received substantial gifts (trips to major sporting events, etc.) from wealthy friends who were undoubtedly interested in cultivating the secretary of agriculture, but there was no evidence of bribery or corrupt influence.

The jurors may have declined to convict Espy because they did not see his violations as genuinely criminal, or because they did not approve of the independent counsel's massive effort to find something worse. (The jurors may have reasoned that if so much investigation turned up so little wrongdoing, Espy was pretty clean.) Nevertheless, Espy's accepting of gifts was certainly inappropriate, and such action should not be permitted. It would help enforcement in such cases if the punishment consisted of reasonable fines without the stigma of criminal conviction or the necessity of removal from office. Proceedings to find the relevant facts and consider the imposition of such fines would neither end an official's useful service nor dominate the news.[7]

Second, investigating and prosecuting high-level public officials should be restructured to institutionalize the idea that the resources devoted to an investigation, the tactics an investigation employs, and, above all, the disruption it causes must be proportionate to the likelihood and seriousness of the suspected crime (Heyman 1998). The country cannot afford Starrism: the attitude that no national interest is higher than that of getting the goods on a high-level public official, even if the offense is minor, harmless, or irrelevant to the conduct of his or her office. In fairness to Starr, we should recognize that he did not invent what I have called "Starrism," he only brought about its fullest expression. In fact, the doctrines surrounding the independent counsel's function never have stressed proportionality (Eastland 1989; Harriger 1991).

In the aftermath of the Clinton–Lewinsky investigation and the impeachment effort, Congress simply allowed the statutory authority

for appointment of independent counsels to lapse when the authorization expired in 1999.[8] Many Republicans had opposed the statute,
especially after Lawrence Walsh's relentless prosecution of Republicans
in the Iran-Contra scandal. In response to Clinton's experience with
Starr and six other independent counsels, many Democrats came to
agree. Attorney General Janet Reno opposed renewal. And, in a surprising turn, so did Starr, arguing that an independent counsel's political separation from the administration lent credibility to partisan
charges that a prosecution was politically motivated. He also recognized the obvious: the statute had not succeeded in ensuring public
confidence. The massive disapproval of the Starr investigation suggests
that there will be little immediate public demand for renewing the
statute.

   If the statute is not renewed, investigation and prosecution of
executive branch wrongdoing reverts to the Justice Department, where
such responsibility resided until the Independent Counsel statute was
first enacted in 1977, in the aftermath of Watergate. Relying on the
Justice Department should reduce the frequency of marginally warranted investigations, and the attorney general will never be compelled
to initiate an investigation through the Independent Counsel statute.
In addition, Justice Department prosecutors should drop unproductive investigations of executive branch officials more quickly, chase
fewer long-shot investigatory leads, and, in the end, bring indictments
more selectively. In effect, the change should lower the priority accorded prosecution of real or imagined executive wrongdoing (Eastland 1989) and, in doing so, should elevate the priority of all other
governmental business. In short, abolishing the independent counsel's
office should help subdue the politics of scandal.

   The solution might not be that easy, however. It would not be
surprising if the public and Congress soon became more concerned
about ensuring integrity and avoiding conflict of interest in investigations of high-level executive branch officials and ended up wanting
to restore the Independent Counsel statute or something similar. Such
a turn of events could conceivably occur soon enough to renew the
statute quickly. But reemergence of the concern for independence is
more likely to result from the first case in which an attorney general,
freed from the law's constraints, declines to prosecute a high-level
presidential appointee widely suspected of wrongdoing. Such a case
is virtually inevitable in the near future, so the passing of the office of
independent counsel, which seems likely now, may be short lived. In

the end, the problem of conflict of interest that the position was designed to overcome cannot be easily dismissed.

If the institution of independent counsel is somehow extended or is reestablished in the future, it should undergo substantial reform. There are a variety of proposals for such reform (Shestack 1998; Harriger 1991). Some would reduce the scope of the independent counsels' jurisdiction by reducing the number of officials or the range of suspected offenses they may be appointed to investigate, while others would raise the evidentiary requirements for triggering their appointment. Both approaches have merit.

The most important objective, however, should be to build in a powerful drive to maintain proportionality in the prosecutorial function when an independent counsel is appointed. An amended independent counsel statute should include an explicit mandate to weigh the cost of potential disruption to government. More important, the statute should establish a new institutional form with strong incentives to take that mandate seriously. As many critics have pointed out, an independent counsel appointed to undertake a single investigation has a strong incentive to make that investigation yield a conviction (Harriger 1991; Heyman 1998). Several independent counsels have undertaken investigations without bringing charges, but no one knows their names. A conviction is the mark of distinguished performance, with all its rewards. Moreover, the normal moderating influences of a limited budget and a caseload do not apply: an independent counsel has one case from which to make a reputation and unlimited resources to use toward that end.

One proposed approach for correcting these institutional defects is to model the independent counsel's office on the inspectors general of the cabinet departments, semi-autonomous civil servants with ongoing responsibility to investigate offenses within particular departments (Heyman 1998). Under this model, for example, a position would be set up similar to an inspector general for the White House. Another possibility might be to model the permanent independent counsel structure and methods and terms of appointment on the independent regulatory commissions, with multiple members who represent both parties, serve fixed terms, and are appointed by the president and confirmed by the Senate. Such a commission would then hire a small staff of prosecutors, assign them to cases, and supervise their operations. The members would be accountable, individually and collectively, to both political parties. Either arrangement would assign the prosecutorial function to an office with substantial independence from the presidential administration and would give its occupants a stake in demonstrating probity, balance, and nonpartisanship over a long period of time.

The Clinton Case and Optimal Enforcement

To make the goal of proportionality more concrete, it is useful to construct a scenario for a more measured and constructive investigatory response to the Tripp tapes—proportionality we should hope for in future investigations by the Justice Department or a reformed independent counsel's office. Stated simply, the tapes presented evidence that the president had committed perjury in the *Jones* trial. Although certainly quite convincing, that evidence was uncorroborated. And in any case, the circumstances of the apparent perjury virtually never would have led to prosecution had the offender been an ordinary citizen. There was also circumstantial evidence of obstruction of justice, although more speculative and again related to the same peripheral issues in the *Jones* case. What was a prosecutor to do in such circumstances? Could a conscientious, yet reasonable prosecutor with jurisdiction in the matter have acted differently than Starr did?

Presumably, a prosecutor in this situation should not simply have ignored the evidence. Congress and the public had the right to know about it. Rather, in my view, the following steps would have been appropriate: First, he should have interviewed each of the main witnesses (Tripp, Lewinsky, Vernon Jordan, and a few others) for a day or so to get a sense of the readily available evidence. Judging from later events, Lewinsky would probably have stuck to her affidavit or refused to talk, leaving the evidence of perjury uncorroborated. Certainly no witness would have offered direct evidence of obstruction; no witness ever did.

Second, Starr should then have decided whether to launch a massive investigation, make a major commitment of time and resources, and most important, create an extraordinary distraction for the political process in an effort to determine the whole truth about these matters. Of course, he could have wished for cooperation from Clinton and Lewinsky, but having this cooperation was not among his options. A balanced assessment would have been clear cut: Because the alleged offenses at this stage were far below a plausible standard for impeachment (even if proved), because they were even below the standards normally employed for criminal prosecution, and because the president, in any case, may not be subject to prosecution even for a serious crime during his term of office, Starr should have concluded that major investigatory effort was not warranted.

Third, Starr should then have turned over all the evidence to Congress.[9] The Republican Congress would have held hearings, which would have been highly embarrassing for Clinton; but with material already passed over by the prosecutor, the investigation would not have occupied the nation's attention for more than a few weeks. If sufficient evidence of Clinton's affair and the civil perjury had turned up (say, if Lewinsky had testified truthfully), Congress might have considered a resolution of censure. If the essential facts had remained in doubt, Congress could have allowed the public to draw its own inferences from the Tripp tapes and Clinton's denials.

Had a prosecutor made these decisions with these results, it would have angered many Republicans; it would have required political courage on the prosecutor's part. But he would have had a strong defense: the crimes possibly committed by the president are beneath the usual standard for prosecution of an ordinary citizen, much less for impeachment of a president. Determining all the relevant facts could take months, during which the nation's crucial business would suffer. We'll be better off leaving the question of what really happened in this episode to the historians.

If Kenneth Starr had taken this course, the nation might never have known whether Clinton actually had had a sexual relationship with Monica Lewinsky, just as it probably will never know whether he actually made a crude sexual advance toward Paula Jones—but it would have had the benefit of an additional year of full-time governing by the president and Congress.

My argument, in this hypothetical exercise, is not that "ignorance is bliss," or that if a president has committed a crime of only modest importance, the nation is better off not knowing it. If we could have all of the facts without incurring excessive costs, we would certainly want them. More generally, if we could have law enforcement that detected and punished every violation by presidents, other officials, or ordinary citizens, we would presumably want that. In the real world, however, law enforcement is costly. Police cannot investigate and prosecutors cannot prosecute every apparent or possible crime, so they use discretion, considering such factors as the seriousness of the offense, the strength of the evidence at the outset, the potential for building a compelling case, the danger of permitting other crimes by the same suspect, the value of deterring others from committing similar crimes, the likely costs of an investigation and trial, and the competing claims upon currently available resources (see Wilson 1990; Holden 1996).

In view of such considerations, there is (in economists' jargon) an *optimal* level of enforcement, and it is usually not *perfect* enforcement (Cooter and Ulen 1997, 20–23). This level does not detect or prevent all crime; some suspected and even known crimes are overlooked. And some people in some circumstances can contemplate committing a crime and getting away with it (even though they often end up disappointed); thus, taking resource constraints and competing goals into account, one can even determine an optimal level of crime.

When enforcing laws upon high public officials, there are special considerations, but limits must be dealt with. It is especially important to try to ensure probity among public officials, at least in matters that bear on their official duties. At the same time, the financial costs of such enforcement hardly matter. (If, for some reason, it required a commitment of $1 million per day to prevent a president from accepting bribes, we would have no hesitancy to spend the money.) Instead, the main cost that must be considered is disruption of government operations. And that cost can be huge. Indeed, with bad luck—for example, a president distracted by an investigation making a bad decision in a foreign policy crisis—such cost can be incalculable. What I am suggesting is that those who decide about investigations of high public officials must take these costs into account. They should not undertake an investigation that will distract such an official for many months unless there is a high likelihood of demonstrating an undeniably serious offense. If the early stages of a highly publicized investigation do not point to an impending decisive result—with or without the target's cooperation—those in charge should pronounce it unproductive and call it off. They should make sure that the likes of the Starr investigation of Whitewater never happens—four years of intensive, massively distracting investigations leading to no charges against the initial targets.

The Inevitability of Scandal Politics

The Lewinsky–Clinton case, especially the impeachment and Senate trial, was the kind of political scandal that the American public loves to hate. Most did not approve of the proceedings, yet they could not bring themselves to turn away from it. In much the same way, the political system as a whole is unable to turn away from the politics of scandal. The causes of such politics are largely beyond manipulation: the attraction of ordinary citizens to the drama and suspense that surrounds scandal, the readiness of the media to cater to this attraction, and the rewards for a politician, interest group, or law enforcement official of exposing and publicizing possible wrongdoing. In the next decade there will undoubtedly be hundreds of public officials prominently accused of serious offenses and subjected to various forms of investigation. In the end, most of the accusations may come to little, but in the meantime, the amount of distraction will be vast. Depending on the frequency and apparent seriousness of the scandal, they may further deepen public cynicism about politics.

To the extent possible, the nation's policies and institutions for preventing corruption and protecting the integrity of governmental processes should also be designed to avoid feeding the politics of scandal. Put simply, they should aim to help public officials stay out of trouble. That is, policies on campaign finance, conflict of interest, and other matters should avoid draconian, career-ending penalties for modest offenses. To ensure that levels of compliance remain high, they should incorporate exceptionally thorough routine auditing. Finally, institutional investigating and prosecuting of public corruption, especially at the highest levels, should be designed to weigh the harm of distracting the public and disrupting government against the probability of discovering and punishing genuine wrongdoing.

Notes

Parts of this chapter were published previously in my article, "Coping with the Politics of Scandal," *Presidential Studies Quarterly* (fall 1998), 898–902.

1. The title of this chapter is inspired by Lillian Hellman's *Scoundrel Time* (1976), about congressional investigations of suspected communists in the 1950s.

2. There are good reasons for not prosecuting perjury in most instances where it has seemed to occur. People's ability to perceive and remember events is radically fallible: seemingly brazen lies are often in reality honest mistakes (Loftus 1996). Fear of prosecution for perjury can sometimes deter witnesses from testifying truthfully—for example, if their truthful testimony would disappoint prosecutors or conflict with other evidence. Nevertheless, failure to prosecute perjury in civil cases, in some reasonable proportion of more serious instances, is a serious deficiency in the legal system. No doubt, unscrupulous lawyers make their clients in civil cases aware of it.

3. For background on the relevant constitutional doctrines and precedents, see Van Tassel and Finkleman (1999) and various sources they cite, especially Berger (1973), Gerhardt (1996), and U.S. Congress (1984). See also Black (1974).

4. A few federal judges were impeached on somewhat similar grounds, but they had been convicted of crimes before their impeachment, and the constitutional standards for impeachment are probably lower in their case. Because judges serve

"during Good behavior," they arguably can be removed for failing to meet that standard. See Van Tassel and Finkleman (1999, 7–8).

5. Contrary to some commentators, the judge's finding does not provide retrospective justification for the impeachment effort. She found Clinton in civil, not criminal, contempt and imposed modest sanctions. Such a ruling certainly does not imply "high crimes and misdemeanors."

6. The article's argument was quite speculative on this point. It was clear that the impeachment debate would have made an earlier use of force, including ground troops, more difficult politically. Because the European NATO countries were not arguing for the use of ground troops, however, it is not clear that the United States would have advocated such action or would have had NATO support, even without the impeachment complication.

7. The idea of decriminalizing certain offenses and some of these observations about the Espy case were suggested in conversation by Katy Harriger.

8. For a variety of views on the substantive issues, see Shestack (1998).

9. To provide a legal basis for such a report, the prosecutor could rely on reporting obligations like those under Independent Counsel statute, or could make a sanitized announcement that he had uncovered evidence of a potential crime that he was not pursuing. Congress could then subpoena that evidence.

References

Berger, Raoul. 1973. *Impeachment: The Constitutional Problems.* Cambridge, Mass.: Harvard University Press.

Black, Charles L. 1974. *Impeachment: A Handbook.* New Haven, Conn.: Yale University Press.

Cooter, Robert D. and Thomas S. Ulen. 1997. *Law and Economics.* 2d ed. Reading, Mass.: Addison-Wesley-Longman.

Eastland, Terry. 1989. *Ethics, Politics and the Independent Counsel: Executive Power, Executive Vice, 1789–1989.* Washington, D.C.: National Legal Center for the Public Interest.

Garment, Suzanne. 1992. *Scandal: The Culture of Mistrust in American Politics.* New York: Anchor Books.

Gerhardt, Michael J. 1996. *The Federal Impeachment Process: A Constitutional and Historical Analysis.* Princeton, N.J.: Princeton University Press.

Ginsberg, Benjamin and Martin Shefter. 1990. *Politics by Other Means: The Declining Importance of Elections in America.* New York: Basic Books.

Harriger, Katy J. 1991. *Independent Justice: The Federal Special Prosecutor in American Politics.* Lawrence, Kans.: University of Kansas Press.

Hellman, Lillian. 1976. *Scoundrel Time.* 1st ed. Boston: Little, Brown.

Heyman, Philip B. 1998. "Four Unresolved Questions about the Responsibilities of the Independent Counsel." In Jerome J. Shestack, ed., "The Independent Counsel Act: From Watergate to Whitewater and Beyond. A Symposium in *The Georgetown Law Journal.*" 86:6 (July): 2119–32.

Holden, Mathew Jr. 1996. "The Lawyers of Power: A Working Paper on Politics and Prosecutorial Discretion." Unpublished manuscript.

Jacobs, Lawrence and Robert Y. Shapiro. 1998. "Politicians Don't Pander: Political Leadership, Public Opinion, and American Politics." Unpublished manuscript.

King, David. 1997. "The Polarization of American Parties and Mistrust of Government." In Joseph Nye, Philip Zelikow, and David King, eds., *Why People Don't Trust Government*. Cambridge, Mass.: Harvard University Press.

Loftus, Elizabeth. 1996. *Eyewitness Testimony*. Cambridge, Mass.: Harvard University Press.

McCarty, Nolan M., Keith Poole, and Howard Rosenthal. 1997. *Income Redistribution and the Realignment of American Politics*. Washington, D.C.: American Enterprise Institute.

Patterson, Thomas E. 1994. *Out of Order*. New York: Vintage Books.

Pious, Richard. 1998. "The Constitutional and Popular Law of Impeachment," *Presidential Studies Quarterly*. 28:4 (fall), 806–15.

Quirk, Paul J. and William Cunion. 1999. "Clinton's Domestic Policy: Lessons of a 'New Democrat.' " In Colin Campbell and Bert A. Rockman, eds., *The Clinton Legacy*. Chatham, N.J.: Chatham House.

Quirk, Paul J. and Joseph Hinchliffe. 1998. "The Rising Hegemony of Mass Opinion." In David Bryan Robertson, ed., *Loss of Confidence: Politics and Policy in the 1970s*.. University Park: Pennsylvania State Press, 19–50.

Quirk, Paul J. and Bruce Nesmith. 1998. "Divided Government and Policymaking: Negotiating the Laws," in Michael Nelson, ed. *The Presidency and the Political System*, 5th ed. Washington, D.C.: Congressional Quarterly Press.

Sciolino, Elaine and Ethan Bronner, 1999. "How a President, Distracted by Scandal, Entered Balkan War," *New York Times,* National Edition. 18 April, A1.

Shestack, Jerome J. 1998. "The Independent Counsel Act: From Watergate to Whitewater and Beyond." A Symposium in *The Georgetown Law Journal*. 86:6 (July).

U.S. Congress. 1984. House of Representatives. Committee on the Judiciary. *Constitutional Grounds for Presidential Impeachment: Report by the Staff of the Impeachment Inquiry*. 93rd Cong., 2nd sess.

Van Tassel, Emily Field and Paul Finkleman. 1999. *Impeachable Offenses: A Documentary History from 1787 to the Present*. Washington, D.C.: Congressional Quarterly.

Wilson, James Q. 1990. *Varieties of Police Behavior: The Management of Law and Order in Eight Communities*. 2d ed. Cambridge, Mass.: Harvard University Press.

EIGHT

The Impeachment and Acquittal of President William Jefferson Clinton

Michael J. Gerhardt

The impeachment and trial of President William Jefferson Clinton are not over. To be sure, roughly two months after the House of Representatives had impeached the president for perjury and obstruction of justice, the Senate fully acquitted him; however, the task remains to assess thoroughly the ramifications of the president's impeachment and acquittal.

Some aspects and significance of Clinton's impeachment proceedings are easy to discern. For instance, the House impeached and the Senate acquitted the president on the basis of votes largely cast along party lines. Moreover, his steady popularity throughout the impeachment proceedings put tremendous pressure on most senators to end the impeachment trial as quickly as possible. The significance of Clinton's impeachment is already evident in several ways: It has already tainted his legacy, marking him as only the second president—and the first popularly elected president—to have been impeached by the House and has also clearly cost the president precious time (and political coinage) in which to achieve policy or constitutional objectives of lasting significance. Nor does anyone seriously doubt or question the impact of media on the impeachment proceedings, a major component that was an incessant reminder to Congress of widespread public opposition to the president's removal, which, ultimately, prolonged the hearings.

Beyond these relatively obvious aspects of the president's impeachment and trial, no systematic analysis has yet been undertaken of the relationship between the proceedings and other impeachment proceedings in American history. Nor is it clear how the Clinton impeachment proceedings fit into the Constitution's general scheme of checks and balances. The purpose of this chapter is to provide such systematic analysis. It examines how Clinton's impeachment proceedings fit with Congress's experiences with other grand inquests and further examines the range of possible explanations for and likely lessons to be drawn from the president's impeachment and acquittal.

The first part of this chapter examines several possible explanations of Clinton's impeachment and acquittal and finds them largely in developments within, interaction between, and impact of several institutions or groups. The latter include Congress, the media, the presidency, the public, and the office of independent counsel.

The second part of this chapter examines several likely consequences of or lessons to be drawn from the president's impeachment and acquittal. First, Clinton's acquittal confirms the aptness of House Judiciary Chairman Henry Hyde's (R-Ill.) prediction at the outset of the House impeachment proceedings that it would not be possible to impeach and remove the president of the United States "without bipartisan support."[1] In every impeachment proceeding, the burden is on those seeking the impeachment and removal of some official to establish the seriousness and nonpartisan basis of their charges. Those seeking to remove the president ultimately failed to carry this burden in the Senate. Second, Clinton's impeachment and acquittal serve as a reminder that the ultimate legitimacy of an impeachment effort turns largely on the procedural choices made by the House and the Senate in the course of conducting those proceedings. The more these choices appear to be expedient, partisan, or unfair, the greater the likelihood that they become the basis for attacking the proceedings as biased or illegitimate. Third, Clinton's impeachment and acquittal exposed several fatal flaws in the Independent Counsel statute, not the least of which is the complete inability of an independent counsel to maintain the impartiality or credibility of his or her investigation in the face of full-scale political attacks waged by a president or presidential defenders. Fourth, the president's impeachment and acquittal sent mixed signals about which, if any, alternatives to impeachment are constitutionally legitimate. Fifth, the Clinton impeachment proceedings clouded the important question about whether there are different standards for impeaching presidents and judges. Last, Clinton's acquittal, contrary to conventional wisdom, is likely to have strengthened the office of the presidency.

The president's acquittal raises serious questions about whether or to what extent Congress has the resolve to conduct lengthy investigations of misconduct by popular presidents. Also, the Clinton impeachment proceedings might have exposed the vulnerability of the federal judiciary to political retaliation: some of the most important factors that helped Clinton survive the threat of removal (i.e., public support and media scrutiny) are absent from lower federal judges' impeachment proceedings. Any defects identified in the impeachment proceedings, should they be discovered, would clearly be exacerbated in a hearing with no media coverage and about which the public is largely indifferent.

Explaining the Impeachment and Acquittal of President Clinton

There has been a lot of speculation about the reasons for President Clinton's impeachment and acquittal, but the most likely explanations put the president's impeachment proceedings in historical, political, and constitutional perspective. The first, most obvious explanation of the outcome is the stated reasons senators have given for casting their acquittal votes. The most serious problem with relying on such statements is that not all senators produced them: Only seventy-two senators published such statements. These seventy-two included only thirty-four of the forty-five Democratic senators who voted "not guilty" on both articles of impeachment, four of the five Republicans who voted "not guilty" on both articles, and three of the five Republicans who voted "not guilty" on the first but "guilty" on the second article. Of those thirty-eight senators who published statements on their reasons for voting "not guilty" on both articles, twenty-seven explained that they did not regard the misconduct alleged in either article of impeachment approved by the House as constituting an impeachable offense. Sixteen of the thirty-eight senators (all Democrats) explained that the partisan zeal of House managers in the Senate proceedings and of Republican leadership in the House affected their votes, while fifteen Democratic senators (and Arlen Specter [R-Pa.]) explained that House managers had not proven the misconduct alleged in either article of impeachment. Two Republican senators indi-

cated that they had voted "not guilty" on the first article of impeachment (and "guilty" on the second) even though they believed all
charges against the president had been proven, while another Republican senator, Fred Thompson (R-Tenn.), explained that he had voted
"not guilty" on the first article based on his belief that the article
was impossible to defend against because it was vague and did not
specify the statements in which the president had allegedly perjured
himself.[2]

These numbers do not tell the full story of the president's impeachment and acquittal. Consequently, one could try to further explain
the event in partisan terms. All thirty-five votes to convict Clinton on
the first article and all fifty votes to convict on the second were cast
by Republicans,[3] and well over 95 percent of the votes cast in the
House to impeach the president were cast by Republicans.[4] Yet, Democrats acted throughout the proceedings in at least as partisan a fashion
as their Republican counterparts. In the House, Democrats cast over
95 percent of the votes in opposition to the president's impeachment.[5]
Moreover, at the outset of the impeachment trial it was clear that if
forty-five Senate Democrats voted in opposition to Clinton's removal
it would be numerically impossible for him to be convicted. In fact,
no Democratic senator bolted from the party to vote for either article
of impeachment, whereas ten senators bolted from the Republican
contingent to vote against the first article, and five voted against
the second.

The president's impeachment and acquittal could also be explained
in light of a significant trend in the federal impeachment process—the
increasing influence of federal prosecutors in triggering impeachment
investigations and proceedings.[6] A telling but overlooked fact about
Clinton's impeachment proceedings is that they marked the sixth occasion in the past twenty-five or so years in which Congress exercised
or contemplated seriously using its impeachment power.[7] No other
comparable period of time in American history has witnessed so much
impeachment activity. One important factor linking all six impeachment efforts is that each was triggered by a referral to Congress from an
external investigative authority. Four of the six impeachment efforts—
involving Judges Claiborne, Hastings, Nixon, and Collins—were referred to the House by the Judicial Conference of the United States.
The other two began with referrals to Congress from two specially
appointed federal prosecutors: Leon Jaworski, who, as a special prosecutor appointed by the attorney general,[8] referred to the House several
boxes of materials relating to possible impeachable misconduct of

President Nixon[9] and former judge and Solicitor General Kenneth Starr, who, as an independent counsel appointed pursuant to the Independent Counsel statute,[10] referred pursuant to a special provision of the act evidence that, his office believed, demonstrated Clinton's commission of possible impeachable offenses.[11] Only one of these referrals resulted in a Senate acquittal (Clinton), three culminated in the removal of the targeted official (Harry Claiborne, Walter Nixon, and Alcee Hastings),[12] and two culminated in forced resignations (Nixon and Judge Robert Collins).

President Clinton's impeachment stands apart from most of these other referrals not only as the one resulting in a Senate acquittal but also the one about which the House failed to undertake any independent fact-finding. In House impeachment proceedings, only twice has it undertaken no independent fact-finding: the first was the impeachment of President Andrew Johnson. The House failed to take evidence because in two prior unsuccessful efforts to impeach Johnson it had undertaken limited fact-finding. The president's firing of Stanton gave the proponents of his ouster something they had not previously had— an act that in their view clearly violated a law and was impeachable. Moreover, President Johnson's impeachment for having fired Stanton has been widely regarded as one of the most intensely partisan impeachments rendered by the House (thereby making it a dubious precedent to follow). Similarly, failure of the House to undertake any independent fact-finding prior to impeaching Clinton provided a basis upon which the House's impeachment judgment could be attacked as partisan or unfair.

The impeachment of Harry Claiborne is the only other instance in which the House failed to undertake any independent fact-finding. The full House impeached Claiborne within a month of the House Judiciary Committee's formal recommendation of impeachment articles against him. The committee had unanimously voted to recommend impeachment articles within three weeks of the House's formal initiation of an impeachment inquiry. Unlike President Johnson before him and President Clinton after, Claiborne did not complain about the House's proceedings (including its failure to undertake any independent fact-finding); he welcomed a quick impeachment because he believed the sooner he had a full trial in the Senate the sooner he would be fully vindicated.[13]

No doubt, the media have had enormous impact on Clinton's impeachment proceedings in several ways. First, the splintering or fragmentation of media into countless outlets (including newspaper, network and public television, cable, the Internet, and radio) over the past two decades has increased competition to get news, particularly breaking news, and to keep or increase audiences. This splintering or fragmentation has made it much more difficult for a single force or group to dominate the news. Nevertheless, the presidency as an institution has several important advantages over Congress in being covered by and in spreading messages through the media. It is much easier to cover a single individual than many people. It is thus easier to cover a president, the embodiment and leader of an entire institution, than Congress, which operates through the actions of several hundred individuals. Moreover, the president has considerably more resources to gain media attention or access than any given member of Congress, more agents available to spread messages, and more media permanently attached to and covering activities. Consequently, Clinton's criticisms of the independent counsel's investigation and of the House's case against him received much more widespread coverage than any counterattacks.

To be sure, the splintering of the media has made it much easier for critics of a president to find an outlet to publicize their charges against him. Such public attacks can service several ends, including deflecting a president's attention or energy and thereby hampering or impeding achievement of certain preferred objectives. In this sense, the media have wreaked havoc by facilitating the destruction of or damage to a president's reputation by a thousand little cuts or attacks. The president can lose popularity or some degree of public support from these assaults, but in the end the office allows a decisive advantage over political foes or attackers because of the unique resources available to gain easy access to and spread messages through the national media. Moreover, recourse to the bully pulpit and the national media enables a president to go over the heads of political opposition in Congress (or elsewhere) to urge people to support either the president personally or the White House agenda.

Second, the media had great impact on the proceedings through coverage that clearly shaped and mobilized public opinion. Indeed the Clinton impeachment proceedings were the first in which public preferences helped to drive the final outcome. Throughout the trial, Clinton's approval ratings held steady at or near 67 percent.[14] Similarly, a majority of Americans steadily opposed the president's removal from office, yet more than 70 percent believed Clinton was guilty of the

misconduct charged in the first article of impeachment,[15] and 55 percent believed that he was guilty of the misconduct alleged in both
articles.[16] These statistics can be reconciled. One poll found 76 percent
of the American people believed the case against the president involved
purely private misconduct that should not have been made the basis
for his impeachment.[17] Another poll found most of the public did not
believe the charges constituted appropriate grounds for his removal.[18]
In other words, most of the public did not feel Clinton's behavior
constituted impeachable misconduct. The Democrats' steady opposition to the president's removal plainly followed the preferences of
most Americans.

Media coverage might have had various other effects on the public
(or at least the 61 percent that regularly followed the hearings) and,
through public opinion, on members of Congress. First, it might have
constantly reminded the public and Congress, particularly senators,
of the House managers' difficulty of arguing convincingly that the
president had breached the public trust—a classic prerequisite for
impeachment—as long as the public did not believe its trust with the
president had been breached. Second, the constant airing of bashing
of Clinton's integrity throughout his presidency might have lowered
public expectations of presidential integrity. New allegations of presidential misconduct would not have surprised much of the public or
perceptively shifted its basic opinion of Clinton. Third, apparent media
obsession with finding the next Watergate might have increased public
skepticism over the likelihood of impeachment proceedings actually
uncovering it. Media rhetoric characterized every new scandal of the
Clinton White House (e.g., Filegate, Travelgate, MonicaGate, Korea-
gate, ChinaGate, Whitewater) to liken President Clinton's scandals to
those of Richard Nixon; the public found the comparisons wanting.
Repeated attempts to liken Clinton's scandals to Watergate, particularly before full investigations had been launched, might have led
much of the public to conclude the president's harshest critics and
the proponents of his impeachment were akin to the boy who cried
wolf. Fourth, comprehensive coverage might simply have bored the
public. Prolonging the hearings held little, if any, prospect that anything new would happen. In virtually every poll, the vast majority of
Americans indicated that they were sick and tired of the trial by the
time it was over. The public's exasperation if not boredom with the
trial, coupled with its steady opposition to removal of the president,
intensified pressure to end the hearings.

The Lessons of Clinton's Impeachment and Acquittal

Moving from possible explanations for Clinton's impeachment and acquittal to the lessons likely to be drawn from the experience, the focus of inquiry shifts from relying primarily on empirical data to determining how successive generations, particularly successive congresses, have understood the significance of each previous grand inquest. Obviously, we can only speculate about the range of possible lessons or consequences of the president's impeachment and acquittal, based on some of the spin already being applied to the event and on the consequences of roughly similar past events. It of course remains to be seen which lessons will stand and which possible consequences will arise.

First, the Democrats' uniform opposition to Clinton's conviction highlights the enormous difficulty (if not impossibility) of securing a conviction as long as senators from the president's party unanimously stand by him. Rarely does a political party dominate more than two-thirds of the Senate seats; hence, the solidity of the Democratic ranks in Clinton's impeachment trial dramatically illustrated that removal of a president is possible only if the misconduct is sufficiently compelling to draw support for a conviction from both sides of the aisle. In the absence of bipartisan support for removal, acquittal is virtually guaranteed. Also the Constitution requires that at least two-thirds of the Senate vote to convict in order for removal to occur.[19] The supermajority requirement makes conviction and removal highly unlikely; it is no easy task to get such a high degree of consensus among senators, particularly when the stakes are so high. When such consensus is achieved, it is likely to be the result of a very compelling and credible case for conviction and removal.

Second, Clinton's acquittal might have shown impeachment to be a relatively ineffective check against the misconduct of a popular president. The acquittal might leave subsequent generations uncertain as to whether Congress has the resolve to conduct impeachment proceedings against a president with high approval ratings. The congressional investigation into Watergate took more than two years before the discovery of the smoking gun (tapes of certain conversations in the White House) that led to President Nixon's resignation. The Clinton impeachment proceedings took roughly six months from start to finish, among the shortest in American history. Impeachment proceedings against Andrew Johnson were the shortest: lasting roughly three months.[20] Even so, the relative shortness of Clinton's impeachment proceedings was too long for most people. Although most people did not believe Clinton's case involved legitimately impeachable offenses, some investigations might not uncover seriously problematic misconduct (insofar as the public is concerned) for some time. Future congresses, for fear of alienating the public, might think twice before engaging in a relatively prolonged investigation of a president's misconduct. (In this respect, the Clinton impeachment proceedings may have strengthened rather than weakened the office of the presidency.) The Clinton impeachment proceedings raise a question: Just how serious must the misconduct of a popular president be to convince a majority of Americans to support removal from office? Impeachment may be effective for only the kinds of misconduct that can galvanize the public to set aside approval of a president's performance to support resignation or formal removal. Indeed, a future Congress might support removal only with direct evidence of very serious wrongdoing and unambiguous consensus (in Congress and among the public) on the gravity of such wrongdoing.

Third, President Clinton's impeachment proceedings might have underscored the greater vulnerability to impeachment and removal of officials who lack a president's resources (e.g., the bully pulpit) or popularity. An unpopular president such as Andrew Johnson might meet a different fate in an age in which media constantly apply pressure to investigate a president's misconduct (or unpopular actions) and in which daily polls can dramatize a loss of popularity and an increase in support for removal; removal or resignation might be extremely likely. (To date, the only such instance occurred during the final days of Richard Nixon's presidency, when the public for the first and only time during the Watergate investigation expressed support for the president's ouster, based on information revealed in the Watergate tapes.) This dynamic is likely to be even more problematic for a federal judge, including a Supreme Court justice, whose hearings will probably not get media coverage nearly as widespread as that of Clinton's, nor the outpouring of public support (or of public opposition to a prolongation of hearings). A federal judge or other low-profile official simply lacks the resources available to a president (particularly a popular one) in defending against political retaliation in the form of an impeachment.

Fourth, the Clinton impeachment serves as a dramatic reminder that the burden in an impeachment proceeding is on the advocates or proponents of impeachment to show that charges have not been based on or motivated by partisanship.[21] No doubt, a proponent of President Clinton's impeachment and removal might claim the charges were not based on partisanship but rather on the need to protect the integrity of the judicial system and to ensure the president's compliance with his oath of office. Yet, those charging Justice Chase and President Johnson with impeachable misconduct argued the very same thing: they claimed the charges against those officials were based on those officials' abuses of authority and not on partisanship. Ultimately, those seeking the removal of President Johnson and Justice Chase failed to carry their burden (for a critical mass of senators and for posterity). Similarly, those seeking Clinton's removal from office have failed (thus far) to convince most Americans (as well as any Democrat in the Senate) that their charges against the president were not based on or motivated to a significant degree by partisanship.

The latter failure increases the chances that subsequent generations will look disfavorably upon the House's impeachment of President Clinton. There have been similar failures in the past (impeachment attempts against Justice Chase in 1805 and President Johnson in 1868), and the majority vote cast in favor of convicting did not preclude either impeachment from being subsequently viewed as lacking political legitimacy. Johnson's and Chase's acquittals have each dissuaded subsequent Congresses from bringing or initiating impeachments based on similar misconduct in part because the outcomes in Chase's and Johnson's trials did not turn on disputes about the underlying facts. Virtually everyone at the time agreed on the facts themselves but disagreed over their significance. Subsequent generations and Congresses, unencumbered with having to resolve factual disputes, have made their own assessments of the legal and constitutional significance of the facts (and thus of Chase's and Johnson's misconduct); they have concluded the misconduct targeted in each impeachment did not warrant removal from office.

By similar reasoning, the Clinton acquittal could be construed by subsequent Congresses as a rejection of the House's judgment on the impeachability of the president's misconduct. The vote to impeach the president was (as in Chase's and Johnson's cases) largely cast along party lines, whereas there has been a relatively widespread perception (at least among the public) that the proceedings generally were conducted and resolved on partisan grounds. Moreover, most people (including most members of Congress) do not disagree much, if at all, about the underlying facts in Clinton's case; they disagree over their legal significance. Subsequent Congresses might conclude that if such misconduct could not merit a conviction in one case (i.e., Clinton's), it would be inconsistent or unfair that it could in another. In addition, future members of Congress could conclude that if a Senate majority vote to convict both Chase and Johnson could not save the impeachment from being regarded as illegitimate, the absence of a Senate majority vote (coupled with other criticisms) for either article of impeachment against Clinton could be viewed as a more resounding rejection of the legitimacy of the House's case for impeachment.[22]

The fifth possible lesson of Clinton's impeachment and trial affirmed the final, nonreviewable discretion of the House and Senate each to conduct its respective impeachment proceedings. In the course of Clinton's impeachment proceedings, both the House and the Senate followed the holding in *Nixon v. United States*,[23] in which the Supreme Court unanimously ruled that challenges to the constitutionality of Senate impeachment trial procedures are nonjusticiable. The Court left to the Senate the final, nonreviewable authority to devise impeachment trial procedures as it saw fit. Consequently, the House and the Senate took great liberties in fashioning their respective impeachment proceedings against Clinton as each saw fit. For example, in relatively controversial decisions, the House decided (for only the third time in history) not to call any live witnesses or otherwise undertake any independent fact-finding, to hold a final vote on the impeachment articles in a lame-duck session,[24] and to forego defining or adopting a uniform standard for defining the impeachability of certain misconduct. House members also decided for themselves such questions as the applicability of the Fifth Amendment due process clause, the appropriate burden of proof, and the propriety of allowing three colleagues to cast votes on the articles even though each had been elected to the Senate and would sit in judgment on the president in his impeachment trial. In the trial, senators decided for themselves such procedural questions as the appropriate burden of proof, the applicable rules of evidence (including need for live testimony), the appropriate standard for determining the impeachability of the president's misconduct, and the propriety of holding closed-door hearings on a variety of issues (including final debates on the president's guilt or innocence.)

A sixth possible lesson of the impeachment proceedings is their underscoring of Congress's inertia in initiating impeachment proceedings in the absence of an external referral or pressure from an independent authority. Generally, members of Congress have little incentive to put aside other pressing business to conduct impeachment proceedings. This reluctance has left a vacuum that prosecutors have filled for several decades. The problem is that criminal prosecutions or convictions that do not result in resignations put enormous pressure on Congress to not only impeach the targeted official(s) but also defer to the findings of an external authority while rushing to judgment in impeachment proceedings.

Seventh, the Clinton impeachment proceedings could be construed as confirming that standards for impeaching presidents are different from standards for impeaching judges. A popular argument made in Congress on behalf of Clinton was that there are different standards based on the officials' different tenure and responsibilities. Judges serve only "during Good Behavior"[25] and thus arguably could be removed for misbehavior that includes but is not necessarily limited to impeachable offenses.[26] Presidents are popularly elected, and thus the electoral process arguably operates as the primary check against a president's abuse of power.[27] A president presumably will return to private life after serving as president and is thus available (in a way a judge is not) to be held accountable for both civil and criminal misconduct at a time when it will not interfere with official duties.

Several factors cut against inferring that Congress endorsed different standards for impeaching different officials. First, the constitutional language is uniform.[28] Second, the assertion counters history; it conflicts with the Founders' obvious intention to adopt the phrase "during Good Behavior" to distinguish judicial tenure (life) from tenure of elected officials (e.g., the president) rather than to establish the particular terms of judicial removal. Moreover, the argument that the Constitution establishes different standards for impeaching presidents and judges is a relatively new one in impeachment history.[29] For instance, President Johnson never made such a claim, although his impeachment had been preceded by four judicial impeachments, including that of Associate Justice Samuel Chase. The most plausible precedents for this point of view are the impeachment and removal of Judges John Pickering (for drunkenness and insanity)[30] and Harry Claiborne (for income tax evasion)[31] because each judge was removed for misconduct arguably unrelated to official duties and thus for basic misbehavior as opposed to official misconduct or the abuse of official power. Yet, neither precedent supports a looser standard for impeaching federal judges. In fact, Pickering was impeached and removed on the basis that he could no longer function as a federal judge and because there was no other alternative for dealing with a federal judge who had, in the estimation of Congress, become completely dysfunctional.[32] This same reasoning led to the ouster of Harry Claiborne, for the House Report on Claiborne indicates a central concern that he had become completely disabled from functioning as a federal judge because of criminal conduct (and conviction).[33]

A third reason for not construing President Clinton's acquittal as signaling different standards for impeaching presidents and judges is this: Allowing judges to be removed for misbehavior that falls short of an impeachable offense undercuts the constitutional safeguards against political retaliation directed toward judges for doing their jobs. The constitutional structure ceases to make much sense if judges can be removed through either the cumbersome, difficult process of impeachment for impeachable offenses or through an easier, looser process (administered by Congress or others, such as judges) for misbehavior that does not rise to the level of an impeachable offense.

Fourth, consequences that might ensue from an attempt to impeach a president might be different from those that might result from an attempt to impeach a judge but should not be a basis for finding different constitutional standards for impeaching presidents and judges. Rather, the consequences of an impeachment of any official are plainly relevant as factors to be taken into account in the course of applying the operative standard. The vesting of impeachment authority in political branches necessarily implies the discretion to take various factors (including possible consequences) into consideration in the course of exercising such authority.[34] Of the seventeen senators who expressed an opinion about this issue in the Clinton impeachment trial, eleven (ten Republicans and one Democrat) upheld the position that the same standard applies for impeaching presidents and federal judges.

Regardless of whether subsequent generations will construe the Clinton impeachment proceedings as confirming that there are different standards for impeaching presidents and judges, they will surely ponder what particular standard, if any, the Clinton proceedings endorsed for determining impeachability of misconduct. To be sure, neither the House nor the Senate formally endorsed a specific standard of impeachment; rather, there appear to have been almost as many standards for determining impeachability of misconduct as there were members of both chambers voting on the articles of impeachment.

Nevertheless, the Clinton impeachment serves as a reminder of the Framers' expectations that Congress would determine on a case-by-case basis the misconduct that constituted "other high crimes or misdemeanors."[35] The constitutional standard was designed to narrow the range of impeachable offenses from that which was available in England (there were no restrictions on the scope of impeachable offenses),[36] but the standard still remains rather broad. The Constitution contemplates that an impeachable offense is a political crime about whose essential elements the Framers agreed only in the abstract (including such general preconditions as serious injury to the republic). Consequently, every impeachment (including the most recent one) has featured a debate over whether the misconduct charged constitutes a political crime. As these debates have shown, it is practically impossible to get the House or the Senate to adopt a uniform standard for determining the impeachability of misconduct. The resolutions of these debates track the historic practice of each member deciding for him or herself the proper resolution of a series of procedural issues.[37] Debates over the proper definition of impeachable offenses in Congress have thus featured tugs-of-war: Those seeking impeachment defend relatively broad, amorphous standards that they can show have been easily met in a given case, and those opposing impeachment support very narrow standards that they claim have not been met in the specific circumstances of the case before them.

Debates over the scope of impeachable offenses in particular cases have not produced any useful guidelines; however, Senate judgments in impeachment trials do reveal an interesting pattern. The seven federal officials the Senate has convicted and removed from office (all federal judgeships) have had in common misconduct that (1) has caused a serious injury to the republic and (2) has had a nexus between the official's misconduct and the official's formal duties.[38] In assessing the nexus, members of Congress have taken into account the degree to which certain misconduct has been either so outrageous or so thoroughly disabling or incompatible with an official's duties as to give Congress no choice but to remove an official.[39] In President Clinton's impeachment trial, several senators explained their acquittal votes on the basis of the absence of one or more of these elements.

Yet another possible consequence of President Clinton's impeachment is the public impression that impeachment is just another political event. Indeed, over 70 percent of the American people believed that the president's impeachment trial had been resolved largely on partisan grounds.[40] This outcome is not what the Framers had wanted. For instance, in Federalist Paper Number 65, Alexander Hamilton expressed the hope that senators in an impeachment trial would rise above the passions of the moment to do what is in the best interest

of the Constitution or the nation. Arguably, Johnson's acquittal is
an example of such altruism. In contrast, the Clinton impeachment
proceedings posed a dynamic different from the one that Hamilton
explained the Founders had tried to guard against. The Founders were
primarily concerned with a circumstance in which the public pressured
Congress to remove a president (and senators resisted), but the Founders did not foresee a situation in which the public largely opposed
removal while many members of Congress intensely supported it.
Interestingly, the Senate's failure to convict Clinton followed popular
sentiment, but it did not win the respect of the American people. The
proceedings generally weakened public confidence in Congress.[41]

It is possible that one facet of the Clinton impeachment proceedings
reduced most people's confidence in government to operate in a neutral manner: censure. Censure was blocked for several reasons put
forward by Republicans in both the House and the Senate. Censure
opponents claimed, inter alia, that it constituted either a bill of attainder
or an illegitimate bypass of impeachment—the only constitutionally
authorized means for dealing with a president's misconduct.[42] Neither
of these arguments is sound. To begin with, a bill of attainder is a
legislative action that seeks to impose punishment on an individual
in the absence of a judicial proceeding.[43] A censure could qualify as a
bill of attainder only if it actually imposed tangible punishment. If a
censure consisted only of the verbal expression of critical condemnation of a president's conduct, the only conceivable damage that would
ensue would be to a president's reputation. Yet, reputation is not
something that the prohibition of bills of attainder was designed to
protect.[44] The prohibition has had the narrower purpose of precluding
fines or physical punishment or imprisonment imposed by a legislature
as a substitute for or instead of a judicial proceeding. Moreover, even
if there were damage to a president's reputation, it is likely to have
resulted from expression on a political subject and as such would
undoubtedly be protected by the First Amendment[45] and the speech
or debate clause.[46]

The argument that censure is illegitimate because impeachment is
the only constitutionally authorized means for Congress to punish a
president might have struck many people as disingenuous (indeed,
throughout the proceedings most Americans supported censure as an
alternative to impeachment).[47] First, the argument that impeachment
is the only means for dealing with a President's misconduct is misguided. The argument for censure held that it was a legitimate option
for dealing with misconduct that did not rise to the level of an impeach-

able offense. Impeachment has no bearing whatsoever on what Congress may do with respect to the latter category of misconduct, for it exists as the exclusive mechanism available to Congress for removing a president for impeachable misconduct. Second, the Constitution can easily be read as allowing, rather than restricting, censure. In particular, Article I, section 7, provides that "Judgments in Cases of Impeachment shall not extend further than to removal from Office, and disqualification to hold and enjoy any Office of honor, Trust, or Profit under the United States. . . . "[48] This clause apparently leaves open the possibility of punishments that fall short of removal of office, such as censure. Third, the Constitution clearly allows senators individually (by virtue of the First Amendment and the speech or debate clause) to announce publicly their own condemnation of a president's misconduct. If the senators may engage in such expression individually, it is not clear why constitutionally they may not do so collectively. There is also nothing in the Constitution that bars a senator from collecting colleagues' signatures on a document that castigates the president and then entering that document into the Congressional Record. A censure is the functional equivalent of the latter action. While one could object that censure might be either a politically futile act or be overused to frustrate or harass a president (or some other official), these objections arise from prudence rather than the Constitution. Whether a censure is constitutional is separate and distinct from whether in any given case it makes political sense to use it.[49]

Another option that clearly seems to have been a casualty in the Clinton impeachment proceedings is the so-called finding of fact that the Senate ultimately refused to formally approve. The proposal was a variation on an intriguing reading of the impeachment clauses given by University of Chicago Law School Professor Joseph Isenberg.[50] Professor Isenberg has suggested that the Constitution allows the House to impeach and the Senate to convict certain kinds of officials for misconduct that do not rise to the level of impeachable offenses.[51] According to Professor Isenberg, only removal (as opposed to conviction) constitutionally requires a two-thirds vote of the Senate and proof or evidence of impeachable offenses. Professor Isenberg based this reading of the Constitution on textual provisions that set forth the House's and Senate's respective authorities regarding impeachment but do not contain within them any express limitations[52] such as confinement to the scope of impeachable offenses or, in the case of the Senate, to removal. In addition, the argument for the finding of fact relies on the earlier impeachment trials of John Pickering in

1803, West Humphreys in 1862, and Robert Archbald in 1913 in which the Senate took separate votes on guilt and removal (i.e., once the Senate had found the official guilty of at least one of the articles of impeachment it then voted on removal).[53] This analysis led several senators to maintain that it was possible for the Senate to find the president guilty of misconduct without removing him from office.[54] This vote would have occurred before, and would have been separate from, a formal vote of conviction or removal. In the view of its supporters, the finding of fact would have been indistinguishable from censure, for it would have embodied nothing more than an expression of opinion about whether an official had done something. As such, a finding of fact conceivably would have been constitutional for many of the same reasons as censure.

The proposed finding of fact proved problematic for several reasons, not the least of which is that it rested on a flawed reading of the impeachment clauses. It was mistaken to read the impeachment clauses in a disjointed or disconnected fashion; rather, they should be read together as a coordinated and coherent whole. When read thus, it is clear that the impeachment clauses all have in common the obvious—impeachment—and impeachment is necessarily defined by its scope. The point of enumerated powers is that powers have limitations, and impeachment has its limits in the constitutional language "treason, bribery, and other high crimes or misdemeanors."[55] To disconnect either the House or the Senate impeachment power from the scope of impeachable offenses not only does damage to the coherence of constitutional text and constitutional structure, but it also opens the door to extraordinary abuse on the part of either the House or the Senate, for each could then be completely unchecked and unbounded—constitutionally—to impeach or convict on whatever basis struck its fancy. Nothing confirms more dramatically that no such door was ever meant to be opened than do the debates on impeachment in the constitutional and ratifying conventions, for, clearly, throughout these debates one of the Framers' most important objectives in designing the impeachment process was to define narrowly—certainly much more narrowly than Great Britain had ever done—the scope of the impeachment power.[56]

Another major problem with the finding of fact was the uncertainty about whether it was meant to be merely an expression of negative opinion about the president or something else. Indeed, its timing—prior to the adjournment of the impeachment trial—made its status as an expression of opinion dangerously ambiguous. As long as the

Senate vote on the finding of fact occurred as part of the impeachment trial, it could easily have been confused with a vote of conviction. And no doubt some senators understood it as tantamount to the latter. Many senators who supported the finding of fact were motivated in part by their desire to prevent the president from claiming vindication or acquittal if the Senate failed to convict for perjury or obstruction of justice. The finding of fact would have allowed these senators to suggest that Clinton had in fact been found guilty of certain misconduct (as defined in the finding of fact) by whatever number of senators had voted in favor of the finding of fact. Consequently, the finding of fact seemed to have represented for some senators a device to bring about a conviction (or the like) without the requisite vote. If the finding of fact were the same as, or tantamount to, a vote of conviction, then at least two-thirds of the senators would have had to vote in favor of it in order for it to have had that effect. Had at least two-thirds of the senators voted in favor of it, it almost certainly would have served as a conviction, and its subject—the president—would have been removed from office; had two-thirds of the senators not voted in favor of the finding of fact, then the president almost certainly would have been entitled to claim that the vote should have counted as an acquittal.

Indeed, if, after having voted on the finding of fact, senators had been required to take another vote on whether to convict (or remove) the president, Clinton would probably have had good reason to claim a violation of fundamental fairness. For a vote on conviction following a vote on the finding of fact would have appeared to allow some senators the chance to try to convict the president on more than one vote—through the vote on the finding of fact and the subsequent vote on conviction or removal. Subjecting the president to a vote of conviction more than once would simply have subjected him to a dubious and arguably spiteful process. The result surely would have been perceived as unfair.

Moreover, the Senate having taken separate votes on guilt and removal in some earlier proceedings does not necessarily show that it may convict for a nonimpeachable offense. First, in each of the earlier trials in which the Senate took such separate votes, it removed the official from office. It is significant that in each of those proceedings the Senate took a single vote on whether to remove the official only after that official had been found guilty of the charges set forth in any single article by more than a two-thirds vote. For instance, the Senate voted 19–7 to find Pickering guilty on each of four articles and then took a single vote 20–6 to remove him from office (with Senator William Wells from Delaware deciding to switch sides for the final vote and go with the supermajority because the outcome was "a fait accompli.")[57] Similarly, after a supermajority had found Humphreys guilty on each of seven articles of impeachment (with the exception of one of the three specifications of misconduct set forth in the sixth article), the Senate voted unanimously to remove Humphreys.[58] In Archbald's trial, the Senate took a voice vote to remove him once a supermajority had found him guilty of the misconduct charged in five of thirteen articles of impeachment passed by the House.[59] These sequences suggest that as long as two-thirds or more of the Senate had found an official guilty of the misconduct charged in at least one article, removal was inevitable. Indeed, in the impeachment trial of Halsted Ritter in 1936 the Senate subsequently took the position that it was not constitutionally obliged to take separate votes on guilt and removal. It concluded then (and has taken the position consistently ever since) that a single vote to convict is all the Senate is required constitutionally to take.[60]

Yet another obvious casualty of President Clinton's impeachment and acquittal is the Independent Counsel statute. Clinton's tangles with Starr unleashed widespread reappraisals and criticism of the statute.[61] In the aftermath of the impeachment proceedings, Congress allowed the act to expire at the end of June 1999.[62]

The Clinton impeachment proceedings demonstrated two major defects in the Independent Counsel statute (apart from any lingering questions about its constitutionality). The first defect was evident in its failure to provide adequate safeguards against aggressive efforts of an independent counsel to influence the course of the impeachment proceedings. Starr attempted such influence through a series of actions, including but not limited to the strong characterizations and a brieflike quality of his office's referral,[63] aggressive advocacy in the wording or characterizations of the referral in his testimony before the Judiciary Committee,[64] submission to the committee in response to White House attacks on the eve of the impeachment vote,[65] public response to criticisms of his testimony by his former ethics adviser (who quit in protest of the tenor of the testimony),[66] and cooperation with House managers on the eve of the conclusion of the impeachment trial to meet informally with Monica Lewinsky to determine her feasibility as a witness.[67] These actions separately and particularly together undermined Starr's claims of impartiality or neutrality. The more that Starr tried to interject his office into the impeachment fray, the less independent and the more partisan he appeared to be. At the very least, such actions highlighted the need to revise the act radically to constrain or preclude such actions in the future.

A second, largely overlooked defect the impeachment hearings exposed was the pragmatic justification for abandoning the Independent Counsel statute (apart from any lingering questions about its constitutionality). An independent counsel has no means by which to effectively defend the integrity of his or her investigation in a public relations battle with the White House. In such a skirmish, the president has unparalleled means to undermine the so-called independence of the independent counsel's investigation. In contrast, the system that preceded the Independent Counsel statute provided a strong disincentive for a president to attack a special prosecutor, because the latter would have been appointed by the president's own attorney general; thus a president's attack on such a special prosecutor would appear to be an attack against the office of president itself. Such was the case with President Nixon's firing of Archibald Cox, a decision that backfired. Firing Cox only made Nixon look guilty, whereas special prosecutors who have been appointed by presidents or attorneys general have largely been immune from presidential public attacks or retaliation.[68]

Last, President Clinton's acquittal hardly qualifies as a personal vindication. During the hearings, virtually every senator published or made public comments but they did not include very strong condemnation of the president's misconduct. Those supporting the president's conviction condemned Clinton in the harshest of terms. With only one exception (Senator Tom Harkin [D-Iowa]), the president's defenders strongly condemned his behavior. His defenders contended repeatedly throughout the impeachment proceedings that his acquittal should not be construed as foreclosing other forums in which to hold him accountable for his misconduct. This widespread condemnation of the president is likely to have some historical if not constitutional significance (beyond the damage to the president's personal reputation and legacy). For example, it might confirm that in our constitutional system impeachment exists only for a very small or rare set of misdeeds, and other forums exist for holding presidents accountable for non-impeachable misconduct, including civil proceedings, criminal prosecution and trial, public opinion, media scrutiny, and history. Indeed, one popular lesson to be derived from Justice Chase's acquittal is that impeachment is an inappropriate device for retaliating against a federal judge's official rulings.[69] The appropriate forum for dealing with a judge's mistaken rulings is the judicial system, particularly through the appeals process. A popular lesson drawn from President Johnson's acquittal is that impeachment is an inappropriate mechanism for redressing a president's mistaken policy judgments.[70] Appropriate forums for dealing with such erroneous judgments include the court of public opinion, elections, and the judgment of history. A critical lesson for subsequent generations to draw from President Clinton's acquittal is that his misconduct did not have a public dimension (or harm) sufficient to warrant his removal from office.[71] The appropriate forums holding him (or others who engage in similar misconduct) accountable include public opinion, the judgment of history, possible censure, civil proceedings (e.g., Judge Susan Webber Wright's contempt citation)[72] and criminal prosecution.

Conclusion

The ultimate significance of President Clinton's acquittal will depend on its meaning to future Congresses and generations. The most likely enduring lessons are those that the Clinton impeachment proceedings reaffirmed. One such lesson is this: It is not possible to remove a president from office without bipartisan support. In other words, presidential impeachment requires making charges against a president and proving misconduct whose seriousness or gravity is sufficiently compelling to draw support from both major parties in Congress. Moreover, what was true about the impeachment process in the nineteenth century seems to be true at the end of the twentieth century—impeachment is not a substitute for criminal or civil proceedings but rather a special mechanism for dealing with abuses or breaches of uniquely presidential powers or privileges and thus serves the very limited function of restoring the constitutional order to full health.[73] Moreover, foreclosing one forum of presidential accountability—impeachment— does not necessarily mean that others, such as civil and criminal proceedings, the court of public opinion, history, or perhaps censure, are unavailable.

Another conceivable lesson is that impeachment proceedings are about more than the fate of some impeached official. Impeachment proceedings, like few if any other political and constitutional events in our system of government, test every institution with which they come into contact. Consequently, President Clinton's impeachment proceedings, like those against Presidents Johnson and Nixon, revealed a great deal about the institutions of the presidency and Congress. There is little or no question that the office of the presidency saved

Johnson from removal in spite of his widespread unpopularity. In the end, enough senators refused to convict Johnson at least in part because of the repercussions such an outcome would have had on the presidency itself.[74] The office did not save Nixon, partly because his conduct was widely regarded as constituting serious abuses of uniquely presidential trusts. In contrast, President Clinton's misconduct, however disreputable, was not perceived by most senators as having a sufficiently public dimension to warrant removal from office. As such, his misconduct is most similar to the income tax fraud for which the House Judiciary Committee refused to pass an impeachment article against President Nixon.[75]

No one seriously questions that in Johnson's impeachment trial and Nixon's impeachment hearings in the House at least a few members of Congress rose above party politics to make a principled judgment about the political and constitutional issues raised. In Clinton's case it is harder to identify such actors or to conclude that Congress as an institution performed on a purely politically neutral or nonpartisan basis. Certainly, most people have not yet been convinced that many (or perhaps any) members of the House or the Senate rose above partisan politics to make principled judgments about the impeachability of President Clinton's misconduct, and the virtual party-line votes in the House and the Senate did reinforce the public's conclusions about the intense partisanship driving the proceedings. Consequently, a major question left open by the Clinton impeachment proceedings is not about the presidency at all, but, rather about whether President Clinton's impeachment proceedings will heighten or lower the confidence of subsequent generations and that of future members of Congress to rise above partisanship to make principled constitutional judgments during impeachment proceedings. In short, only time will tell if President Clinton's impeachment proceedings set a model to follow or a model to avoid.

Notes

1. Ronald Brownstein, "The Senate Verdict," *Los Angeles Times,* 13 February 1999, A18.
2. See senators' statements in *Congressional Record* (daily ed. Feb. 12, 1999); see also Fred Thompson, "Senate Trial of Clinton Is Over, and It's Time to Move On," *Knoxville News-Sentinel,* 15 February 1999.
3. Only nineteen of the Senate's fifty-five Republican members are up for reelection in the year 2000, but thirteen of the nineteen come from states that Clinton carried in the 1996 presidential election. See Fred Brown, "Senators to Watch," *Denver Post,* 10 February 1999, B11. Of these thirteen, the following nine senators

voted to convict the president on both articles of impeachment: Spencer Abraham (Mich.), Rod Grams (Minn.), William Roth (Del.), Rick Santorum (Pa.), John Ashcroft (Mo.), Mike DeWine (Ohio), Bill Frist (Tenn.), John Kyl (Ariz.), and Connie Mack (Fla.). (Shortly after the trial, Connie Mack announced that he would not run for reelection.) Of the thirteen, three voted to acquit the president on both articles of impeachment: Olympia Snowe (Maine), Jim Jeffords (Vt.), and John Chafee (R.I.) (who announced shortly before the end of the trial that he would not run for reelection). One of the thirteen, Slade Gorton (Wash.), split his vote on the articles, finding the president not guilty on the first but guilty on the second article of impeachment.

4. More than one-third of Republicans who voted for the first article of impeachment (i.e., 88 of 223) represent districts that Clinton carried in 1996. See Chuck Raasch, "Votes to Impeach Could Haunt House GOP," *USA Today,* 29 December 1998, A1. Nevertheless, the 223 Republicans who voted to impeach Clinton on the first article represented districts that, on average, gave him 43 percent in 1996. Moreover, Clinton's share of the 1996 vote averaged only 40 percent in the districts of Republican members of the House Judiciary Committee. Only two of the thirteen House managers won reelection in 1998 by close margins. In contrast, four of the five Republicans who voted against impeachment represent districts that Clinton won in 1996. Ibid.

5. Only 14 of the 201 Democrats who voted against represent districts that Republican presidential nominee Bob Dole carried in 1996. Ibid. Indeed, the 201 Democrats who voted against impeachment represented districts in which Clinton received an average of 59 percent of the vote in 1996. Four of the five Democrats who voted for impeachment came from districts that Dole carried in 1996; the fifth, Paul McHale, was the only one of the five who did not stand for reelection in November 1998.

6. Several related factors helped to explain this trend, including but not limited to the expansions of the federal judiciary, federal criminal law, and federal prosecutors' offices. See generally Michael J. Gerhardt, *The Federal Impeachment Process: A Constitutional and Historical Analysis* (Princeton, N.J.: Princeton University Press, 1996), 58–60.

7. Besides the impeachment and removal attempt against the president, other impeachment efforts were undertaken against Nixon (who resigned from office in 1974); Harry Claiborne (impeached and removed from a federal district judgeship for tax evasion in 1986); Alcee Hastings (impeached and removed from a federal district judgeship in 1989 for perjury and bribery); Walter Nixon (impeached and removed from a federal district judgeship in 1989 for making false statements to a grand jury); and Robert Collins (who resigned from a federal district judgeship in 1993 after having been convicted and imprisoned for bribery and threatened with impeachment). A seventh official, Robert Aguilar, had had his conviction for illegally disclosing a wiretap and attempting to obstruct a grand jury investigation overturned by the U.S. Court of Appeals for the Ninth Circuit en banc but resigned from his federal district judgeship as part of a deal to avoid being reprosecuted. See David Dietz, "No Retrial But No Job for Aguilar: Judge Resigns to Get Last Charge Dropped," *San Francisco Chronicle,* 25 June 1996.

8. See Katy J. Harriger, *Independent Justice: The Federal Special Prosecutor in American Politics* (Lawrence, Kans., University Press of Kansas, 1992), 19.

9. Stanley J. Kutler, *The Wars of Watergate: The Final Crisis of Richard M. Nixon* (New York: W. W. Norton, 1990), pp. 461–63.

10. Independent Counsel Reauthorization Act of 1994, Pub. L. No. 103-270, 108 Stat. 732 (1994) (codified at 28 U.S.C. sections 591–99).

11. 28 U.S.C. section 595(c) (1994).

12. See generally Appendix, United States Impeachments 1789 to Present, *Special Hearing on the Background and History of Impeachment, before the Subcommittee on the Constitution of the Committee on the Judiciary*. House of Representatives, 105th Congress, 2d sess, November 9, 1998, at 368–71.

13. See Eleanore Bushnell, *Crimes, Follies, and Misfortunes: The Federal Impeachment Trials* (Urbana, Ill.: University of Illinois Press, 1992), 134–37, 251–52, 293–94.

14. See, for example, Mark Z. Barabak, "The Times Poll," *Los Angeles Times*, 31 January 1999, A1.

15. Ibid.

16. Ibid.

17. Ibid.

18. See ABC News poll (February 12, 1999).

19. U.S. Const. Art. I. section 3, clause 6.

20. Bushnell, 135–57.

21. Federalist No. 65.

22. This rejection could be construed as the Senate's performing, as expected by the Framers, an important checking or balancing function. See Gordon Wood, *The Creation of the American Republic.* (Chapel Hill, N.C.: University of North Carolina Press, 1969), 513, suggesting that the Framers expected that the Senate "would function with more coolness, with more system, and more wisdom, than the popular branch," because its members would be drawn from the elite of society and as a result of its longer term and insulation from direct public pressure. Yet some argued that the balancing was achieved in Clinton's trial only because of the uniform partisanship of the Democrats in opposing removal.

23. 113 S.Ct. 732 (1992).

24. In his testimony before the House Judiciary Committee, Yale law professor Bruce Ackerman made the provocative argument that by impeaching the president in a lame-duck session the House had violated the 20th Amendment. See *Impeachment Inquiry: William Jefferson Clinton, President of the United States: Presentation on Behalf of the President: Hearing before the House Comm. on the Judiciary*, 105th Cong. 37 (1998) (testimony of Bruce A. Ackerman). The argument got a lot of attention from the media but for several reasons won no supporters in Congress. First, the text of the amendment does not clearly forbid such actions. Second, Professor Ackerman's argument is undercut by several earlier impeachments (one as recently as 1988–89) having been carried over from one Congress to the next. These two factors led Professor Ackerman to shift his argument to

maintaining that (1) lame-duck impeachments are generally a bad idea and (2) a lame-duck impeachment might be legitimate only if, like a piece of legislation passed in an earlier Congress, the House were to reaffirm it in a subsequent Congress prior to the Senate's acting upon it. The second argument is also undercut by several impeachment trials involving "carryover" impeachments. Moreover, impeachment is arguably a more complete act than legislation passed only by a single house. Last but not least, Thomas Jefferson, in his influential manual on parliamentary practice drafted while he was vice president, maintained that the American system followed the British practice in which impeachments carried over from one Parliament to the next. See Thomas Jefferson, *Jefferson's Manual of Parliamentary Practice*, Section 620, reprinted in H.R. Doc. 104-272, at 13 (1997). Nevertheless, Ackerman's argument served as a reminder that by impeaching the president in a lame-duck session the House arguably had put at risk some of the political (as opposed to constitutional) legitimacy of its impeachment judgment.

25. U.S. Const. Art. III, section 1.

26. For a more elaborate articulation of this argument (and the counterargument) *see* Gerhardt, 83–86.

27. See, for example, *Special Hearing on the Background and History of Impeachment, before the House Subcommittee on the Constitution*, 231, oral testimony of Professor Susan Low Block; 243, oral testimony of Professor Jack Rakove.

28. See U.S. Const., Art. II, section 4. "The President, the Vice-President, and all civil officers of the United States, shall be removed from office on Impeachment for and Conviction of Treason, Bribery, or other high Crimes and Misdemeanors."

29. See *Closed Door Impeachment Statement of Senator Paul Sarbanes* (released into the *Congressional Record* on February 12, 1999). "Judges must be held to a higher standard of conduct than other officials. As noted by the House Judiciary Committee in 1970, Congress has recognized that Federal judges must be held to a different standard of conduct than other civil officers because of the nature of their position and the tenure of their office." Quotation from House Judiciary Committee majority report accompanying recommended articles of impeachment against Walter Nixon in 1989; citation omitted in original.

30. See *Special Hearing on the Background and History of Impeachment, before the House Subcommittee on the Constitution*, 358.

31. Ibid., 368.

32. See 13 *Annals of Cong.* 319–22 (1804) [1803–04].

33. See House Committee on the Judiciary, Impeachment of Judge Harry E. Claiborne, H.R. Rep. No. 96-688, at 23 (1986); 132 *Cong. Rec.* 30,251–58 (1986).

34. Cf. *Impeachment Staff Inquiry, House Committee on the Judiciary*, Memorandum: Constitutional Grounds for Presidential Impeachment 4 (Feb. 20, 1974); Joseph Story, *Commentaries on the Constitution of the United States*, rev. ed. (New York: Fred Rothman & Co., (1991) sec. 780, 252, ibid., sec. 744, at 218. See also Albert Broderick, "Citizens' Guide to Impeachment of a President: Problem Areas," 23 Cath. U. L. Rev. 205, 229–34 (1973); Alex. Simpson Jr., "Federal Impeachments," U. Pa. L. Rev. 651, 676–77, 803 (1916).

35. U.S. Const., Art. II, section 4.

36. Prepared Statement of Professor Michael J. Gerhardt, Professor of Law, The College of William & Mary, *Special Hearing on the Background and History of Impeachment before the House Subcommittee on the Constitution,* 47–49.

37. See Gerhardt, *Federal Impeachment Process,* 115–16.

38. Ibid., 54–56.

39. See *Special Hearing on the Background and History of Impeachment, before the House Subcommittee on the Constitution,* 55–56 (written statement of Professor Michael J. Gerhardt).

40. ABC News poll (February 12, 1999) indicated that 71 percent of those polled believed that the Senate voted on the basis of partisan politics rather than the facts; ABC "Nightline" poll (February 8, 1999) indicated that 74 percent of Americans expected senators not to vote their consciences but rather on the basis of partisan politics.

41. ABC News poll (February 12, 1999).

42. See Robert H. Bork, "Read the Constitution: It's Removal or Nothing," *Wall Street Journal,* 1 February 1999, A21. "Senators Exploring Censure Hit Obstacles," *Washington Post,* 28 January 1999, A17.

43. See *Selective Service System v. Minnesota Public Interest Research Group,* 468 U.S. 841, 844, 848 (1984); *Nixon v. Administrator of General Services,* 433 U.S. 425, 470–72 (1977); *United States v. Lovett,* 326 U.S. 303 (1946); *Ex Parte Garland,* 71 U.S. (4 Wall.) 333 (1866); *Cummings v. Missouri,* 71 U.S. (4 Wall.) 277, 323 (1867); *Fletcher v. Peck,* 10 U.S. (6 Cranch) 87, 138 (1810).

44. See Erwin Chemerinsky, "Constitutional Law, Principles, and Policies", Section 6.2.2 (Rev. Ed. 1999); Thomas B. Griffith, Note. "Beyond Process: A Substantive Rationale for the Bill of Attainder Clause," 70 Va. L. Rev. 475, 476 (1984).

45. U.S. Const., amend. 1.

46. Ibid., Art. I, section 6, cl. 1.

47. See, for example, ABC News poll (February 6–7, 1999); ABC News poll (January 8–10, 1999).

48. U.S. Const. Art. I, section 7.

49. Prior to the House's vote to impeach President Clinton, Representative William Delahunt (D-Mass.) sought opinions regarding the constitutionality of censure from the nineteen constitutional scholars and historians who testified about the background and history of impeachment in the special hearing held by the House Subcommittee on the Constitution on November 9, 1999. See letter from Representative William D. Delahunt to Representative Henry J. Hyde, Chair, House Judiciary Committee (Dec. 4, 1998), on file with the author. Fourteen of the nineteen constitutional scholars indicated that they thought censure was constitutional. See letter from Representative William D. Delahunt & Frederick C. Boucher to members of the U.S. House of Representatives (Dec. 15, 1998), on file with author.

50. See Joseph Isenberg, "Impeachment and Presidential Immunity from Judicial Process, University of Chicago School of Law Occasional Paper No. 39 (Dec. 31, 1998). See also Joseph Isenberg, "Note, The Scope of the Power to Impeach." 84 *Yale Law Journal* 1316 (1975).

51. Isenberg, "Impeachment and Presidential Immunity," p. 14.

52. Compare, for example, U.S. Const., Art. I, section 2, cl. 5 ("The House shall . . . have the sole Power of Impeachment"); ibid., Art. I, section 3, cl. 6 ("The Senate shall have the sole Power to try all Impeachments"); ibid., Art. I, section 3, cl. 7 ("And no Person shall be convicted without the concurrence of two thirds of the Members present").

53. See Appendix, United States Impeachments 1789 to Present, *Special Hearing on the Background and History of Impeachment, before the House Subcommittee on the Constitution,* supra note 22, at 358 (Pickering), 360 (Humphreys), and 364–65 (Archbald).

54. See, for example, Gary Osen and Patrick Morrisey, "Finding of Fact Is Constitutional," *Wall Street Journal,* 1 February 1999, A20; Douglas W. Kmiec, "Convict But Don't Censure Clinton," *Wall Street Journal,* 29 January 1999, A14. See also Editorial, "Censure and the Constitution," *Washington Post,* 16 December 1999, A30; Benjamin Wittes, "Congress Can Censure Anything," *Washington Post,* 2 December 1998, A29.

55. U.S. Const. Art. II., section 4.

56. See Gerhardt, *Federal Impeachment Process,* 3–21.

57. Bushnell, 52.

58. Ibid., 123.

59. Ibid., 237–39.

60. Appendix, United States Impeachments 1789 to Present, *Special Hearing on the Background and History of Impeachment, before the House Subcommittee on the Constitution,* supra note 22, at 368.

61. See, for example, "Symposium: The Independent Counsel Act: From Watergate to Whitewater and Beyond," 86 Geo. L.J. 2011 et seq. (1998); "*Symposium on the Future of the Independent Counsel Act,*" 49 Mercer L. Rev. 427 et seq. (1998); "Sixty-Seventh Judicial Conference of the 4th Circuit: The Independent Counsel Process: Is It Broken and How Should It Be Fixed?" 54 Wash. and Lee L. Rev. 1515 (1997). See also Ken Gormley, "Impeachment and the Independent Counsel: A Dysfunctional Union," 51 Stan. L. Rev. 309 (1999); Ken Gormley, "An Original Model of the Independent Counsel Statute." 97 Mich. L. Rev. 601, 639–92 (1998).

62. Ethan Wallison, "Starr Testimony May Seal Fate of Censure Law," *Roll Call,* April 15, 1999; Penny Bender, "Reno Supports Dismantling Independent Counsel Act," Gannett News Service, March 18, 1999; Marc Lacey and Eric Lichtblau, "Independent Counsel Law Faces Reform—or Demise." *Los Angeles Times,* 24 February 1999, A1.

63. See Referral from Independent Counsel Kenneth W. Starr in Conformity with the Requirements of Title 28, United States Code, Section 595(c), H.R. Doc. No. 105-310 (1998).

64. See Independent Counsel Kenneth Starr's Prepared Testimony for Delivery before the House Judiciary Committee, 1998 West Law 801023 (F.D.H.C. Nov. 19, 1998).

65. See letter from Independent Counsel Kenneth W. Starr to Henry J. Hyde, Chair of the House Judiciary Committee, and John Conyers Jr., Ranking Minority

Member of the Committee on the Judiciary, December 11, 1998; copy on file with the author.

66. See "Letter of Resignation from Samuel Dash and Kenneth W. Starr's Letter in Response," *New York Times,* 21 November 1998, A10. See also Samuel Dash, "Letters to the Editor: Sam Dash Replies," *Washington Post,* 24 November 1998, A18.

67. See, for example, Kurt Royce and Shirley E. Perlman, "The Impeachment Trial/ Scholars Criticize Starr Move," *Newsday,* 26 January 1999, A20; Bob Hohler, "Lewinsky Summons Ignites a Firestorm," *Boston Globe,* 24 January 1999, A1.

68. Six presidents appointed ten special prosecutors during the period from 1875 until Archibald Cox's appointment in 1973. Of these ten, two were fired—the first by President Grant in 1875 (lending further credence to the widespread perception of corruption in the Grant administration) and the second by President Truman in 1952 (because the president believed that the special prosecutor had become a nuisance to his Justice Department). See generally Donald C. Smaltz, "The Independent Counsel Statute: A View from Inside," 86 Geo. L.J. 2307 (1998).

69. See William Rehnquist, *Grand Inquests: The Historical Impeachment Trials of Justice Chase and President Johnson* (New York: Quill Press, 1992) 114, 277–78.

70. Ibid., 251–52, 261, 274, 277–78. To be sure, the view set forth, for example, by Chief Justice Rehnquist of the significance of President Johnson's impeachment as a thoroughly partisan effort by some members of Congress to increase congressional power at the expense of the presidency is not one on which all historians would agree. For instance, Michael Les Benedict, in his well-regarded study of the Johnson impeachment, suggested that the effort to impeach and remove Johnson from office was not necessarily illegitimate in view of Johnson's repeated violations of statutes that had been passed by the Congress over his veto and Johnson's efforts to weaken the enforcement of the 14th Amendment. See Michael Les Benedict, *The Impeachment and Trial of Andrew Johnson* (New York: W. W. Norton, 1973).

71. To the extent that President Clinton's acquittal turns on the belief of a critical mass of senators that his misconduct did not rise to the level of an impeachable offense, see supra note, the outcome of his trial dovetails with an important strain in the discourse of the Framers that a president is impeachable for his abuses of uniquely presidential powers (that could not be easily redressed in other legal proceedings).

72. See *Jones v. Clinton,* 1999 U.S. Dist. Lexis 4515 (W.D. Ark. April 12, 1999). In her contempt citation of President Clinton, Judge Susan Webber Wright concluded that "the President's deposition testimony regarding whether he had ever been alone with Ms. Lewinsky was intentionally false, and his statements regarding whether he had ever engaged in sexual relations with Ms. Lewinsky likewise were intentionally false . . ." ibid., 4539. Consequently, Judge Wright fined the president for the reasonable expenses incurred by the plaintiffs' attorneys as a result of his testimony and by the judge in attending to the deposition. She also referred the matter "to the Arkansas Supreme Court's Committee on Professional Conduct for review and any disciplinary action it deems appropriate . . ." ibid., 4544.

73. See Sullivan at 2206 n. 53 citing and quoting from a wide variety of primary and secondary sources on the unique functioning of impeachment as a means not of punishment but rather of protecting the integrity and well-being of the constitutional order.

74. See, for example, Rehnquist, at 248 (quoting letter from Senator Dixon to Senator Fessenden in which Dixon emphasized, "Whether Andrew Johnson should be removed from office, justly or unjustly, was comparatively of little consequence—but whether our government should be Mexicanized, and an example set which would surely, in the end, utterly overthrow our institutions, was a matter of vast consequence. To you and Mr. Grimes it is mainly due that impeachment has not become an ordinary means of changing the policy of the government by a violent removal of the executive" (citation omitted in original).

75. See The U.S. House of Representatives Committee on the Judiciary Hearing on the Impeachment of the President, 105th Cong. (1998), available in 1998 WL 846820, statements of former Representatives Elizabeth Holzman (D-N.Y.), Robert Drinan (D-Mass.), and Wayne Owen (D-Utah), noting that because it was personal rather than official misconduct.

Public Opinion: The Paradoxes of Clinton's Popularity

Molly W. Andolina and Clyde Wilcox

In January 1999 President Bill Clinton was the most publicly shamed president of modern time, and paradoxically, one of the most popular. He had admitted an improper sexual relationship with a young White House intern, the details of which were widely available in published form. He had been impeached by the House of Representatives for allegedly lying about that relationship to the grand jury and for trying to obstruct the investigation of that affair. The media were full of the story, comedians made jokes about some of the racier details of the affair, and the Internet hummed with Clinton jokes.

Most importantly, the Senate was in the midst of a trial to determine if he should be removed from office—only the second time this had happened in the nation's history.

Yet in the beginning of the seventh year of his presidency, Clinton had the solid support of a public tired of scandal politics. His job approval ratings were over 60 percent, especially after delivering a State of the Union speech in which his appeals for passage of popular programs left some Republicans smirking and squirming. Most models of presidential popularity take into account the effects of scandals, which inevitably lower a president's job approval ratings. Yet from the spring of 1998 through the end of the Clinton impeachment, the public remained remarkably stable in its support of the president and its belief that he should not be removed from office. Clinton's job approval rating presents a puzzle: Why in the midst of a rather tawdry scandal were his approval ratings so high? Why did his approval ratings go *up* as the story unfolded?

Clinton's resilient popularity surprised many analysts who thought that his support was a mile wide and an inch deep and would disappear immediately after the next details were revealed. It surprised many in the news media who either called for his resignation or spent hours pontificating about his imminent demise (Connolly and Edsall 1998). It also surprised Republican members of the House and Senate, most of whom were immune to Clinton's appeal and therefore kept waiting for the public to see him through their eyes. Indeed, the hasty release of various materials—the Starr report and Clinton's videotaped testimony before the grand jury—and the push for live witnesses were all part of an effort to change public opinion, but one of the most remarkable aspects of public sentiment about Clinton, the scandal, and impeachment was its stability.

The public wavered in its support for Clinton only once—immediately after the scandal broke in January 1998. As the media rushed to judgment, the public followed suit, and polls showed that a clear majority thought Clinton had engaged in a sexual affair with Monica Lewinsky and lied to cover it up. A slim majority in some polls called for the president to resign. Clinton's State of the Union speech in 1998 reminded the public how much they liked his policies, and his forceful denial of the affair served to create a public opinion backlash against the media. Polls in late January 1998 showed that although a narrow majority of Americans did not believe the charges against Clinton, they also thought that *if* these charges turned out to be true, he should leave office.[1]

Later in 1998, the public had to come to grips with the reality that the president had sexual relations with Lewinsky and that he had testified in a misleading manner about that affair. The public was forced to choose between strong approval of Clinton's performance as president and a belief that this behavior was sufficiently immoral to remove him from office. Overwhelmingly the public chose to support Clinton and came to believe that the charges did not justify his being removed from office.

In this chapter we will examine public attitudes toward Clinton during the unfolding scandal. We begin with a chronology of public response to the crisis, which focuses on different components of attitudes toward Clinton and the dynamics of these attitudes; second, we look at group differences in attitudes over time; third, we consider a series of explanations for Clinton's continued popularity; and finally, we speculate about the lingering impact of the scandal on Clinton's popularity, on evaluations of the two parties, and on electoral politics for the next decade.

The Public Stands by Their Man: Popular Response to the Clinton Crisis over Time

Prior to the news of the Lewinsky affair, President Clinton's approval rating stood at about 60 percent in several polls, on par with those of Eisenhower in 1958 and lagging only slightly below Reagan's 1986 numbers. After the charges were first plastered throughout the press, the public briefly soured on the president but then quickly bounced back, remaining steadfast and loyal throughout the twists and turns of the scandal and news reports of cigars, stained dresses, and exchanged gifts.

When the story broke on Wednesday, January 21, 1998, news organizations rushed to take the public pulse, conducting a flurry of overnight and two-day polls. Although Americans responded to the story with limited interest—only one-third of the public was following the story very closely—they did become less supportive. Throughout the rest of the week and into the weekend, Clinton's job approval rating began to falter, dropping to 51 percent in one ABC News/ *Washington Post* poll.

As Clinton responded to charges with steely silence, the public expressed doubts about his innocence. Most Americans believed he had had an affair with the young intern, and substantial numbers thought he was guilty of asking her to lie under oath as well. In one ABC News poll conducted on Friday, January 23, 62 percent of the public said they thought he had had a sexual relationship with Lewinsky, and 51 percent thought that he had asked her to lie in a legal document.

After several days of All-Monica, All-the-Time news, Americans began to question Clinton's fitness for office. Although most did not believe that the affair alone was a sufficient reason for him to step down, public judgment was harsher about lying in legal proceedings. A solid majority thought that he should resign if he had lied under oath (63 percent in a *Washington Post* poll) or if he had encouraged Ms. Lewinsky to lie (64 percent in an ABC News poll). If he was unwilling to take such action himself, fully 55 percent of the public said that his lying under oath should result in his impeachment (*Washington Post*, January 25).

Clinton's job performance was not the only indicator to take a hit; his personal ratings tumbled as well. By Monday, January 26, Americans were divided 51 percent to 47 percent on whether Clinton had the honesty and integrity to serve effectively as president, and only 33 percent of the nation said that the phrase "honest and trustworthy" applied to him, a drop of 16 percentage points since February 1997.

Finally, amid this weakened public support and a relentless barrage of punditry declaring the presidency in crisis, Bill and Hillary Clinton started to fight back (Zaller 1998). Clinton issued a forceful denial, shaking his finger at the camera and declaring, "I did not have sexual relations with that woman, Miss Lewinsky. I never told anybody to lie, not a single time." The following morning the first lady appeared on the "Today Show," defending her husband and blaming the accusations on a vast "right-wing conspiracy." That same night Clinton did what he does best, he delivered a skillful State of the Union Address to cheering crowds of Democratic supporters in Congress. With 36.5 million houses tuned in to this highly ritualized event, he reminded Americans of their current economic prosperity, offered them popular programs for the future, and ignored the lingering scandal.

The public responded accordingly. Clinton's job approval ratings rebounded, Americans became more skeptical of his guilt, and support for impeachment dropped. By the end of the week, most polls indicated that Clinton's job performance was at the highest point in his presidency, hovering around 70 percent. An ABC News poll found that the percentage of Americans who believed he had the honesty and integrity to serve as president was back up to 59 percent from its earlier low at 51 percent. A Gallup survey showed 43 percent of the public very confident in Clinton's abilities to carry out his duties as president, up from 29 percent who had felt this way before the speech.

Americans did not simply react to the president playing the role of rhetorical leader; some found his strong denial of an illicit relationship convincing. In the days following his statement, Americans were less likely to think that Clinton had had sexual relations of any kind with Lewinsky, less inclined to think he had lied about it under oath, and significantly less supportive of the charge that he had encouraged Lewinsky to lie about it.

And Americans' strong support for Clinton's job performance and their confidence in his abilities were accompanied by a rise in support for his continued presidency. Prior to the speech, almost two-thirds of Americans said Clinton should resign if he had lied under oath or if he had encouraged Lewinsky to lie. Following his address, support for resignation fell to just over 50 percent for each of these allegations. Even fewer Americans wanted Clinton to be impeached. Before the speech, a *Washington Post* poll found 55 percent of the public favoring impeachment for perjury; by Saturday, January 31, this number had dropped to 40 percent. The public was growing weary of the issue and wanted the entire investigation to stop. In a Pew Research Center poll a 55 percent majority favored dropping the matter altogether, compared with 43 percent who supported carrying on the investigation. Many analysts argued at this time that once the public was forced to confront Clinton's guilt, they would turn on Clinton. Instead, the public increasingly believed that even if the allegations were true, they did not justify removing the president.

By mid-February, more Americans doubted Clinton's innocence, but fewer seemed to care. While television news programs labeled their coverage "Crisis in the White House," and "Is He Finished?" screamed out from the cover of *U.S. News & World Report,* a Pew Research Center poll found that only 30 percent of the public was following the story very closely.

And, as the scandal progressed, a pattern set in. With each new revelation, Americans became more convinced of Clinton's guilt but less supportive of his removal—and his popularity remained steady. In March, "60 Minutes" aired an interview with Kathleen Willey, a former White House volunteer, in which she accused the president of sexual assault—Gallup recorded his job performance rating at 67 percent.

By July, the public had simultaneously reached two strong judgments: Clinton had lied under oath and he should remain in office. In a Pew Research Center survey, fully 70 percent of the public said he probably had sexual relations with Lewinsky, and two-thirds said he probably had lied about it under oath—in February, only 52 percent had thought so. Almost half (48 percent) thought he probably had pressured Lewinsky to lie, up from 40 percent in February. But the same survey showed that just 31 percent of the public supported impeachment and removal from office if Clinton lied under oath; in February fully half of the public wanted him ousted for perjury. Only 41 percent supported impeachment for suborning perjury, down from 48 percent in February. The public had adjusted its moral judgment to fit a more basic judgment: retain a president who was doing a good job.

On August 17 Clinton testified before the grand jury and then publicly addressed the American people, admitting an "improper" and "wrong" relationship with Lewinsky, apologizing to his wife and daughter, and denying any illegal actions. Yet Clinton's public acknowledgement of the affair and the charges of his critics had little effect on the American people, who continued to stand by the president. A Pew Research Center poll found that 62 percent of the public approved his job performance, 66 percent were opposed to his resignation, and 75 percent were against his impeachment and removal. Although 83 percent also said that he probably lied about the affair under oath, fully 61 percent believed that his public statement was sufficient to end the matter. (Several days later American planes struck terrorist sites in Sudan and Afghanistan, and critics of the president began to make references to the film, "Wag the Dog," suggesting that he launched the attacks to distract attention from the scandal, a ploy that was featured in the film.)

Congressional Republican leaders were taken aback by Clinton's continued popular support and sought to publicly discredit him by releasing damaging documents and videotapes throughout the fall. In September, the Starr report was published on the Internet, providing millions of Americans immediate access to many of the salacious details of Clinton's relationship with Lewinsky. But while half of the public read some or part of the narrative, only 29 percent of Americans were convinced that the charges were serious enough to warrant impeachment and removal, and support for Clinton remained strong.

Later in the month, Congress voted to release copies of the president's videotaped testimony before the grand jury, and Clinton's approval ratings turned down slightly, falling to 55 percent in a Pew Research Center poll. But the actual testimony turned out to be less damning than Clinton's accusers had hoped; Clinton spoke forcefully to the camera and seemed to explain to many Americans why his testimony had been misleading. After the tapes were aired, Clinton's job performance ratings rose again, rebounding to 62 percent, and those who wanted him to resign fell back to 26 percent from a brief high of 34 percent.

After much internal debate, GOP congressional leaders agreed to an electoral strategy that involved an attack on Clinton's integrity and an emphasis on the scandal. The Democrats however, picked up five seats in the election—only the second time in this century that the president's party had gained ground in a midterm election. Amid embarrassing election day losses for the Republican Party and polls showing the public resoundingly opposed to impeachment, the GOP leaders in the House marched forward into committee hearings, full

House debate, and, ultimately, impeachment itself. At the same time, Clinton authorized military strikes against Iraq—a move supported by three-quarters of the American public. And, once again, the people stood by their man: the president's job approval ratings rose to 71 percent in Pew Research Center survey.

Throughout Clinton's trial in the Senate, Americans' support for his job performance and their opposition to his impeachment remained unchanged. His approval ratings stayed in the low-to-mid-60s; support for his removal never rose above 35 percent. Indeed, the public largely ignored the historic trial; only a small minority, less than 30 percent, followed news of the trial very closely, and even fewer actually talked about it with friends or family. When the Senate voted to acquit him in February, 63 percent of the public voiced their approval of this decision.

Group Differences

Not all Americans responded to the scandal in the same way. Table 1 shows group differences over time in support of impeachment and removal of the president. Throughout the crisis, while assertive Republicans continued to call for Clinton's impeachment, Democrats stayed staunchly opposed and Independents and more passive Republicans remained resistant to arguments for removal. Clinton's popularity during the scandal was anchored in a strong reservoir of support among traditionally Democratic groups—a support that grew over time.

Clinton was helped early on by women's resistance to impeachment. Before the news of the illicit affair became public, 63 percent of women said that they approved of Clinton's job performance, and 62 percent of men agreed. After Clinton's State of the Union address, support rose to 73 percent among women and 69 percent among men. Not much later, in early February 1998, a narrow majority of men (53 percent) supported impeachment, a sentiment shared by only 46 percent of women. By March, however, support for impeachment had dropped for both groups: 43 percent among men and 37 percent among women. By summer, only one-third of men and women favored impeachment, a statistic that would scarcely change throughout the ensuing months. A full year after the controversy first erupted, only 35 percent of men and 28 percent of women favored removing Clinton from office.

Clinton's support among women pales in comparison to the fidelity demonstrated by African Americans and senior citizens. As the most loyal of the Democratic constituencies, African Americans remained

Table 1. *Support for Impeachment and Removal of Clinton*

	1998		1999
	Jan. 30–Feb. 2 %	Aug. 27–Sept. 8 %	Jan. 14–17 %
Total	50	31	32
Gender			
Male	53	33	35
Female	46	29	28
Race			
Caucasian	53	33	35
African American	22[1]	17	8
Age			
<30	52	36	28
30–49	53	29	34
50–64	45	31	34
≥65	41	24	30
Education			
College graduate	52	33	37
Some college	54	31	33
High school graduate	46	29	31
<High school	48	31	23
Income			
≥$75,000	55	36	37
$50,000–$74,999	51	32	33
$30,000–$49,999	61	30	33
$20,000–$29,999	47	28	32
<$20,000	40	28	24
Party identification			
Republican	71	54	60
Democrat	31	12	11
Independent	55	30	31
Religion			
Nonevangelical Protestant	57	29	39
Evangelical Protestant	57	44	45
Nonhispanic Catholics	52	28	29

Note: The first two surveys asked, "If it turns out that President Clinton lied under oath about having a sexual relationship with Monica Lewinsky, do you think he should be impeached and removed from office, or not?" The last survey asked, "Based on what you know at this point, do you think Clinton should or should not be removed from office?" All surveys were conducted by The Pew Research Center for the People & the Press.

[1] The sample size for this group is small, $n = 73$.

steadfast in their support of the president, bestowing performance ratings that averaged in the mid-eighties throughout the scandal and ending the year with a stellar 94 percent registering approval of his presidency. And, not surprisingly, African Americans were over-whelmingly opposed to impeachment for all charges, particular and general.

The story is the same, albeit to a lesser degree, for senior citizens. This Democratic Party faithful, to whom Clinton had promised to "save Social Security," resisted all calls for impeachment. In early February, just 42 percent of those sixty-five and older supported im-peachment if Clinton had lied under oath, and even fewer (38 percent) supported ousting him for subornation of perjury—both measures were ten percentage points below the national average. Seniors re-mained loyal as the scandal progressed. When Clinton admitted to the affair on national television, support for his removal dropped even further: just two in ten seniors believed he should be impeached for perjury; fewer than three in ten thought that encouraging Lewinsky to lie was sufficient to end his presidency. Indeed, even the embar-rassing trivia surrounding Clinton's infidelity failed to sway older Americans. By January 1999, less than one-third of them favored impeachment.

A Party Divided
Unlike their Democratic adversaries, Republican House managers leading the charge for removal were unable to garner majority support from their key coalitions—white Evangelical Protestants, the wealthy, and the well educated. Indeed, although these groups were less im-pressed by Clinton's job performance than was the average American, their initial support for impeachment stumbled, wavered, and then almost fizzled out.

In the first few months of polling on the crisis, slim majorities of each group said that lying under oath and advocating perjury by another were impeachable crimes. Yet, by early fall 1998 only about one-third of those making over $50,000 a year and an equal number of college graduates favored impeachment for perjury. Support among white evangelicals dropped to 44 percent from 57 percent over this same time. And, although narrow majorities of all three groups con-tinued to view subornation of perjury as an impeachable offense, support for removing Clinton eventually fell below the 50 percent mark. By January 1999, fewer than four in ten of the well off and well educated and just 45 percent of white Evangelical Protestants en-dorsed impeachment.

Indeed, the only group that consistently supported impeachment was self-identified Republicans—roughly six in ten favored removing Clinton from office; yet, only among strong Republicans was this feeling deeply held. Prior to the House vote, only 27 percent of rank-and-file GOP loyalists said that they would have a better opinion of their party if they impeached Clinton.

Explaining Clinton's Popularity

Given widespread disapproval of Clinton's conduct with Lewinsky and the majority sentiment that he lacked critical moral judgment, why did the public continue to support him? The available data do not permit a definitive explanation, but we believe that the answer lies in five areas. First, the strong economy and good news in other policy areas served to bolster Clinton's support. Had the country faced double-digit inflation and high unemployment, he might well have been removed from office. Second, Clinton's policies remain generally popular. More than most modern presidents Clinton has shifted his policy priorities to reflect prevailing public sentiments, and, as the endgame in the impeachment crisis neared, Clinton's positions were far more popular than those of the GOP Congress. Third, Clinton has an intangible ability to connect with the American public—to "feel their pain" and to project an ability to understand the problems of the average American. Fourth, Clinton's enemies were unpopular, and the public saw no real heroes or victims in the story that might have lead them to desert Clinton. Finally, the public considered the Lewinsky matter to be a matter of private moral conduct, and although they disapproved of Clinton's behavior, they did not see it as being relevant to his job performance. Let us consider each of these in turn.

Let the Good Times Roll

One of the strongest predictors of aggregate presidential popularity is the performance of the economy (Monroe 1981; Kernell 1978; Hibbs, Rivers, and Vasukatis 1982; Ostrom and Simon 1985; Chappell and Keech 1985). Simply put, presidents are generally popular when the economy is strong and much less popular when the economy is weak. A significant portion of the public appears to view politics through the lens of the "nature of the times"—if times are good, keep the leadership team; if times are bad, hire someone else. Jimmy Carter attacked Gerald Ford in 1976 for the "misery index," but it was Ronald Reagan who captured the sentiment in grand style when he told voters to "ask yourself if you are better off than you were four years ago."

In 1999, the answer to that question for most Americans was "yes." Throughout the course of the scandal, a strong economy served as a major source of Clinton's popularity. Had Clinton's confrontation with impeachment occurred during a period of economic stagnation (or the recession that preceded his tenure in office), the outcome might well have been different. Indeed, when survey researchers asked respondents why they approved of Clinton's job approval, the most frequent answer was the economy was good. The economy was considerably stronger in 1999 than it had been in 1993, when Clinton took office, (see table 2).

Wealthy Americans benefited from an enormous surge in stock prices, pushing the Dow up almost 200 percent in six years. Increases in real income for average Americans had been more modest, but were nonetheless significant. Economic growth was considerably stronger in 1998 than it was when Clinton took office, and unemployment and inflation were both at long-time lows. Interest rates were also at a long-time low, allowing many Americans to refinance their mortgages or to move into larger homes. Gasoline prices (in real dollars) were lower than they had been in forty years. Inflation was practically nonexistent.

Table 2. *Economic and Social Indicators*

Indicators	1993[1]	1999[2]
Dow Jones Industrial Average	3242	9340
Median income, 1997 dollars	$16,665	$19,241
Economic growth	2.7%	3.5%
Unemployment	7.3%	4.5%
Inflation	4.2%	1.4%
Average mortgage interest rate	8.0%	6.8%
Federal budget (in billions)	−$290	+$70
Welfare recipients (in millions)	14.1	8.4
Violent crime (per 100,000)	757.5	610.8
Abortions (per 1000 women)	25.9	22.9
Satisfied the way things are going	39%	59%[3]
Country on right track	35%	51%

[1] 1993 when Clinton took office.
[2] January 1999.
[3] As of February 1999.

For most Americans, the strong economy meant slightly higher incomes, lower mortgage payments, considerably higher values for their mutual funds and retirement savings, greater job security, and more buying power. Perhaps more importantly, they were able to feel confident and secure for the first time in many years. In the late 1980s and early 1990s, many Americans believed their children would experience a lower standard of living than they had enjoyed; by 1999 this feeling had disappeared and more Americans were optimistic about their children's future.

The precise mechanism by which the economy influences presidential approval is still a subject of considerable debate (MacKuen, Erikson, and Stimson 1992; Clarke, Rapkin, and Stewart 1994; Clark and Stewart 1994; Brody 1991; Edwards 1991; Hibbs, Rivers, and Vasukatis 1982; Kinder 1981; Lau and Sears 1981; Monroe 1981; Monroe and Laughlin 1983; Norpoth and Yantek 1983; Peffley and Williams 1985; Sigelman and Knight 1985). The current consensus is that presidential approval is influenced by three factors: (1) retrospective evaluations of how the economy has performed, including a comparative judgment of past administrations; (2) prospective forecasts of the direction of the economy; and (3) objective economic conditions. By the time Congress got down to impeaching the president, each of these sets of indicators was strong and the public was increasingly confident of the future. In a survey conducted by the Pew Research Center in late February 1999, 48 percent of Americans indicated that their current circumstances were very good, 29 percent recalled that their circumstances five years earlier were very good, and 72 percent indicated that their circumstances would be very good five years hence. A CNN/USA Today/Gallup poll taken just before the 1999 State of the Union address showed that 60 percent thought the economy was the best it had *ever* been in their lifetime. Small wonder that the same poll showed that 81 percent approved of Clinton's handling of the economy, the highest figure *ever* recorded by Gallup in the thirty-year history of this question.

Despite Republican claims that Clinton's job approval ratings were entirely the result of a strong economy, Clinton's popularity was actually even greater than the good economic times would normally predict. Political scientist Robert Erikson estimated that economic performance and confidence would predict job approval ratings for Clinton in early 1999 of 59 percent, but in fact his scores ranged from 65 percent to 72 percent (Robert Erikson, personal communication).

The good social indicators extended beyond the economy. In early 1999, the welfare rolls were down and newspapers were full of stories of former welfare recipients working. Drug use had declined, as had violent crime, especially in major urban areas. By some measures violent crime in 1998 was at its lowest level in twenty-five years. Teenagers were waiting longer to have sex and becoming pregnant less often. The abortion rate had declined. A decade earlier, most Americans had believed that large welfare rolls, high rates of teenage pregnancy, drug use, and violent crimes were permanent fixtures in modern American life. The positive changes were a welcome surprise.

Although the economy is the most reliable predictor of presidential popularity, foreign policy can also influence job approval ratings (Bruce, Wilcox, and Allsop 1994; Edwards, Mitchell, and Welch 1995; Hurwitz and Peffley 1987; Krosnick and Brannon 1993; Wilcox and Allsop 1991). In 1998 and early 1999, America was at peace, its major military enemy of the past half-century had collapsed, and its major economic rival was in a deep recession. As Asia slumped and Brazil devalued its currency, the U.S. economy seemed immune to world forces. The Kosovo crisis was months away. Indeed, one Gallup poll in March 1999 showed that a majority of Americans thought that Clinton was the greatest *foreign policy* president in their lifetime.[2]

Americans knew that Bill Clinton was not personally responsible for all of these positive trends, but they could remember when times had been worse and when they had held little hope that times would ever get better. With most trends tilting in a positive direction, they were loath to rock the boat. They had believed that George Bush was a decent man who could not manage the country; they now believed that Bill Clinton was a flawed man who could do the job.

Talking the Talk

Clinton's popularity was also buoyed by his generally popular positions on public issues (Zaller 1998). A Pew Research Center survey conducted in February 1999 revealed that some 69 percent of respondents liked Clinton's policies. The president's ability to cut right or left, depending on prevailing sentiments, had long frustrated his opponents. Clinton campaigned in 1992 from the center, pushing a middle-class tax cut, promising more police on the streets, and returning to Arkansas to oversee a controversial execution. Early in his presidency Clinton steered left, pushing for gays in the military and national health insurance; his approval ratings after his first one hundred days in office were the lowest of any modern president. After the 1994 elections, which created a Republican majority in Congress, Clinton moved quickly to the center, both in rhetoric and policy. Clinton staked rhetorical positions on issues such as school uniforms, discipline in the classroom, and an end to social promotion. He endorsed values such as responsibility, hard work, and playing by the rules. Presidents do not actually *do* anything about most of these issues, but Clinton learned an important lesson from Ronald Reagan: articulating the values of the American people in public speeches is an important component of building popular support.

Clinton's policies have also been generally popular, in some cases more popular with the overall public than among Democratic activists. He pushed welfare reform, spending cuts to create a balanced budget, more police on the beat, fewer appeals from death-row inmates, and NAFTA—all over the muted cries of liberal Democrats. Clinton co-opted so many Republican policies that cartoonists joked in 1996 that the Republicans would also nominate Clinton because he was the most articulate politician who shared their values.

As the Senate discussed the removal of the president, Clinton delivered a masterly State of the Union speech, in which he addressed all of the major issues on the public agenda with a mix of conservative and liberal programs. He called for devoting most of the budget surplus to saving Social Security and Medicare, with some money going to other programs. His education program combined conservative rhetoric about ending social promotion and providing parents with report cards on schools with more liberal plans to hire more teachers and reduce class sizes. His discussion of programs for families and communities included a boost in the minimum wage, expanding child-care tax credits, and extending the Family and Medical Leave Act. He proposed hiring up to 50,000 more police officers and providing aid to communities to save open spaces.

The Republican response to Clinton's speech tells volumes about why, at the end of the impeachment process, Clinton was far more popular than the GOP leaders in Congress. The television cameras caught House majority leader Dick Armey smirking and whispering while Clinton called for extending the Family and Medical Leave Act to include more businesses—a wildly popular program with women and families with small children or ailing grandparents. Republicans sat on their hands as the president called for hiring more teachers and striving for smaller class sizes—a program of great interest to parents of school-aged children. In the official GOP response, the party spoke with two voices, one that called for an end to the IRS, the other that called for a 10 percent across-the-board tax cut at a time when Americans were feeling prosperous and wanted better schools and infrastructure. Republicans attempted to rally the American public behind the tax cut—the one issue that helps unite the two wings of the GOP—but found little interest. A Pew survey conducted in February 1999 showed that 50 percent of the public preferred to use the surplus to save Social Security, while 14 percent wanted the money to go to a tax cut. When asked to choose between tax cut proposals, only 37 percent of the public preferred the across-the-board cut, while 58 percent preferred Clinton's targeted approach. Among Republicans, support for a 10 percent tax cut reached only 50 percent.

The inability of the Republicans to develop a positive message that went beyond cutting government enabled Clinton to seize the middle ground on policy issues. Ironically, Clinton emerged from the Senate trial with clear control of the domestic policy debate. Surveys repeatedly showed that the public preferred that Clinton take the lead on policy, rather than the GOP Congress; one Pew survey from November 1998 put those numbers at 49 percent for Clinton and 26 percent for the GOP Congress. A Pew survey from February 1999 showed that 54 percent of the public preferred that the next president pursue policies similar to those of Clinton. Clinton's policies were clearly part of his ability to maintain high job-approval ratings in the midst of personal scandal. Indeed, in repeated Pew polls over the course of the scandal, two-thirds of the public repeatedly said they did not like Clinton as a person, but over 60 percent consistently said they did like his policies.

Taken together, the state of the economy and Clinton's popular policies explain most of the president's resilient popularity. Yet they do not tell the entire story.

There's Something about Bill

Presidential personalities are one of the great intangibles of politics—easy to talk about but difficult to measure. There is a consensus among political observers, however, that Bill Clinton is an extremely talented politician who communicates well with the American public. His ability to feel the pain of the average American was the subject of much ridicule, yet that ability helped establish a rapport with the public that provided him with a cushion of goodwill. Clinton evinced an understanding of the problems that faced ordinary Americans; one *Washington Post* poll in September 1998 showed that while only slightly more than one in five respondents thought Clinton was honest and trustworthy, nearly three in five thought he understood their problems.

Clinton's skill in projecting a compassion and understanding of average Americans stood in sharp contrast to that of President Bush. In the 1992 presidential campaign Bush had demonstrated his unfamiliarity with the details of everyday life and a complete lack of understanding about how downturns in the national economy might create hardship for a particular family. He vetoed a bill to extend unemployment benefits as he came off a private golf course on his way to a $1,000-a-plate fundraising dinner. Many Americans believed that Bush was a decent man but that he did not understand or care about average citizens.

In some ways, Clinton's connection with the American public resembled that of Ronald Reagan. Reagan communicated that he shared many basic values with the public, and voters forgave his inattention to detail and inability to control the foreign policy process. Both Reagan and Clinton were skilled communicators, but their relationship with the public goes deeper than that. Both men were raised in very modest backgrounds and appear to have made good by their skills and hard work. Both were able to draw on their roots in their rhetoric and convey that they remembered where they came from.

This does not mean, of course, that the public approved of Clinton or thought he had strong moral character. As we noted previously, polls consistently showed that a very large majority of the public thought Clinton was dishonest and lacked critical moral qualities. After he admitted to an improper relationship with Lewinsky, fully 70 percent of Americans described his actions as "very wrong," in a Pew Research Center poll. Yet William Dalbec of the Wirthlin Group noted that "President Clinton's ability to connect with personally relevant messages and policies blunts much of the concerns people have about his personal life. . . . Not since Ronald Reagan has a president understood the power of a values-laced message when communicating with the nation."[3]

After Clinton's State of the Union address in 1999, he was surrounded by African American members of Congress who proudly showed their loyalty to a president who had understood the problems of their community. Novelist Toni Morrison went so far as to write, "Years ago, in the middle of the Whitewater investigation, one heard the first murmurs: white skin notwithstanding, this is our first black President. . . . Clinton displays almost every trope of blackness: single-parent household, born poor, working-class, saxophone-playing, McDonald's-and-junk-food-loving boy from Arkansas." (In the *New Yorker*, October 5, 1998, p. 32).

One other factor shielded Clinton from the full impact of the public's harsh moral judgments: their evaluations of his opponents.

With Enemies Like These

Political judgments are necessarily comparisons. If Clinton were removed from office, someone else would be president. If the president were weakened and unable to conduct the nation's business, the Republicans in Congress would dominate the policy agenda—Clinton benefited in this crisis from widespread public dislike of his enemies and skepticism of their motives.

Clinton's nemesis was Kenneth Starr, a prosecutor who appeared to many to be willing to do anything to convict the president. As the investigation unfolded, Starr repeatedly asked for permission to investigate new issues and problems, creating the impression that he was fishing for a scandal. His investigation of Whitewater—repeated prosecutions of Webb Hubbell and Susan McDougal languishing in jail and appearing in public in chains and manacles—made him seem overly zealous. His handling of the investigation—holding Lewinsky without her lawyer, forcing her mother to testify against her, the repeated leaks from his office to the press—all served to undermine his legitimacy in the eyes of the public. The Starr report, full of explicit details of Clinton's sexual encounters and charging Clinton with misuse of power for defending himself against Starr's probe, struck many Americans as overkill. By the fall of 1998 a substantial majority of Americans had a negative view of Starr and, according to a *Newsweek* poll, fully 58 percent disapproved of his methods. They believed that he was more interested in removing the president than in finding the truth and that he had included licentious details of Clinton's sexual encounters with Lewinsky in his report in order to embarrass the president.

Clinton's partisan nemesis during 1998 was GOP Speaker Newt Gingrich (R-Ga.), who was also generally unpopular. In the fall of 1998 as Gingrich finally agreed to conservative demands that the party focus part of the congressional campaign on Clinton, Gingrich's approval ratings lagged behind those of the president by more than twenty points. After the election, the same conservatives who pushed Gingrich to attack the president blamed him for doing so, and he was forced to resign as Speaker.

Not only were Clinton's antagonists unpopular, but there were no likable characters in the entire drama. Despite Lewinsky's youth, few Americans sympathized with her or saw her as a victim. Media reports of her previous affair with a married man, her claim to her friends that she was bringing her "Presidential kneepads" to Washington, details of her conversations with Linda Tripp, and perhaps a lingering double standard about sexual affairs led many Americans to view Lewinsky unfavorably. Tripp, who tried to convince the public that when she turned her "friend" over to Starr's prosecutors she was doing her duty to the country and had Monica's best interests at heart, was seen by most Americans as mean spirited. Paula Jones was widely perceived as a woman motivated by a desire for financial gain and a pawn in the hands of Republican activists bent on bringing down the president.

The House GOP leadership was generally perceived by the public as engaged in a partisan vendetta. Although Judiciary Committee chair Henry Hyde (R-Ill.) promised a bipartisan hearing, the committee's deliberations were more like a partisan circus. Although few Americans were watching, the committee council's drafting of the articles of impeachment while the president's team was presenting their case was merely emblematic of what appeared to many Americans as a hurried, partisan endeavor. The angry rhetoric of Bob Barr (R-Ga.) and Tom DeLay (R-Tex.) made it clear that many Republicans truly hated Clinton, and the tight smile on Hyde's face suggested that media reports that he really despised Clinton were on the mark. A CBS News poll found that 61 percent of the public characterized the investigation as a partisan affair.

In April 1998, in the midst of the investigation, a Pew poll showed that 62 percent of the public had a favorable impression of Clinton, 36 percent were favorable toward Gingrich, 22 percent toward Starr, 17 percent toward Lewinsky, 10 percent toward Tripp, and 17 percent toward Paula Jones. If the story had had a clearly likable victim, or if the prosecutors and House GOP leadership had seemed more balanced and judicious, it is possible they could have chipped away at Clinton's approval ratings.

When They Say It Isn't about Sex . . . It's about Sex

The public finally saw at the heart of this scandal a man lying about an extramarital affair. Because this testimony had been ruled irrelevant to the Jones trial, Clinton's lying was presumably to save face with the public and to prevent his wife and daughter from learning of the affair. Although surveys show that substantial majorities of Americans disapprove of extramarital affairs, many engage in them and many more contemplate them. Almost all Americans who have affairs lie about them, and those who contemplate them realize that, if acted upon, they would lie about the affairs. Thus, unlike lying about politics or the conduct of government, lying about sex is something that most Americans understand, and many can imagine themselves engaged in at some point in their lives.

For many Americans, Clinton's affair with Lewinsky was a private matter between the two of them and between Bill and Hillary Clinton. In an ABC News poll, two-thirds of the public said that the affair had nothing to do with Clinton's job as president. Few worried about the details of why Clinton was asked questions about the affair or how Jones's lawyers came to know of the affair; those who did express concern were even more likely to believe that Clinton should never have been questioned about the matter in the first place.

This does not mean that the public believed that lying about the affair was proper, merely that they believed that it was a private matter— 63 percent saying so in an NBC survey conducted in August 1998. By defining this as a private matter, many Americans compartmentalized their judgments about the moral conduct, allowing condemnation of the behavior while supporting the president's policies. The issue could have been defined differently—Lewinsky was an intern in Clinton's office, and the affair occurred in the office—but the public framed the issue as private consensual sexual conduct.

Americans believed that many public officials have sexual affairs and lie about them, a belief that was confirmed by a spate of confessions by Republicans of their own sexual escapades. Judiciary Committee chairman Hyde confessed to a "youthful indiscretion" when he was in his forties that broke up a marriage with children, yet he seemed curiously unconcerned or unrepentant of the affair. Helen Chenowith (R-Idaho) admitted to an extramarital affair but denied lying about it until she was confronted with her previous denial captured on videotape. Clinton antagonist Dan Burton (R-Ind.) admitted to having fathered a child out of wedlock but claimed that he had done right by "the child" by sending regular support checks (when many Americans might have thought that his son deserved more than merely money). Most dramatically, House Speaker-elect Bob Livingston (R-La.), to the shock of most party members, admitted to multiple sexual affairs and renounced his elected position and resigned from Congress.

Many Americans believe, moreover, that government officials lie to them regularly about important policy matters. In seven polls conducted between June 30, 1987, and January 15, 1989, a majority of Americans in each survey believed that Ronald Reagan had lied about Iran-Contra.[4] A substantial majority of Americans believed that George Bush lied about Iran-Contra as well, and this number grew over time. Nearly one-third of Americans believed that Bush lied when he denied allegations of his own sexual affair, although a somewhat higher number believed him.

Americans would prefer that their politicians not lie to them. Yet overall, they think that it would be easier to simply not invade their privacy. One Pew poll in December 1998 found by a margin of 60 percent to 34 percent that Americans believe that the best way to avoid scandals like this in the future is to make sure a president's private life remains private, rather than to elect a president with high moral character.

Thus, cynicism about government officials helped to prop up Clinton's popularity because the public believed that many Republicans were having sex, lying about it, and then hypocritically prosecuting the president. Given the strong economy and the popularity of Clinton's policies, it is unlikely that the public would have responded very differently to a Clinton lie about policy. Nevertheless, the public did appear to distinguish in this case the nature of the lie and to relegate it to a matter of private morality.

Future Implications of the Crisis

When the Republicans lost five House seats in the 1998 midterm elections, the exit polls showed that a substantial majority of Americans wanted the GOP to drop the matter and move on. This sentiment persisted throughout the entire impeachment process: the public opposed a Senate trial and opposed calling witnesses and mostly wanted the story to go away. It is still too early to determine whether the scandal will have any lasting impact on American politics and public opinion.

On the one hand, polls showed that at least some Americans planned on changing their party registration to protest the GOP action and believed in early 1999 that they would support Democratic candidates in 2000. Generic ballot questions for the 2000 House races showed substantial Democratic advantages in early 1999—far larger than normal. A survey by ABC News showed that 31 percent of respondents said they would be more likely to oppose a Senator who voted to remove the president, compared with only 19 percent who would be more likely to support such a representative.[5]

Although the numbers involved were relatively small, aggregate House elections often hinge on 1 to 2 percent of the popular vote, and even small shifts in public sentiment might make a difference. Moreover, an interest group called "Censure and Move On" collected a number of signatures and pledges for millions of dollars in contributions to help defeat Republicans who voted for impeachment, and other liberal groups found that the impeachment effort was at least a temporary boon to their fund-raising.

There was scattered anecdotal evidence that in early 1999 the public was truly angry. In Henry Hyde's conservative Republican suburban district, Bill Clinton's job approval ratings were higher than those for Hyde. In California, election officials reported unusually high levels of changed voter registration. Yet in politics, two years is an eternity. It is likely that that anger will dissipate over time as other issues become more salient. The lasting impact of the impeachment hearings on public opinion depends on events that occur throughout 1999 and 2000 that either keep the impeachment process in the public mind or distract the public's memory.

Generic ballot questions and vote intention questions are meaningless two years before an election; but even more damaging for the GOP is the sharply negative public image of the party. Private surveys conducted in mid-1997, *before* the Lewinsky story even broke, showed that *the* most negative aspect of the Republican image was the party's efforts to "force Bill Clinton out of office." Obviously the events that transpired in 1998 and 1999 only added to this view. Going into the 1998 elections, the GOP faced the problem that Congress had accomplished little. Before the 2000 contests, the Republican party needs to accumulate accomplishments that it can trumpet during the campaign.

As of spring 1999, the GOP appears in disarray, with the public seemingly indifferent to the party's long-standing promise of tax cuts, the only policy that the party seems to be able to focus on. Republicans hope that the "compassionate conservatism" of the current GOP presidential nomination front runner, George W. Bush, might reshape the public view of their party. If the public forgets about impeachment, enjoys prosperity, and rewards incumbents for it, then the impeachment story will not influence electoral behavior in 2000. Yet the campaign itself might keep it in the public eye.

First, a dozen candidates are currently contemplating a run for the GOP presidential nomination, and several of them will cater to the conservative wing of the party that hates Clinton. If these candidates spend a good deal of time and money attacking Clinton during the campaign, it will remind voters of the seemingly irrational hatred party activists feel for the president. At the 2000 convention, it will be difficult to deny that wing of the party access to the microphone, yet if the convention roars with approval at anti-Clinton rhetoric, many voters will remember impeachment.

Second, the current Democratic front-runner, Vice President Al Gore, may suffer from his loyalty to his boss. Americans are already expressing scandal fatigue; in an April 1999 Pew poll, 74 percent of the public agreed with the statement, "I'm tired of all the problems of the Clinton Administration." In the same survey, Gore's favorability ratings dipped below 50 percent for the first time since the allegations of improper fundraising by the vice president in September 1997.

Although Clinton emerged from the impeachment scandal more popular than Congress and apparently in control of the domestic agenda, he soon found himself distracted by an air war in Kosovo and the possibility of ground troop deployment by summer 1999. Critical events like wars have a way of focusing the public's mind on what is truly important. The partisan impact of a protracted war is unpredictable at this time, but it is clear that the events that occur immediately before the 2000 elections will be important in voters' minds, whereas the Lewinsky scandal may be long forgotten.

Notes

1. The authors acknowledge estimates from political scientist Robert Erikson of early 1999 job approval ratings for President Clinton. Surveys used in this analysis were conducted by The Pew Research Center for the People & the Press between January 1998 and February 1999. Copies of the results are available from their website: <www.people-press.org>

2. <www.msnbc.com/news/250154.asp> March 22, 1999.

3. Personal communication via e-mail, March 31, 1999.

4. The surveys include a Roper poll from June 30, 1987, and CBS/NYT 1987 surveys on July 9, July 16, July 22, August 22, and November 24, and on January 15, 1989.

5. <www.abcnews.com/poll990111.html>

References

Brody, Richard. 1991. *Assessing the President: The Media, Elite Opinion, and Public Support*. Stanford, Calif.: Stanford University Press.

Bruce, John M., Clyde Wilcox, and Dee Allsop. 1994. "Presidential Evaluations, Domestic and International Influences, and the Mass Media." Paper presented at the annual meeting of the American Political Science Association, New York.

Chappell, Henry and William Keech. 1985. "A New View of Political Accountability for Economic Performance." *American Political Science Review* 79:10–27.

Clarke, Harold D., Jonathon Rapkin, and Marianne C. Stewart. 1994. "A President out of Work: A Note on the Political Economy of Presidential Approval in the Bush Years." *British Journal of Political Science* 24:535–61.

Clarke, Harold D., and Marianne C. Stewart. 1994. "Prospections, Retrospections, and Rationality: The 'Bankers' Model of Presidential Approval Reconsidered." *American Journal of Political Science* 38:1104–23.

Connolly, Cecil, and Thomas B. Edsall. 1998. "Political Pros Looking for Explanations: Public Reaction Seems to Rewrite the Rules." *Washington Post*. 9 February, A6.

Edwards, George C., III. 1991. *Presidential Approval.* Baltimore: Johns Hopkins University Press.

Edwards, George C., III, William Mitchell, and Reed Welch. 1995. "Explaining Presidential Approval: The Significance of Issue Salience." *American Journal of Political Science* 39:108–34.

Hibbs, Douglas, Douglas Rivers, and Nicholas Vasukatis. 1982. "The Dynamics of Political Support for American Presidents among Occupational and Partisan Groups." *American Journal of Political Science* 26:312–32.

Hurwitz, Jon, and Mark Peffley. 1987. "The Means and Ends of Foreign Policy as Determinants of Presidential Support." *American Journal of Political Science* 31:236–58.

Kernell, Samuel. 1978. "Explaining Presidential Popularity." *American Political Science Review* 72:506–22.

Kinder, Donald R., 1981. "Presidents, Prosperity, and Public Opinion." *Public Opinion Quarterly* 45:1–21.

Krosnick, Jon A., and Laura Brannon. 1993. "The Impact of the Gulf War on the Ingredients of Presidential Evaluations: Multidimensional Effects of Political Involvement." *American Political Science Review* 84:497–512.

Lau, Richard, and David Sears. 1981. "Cognitive Links between Economic Grievances and Political Responses." *Political Behavior* 3:279–302.

MacKuen, Michael B., Robert S. Erikson, and James A. Stimson. 1992. "Peasants or Bankers? The American Electorate and the U.S. Economy." *American Political Science Review* 86:597–611.

Monroe, Kristin. 1981. "Presidential Popularity: An Almon Distributed Lag Model." *Political Methodology* 6:43–69.

Monroe, Kristin, and Dona Metcalf Laughlin. 1983. "Economic Influences on Presidential Popularity among Key Political and Socio-Economic Subgroups." *Political Behavior* 5:309–45.

Norpoth, Helmut, and Thom Yantek. 1983. "Macroeconomic Conditions and Fluctuations of Presidential Popularity." *American Journal of Political Science* 27:785–807.

Ostrom, Charles W. Jr., and Dennis M. Simon. 1985. "Promise and Performance: A Dynamic Model of Presidential Popularity." *American Political Science Review* 79:334–58.

Peffley, Mark, and John Williams. 1985. "Attributing Presidential Responsibility for National Economic Problems." *American Politics Quarterly* 13:393–425.

Sigelman, Lee, and Kathleen Knight. 1985. "Public Opinion and Presidential Responsibility for the Economy: Understanding Personalization." *Political Behavior* 7:167–89.

Wilcox, Clyde, and Dee Allsop. 1991. "Economic and Foreign Policy as Sources of Reagan Support." *Western Political Quarterly* 44:941–58.

Zaller, John R. 1998. "Monica Lewinsky's Contributions to Political Science." *Political Science and Politics* 31:182–89.

T E N

The Media:
The New Media and the
Lure of the Clinton Scandal

John Anthony Maltese

On January 17, 1998, President Clinton videotaped a deposition for the Paula Jones sexual harassment lawsuit against him. The next day, former White House adviser George Stephanopoulos appeared on the Sunday morning ABC News program "This Week." Discussion turned to the Jones lawsuit, and Stephanopoulos confidently predicted that Clinton would win in court. ABC correspondent Sam Donaldson asked why the president did not settle out of court with Jones to avoid damaging revelations at the trial. "But Sam," Stephanopoulos replied incredulously, "What worse can come out than already has been out? . . . What else can come out?"[1]

Three days later, America woke up to startling reports that the president had had an affair with a 24-year-old White House intern, had lied about it under oath the previous Saturday, and had urged her to lie about it as well. *Newsweek* reporter Mike Isikoff had been investigating the Lewinsky story for a year and had been on the verge of publishing it the weekend of the president's deposition. Over Isikoff's objections, *Newsweek* editors chose not to run the story, in part because Kenneth Starr, the independent counsel investigating the president, had asked them not to.[2] But gossip columnist Matt Drudge posted details of the story on his Internet site, which, in turn, prompted the *Washington Post* to run the story in its Wednesday morning edition (preceded by an early-morning posting on its Web site).[3] Sources also revealed that the president—contrary to his previous denials—had admitted in his deposition to having an affair with Gennifer Flowers.

At 9:45 A.M., Press Secretary Mike McCurry sat down for his daily off-camera session with reporters in his office. In a rare move, he read a two-sentence statement carefully crafted by aides in the early morning hours: "The president is outraged by these allegations. He's never had any improper relationship with this woman and he's made clear from the very beginning that he wants people to tell the truth in all matters." McCurry's daily on-camera briefing was scheduled for 1:00 P.M., but he did not appear until 1:24 P.M. Mindful of the president's history of evasive answers, reporters asked over and over again what the White House meant by an improper relationship. . . . Why didn't the White House say that there was no sexual relationship? McCurry refused to elaborate: "I'm not going to parse the statement. You all got the statement I made earlier . . . so, I'm not going to parse the statement."[4]

At 3:15 P.M., President Clinton sat down for a previously scheduled interview with Jim Lehrer for the PBS news program *The News Hour with Jim Lehrer*. Questioning began with the allegations:

Jim Lehrer:	The news of this day is that Kenneth Starr, the independent counsel, is investigating allegations that you suborned perjury by encouraging a 24-year-old woman, a former White House intern, to lie under oath in a civil deposition about her having had an affair with you. Mr. President, is that true?
President Clinton:	That is not true. That is not true. I did not ask anyone to tell anything other than the truth. There is no improper relationship. And I intend to cooperate with this inquiry. But that is not true.
Jim Lehrer:	No improper relationship. Define what you mean by that.
President Clinton:	Well, I think you know what it means. It means that there is not a sexual relationship, an improper sexual relationship, or any other kind of improper relationship.
Jim Lehrer:	You had no sexual relationship with this young woman?

President Clinton: There is not a sexual relationship. That is
                      accurate.[5]

Reporters immediately pounced on the president's use of the present tense: there *is* no sexual relationship. As Mara Liasson of National Public Radio put it the next day: "Everybody thought, oh, he's pulling a Clinton. He's saying there was one but there isn't now."[6] Later in the day, *Roll Call* magazine interviewed the president. This time he did not rely on the present tense. When asked, "What exactly was the nature of your relationship with her?" the president responded, "The relationship was not improper and I think that is important enough to say." Then he added what appeared to be a more categorical denial: "The relationship was not sexual."[7]

Even that did not satisfy reporters. Recorded telephone conversations between Lewinsky and Linda Tripp suggested that the president drew a distinction between oral sex and adultery, and Lewinsky said on the tapes that there had been only oral sex. Chris Bury reported on ABC's "Nightline" that "such distinctions may prove important in the context of what constitutes an improper relationship."[8] To illustrate why such careful parsing was necessary, Bury ran a segment showing Clinton responding to charges in 1992 that he had had a twelve-year affair with Gennifer Flowers. Asked in 1992 about the story alleging the affair, Clinton said: "I read the story. It isn't true. It isn't a true story."

That was the line that Clinton maintained for the next six years. He admitted in a famous 1992 interview with his wife on CBS's "60 Minutes" that he had caused pain in his marriage, but when asked during the same interview whether the supermarket tabloid story of a twelve-year affair was true, Clinton again responded, "That allegation is false." Six years later, in his January 17, 1998, Paula Jones deposition, Clinton finally admitted to an affair with Flowers. As Bury told his television audience, "That precise allegation, a *twelve-year* affair, may indeed have been false. But [prior to the deposition] Bill Clinton carefully avoided answering or denying the fundamental question, did he have an affair with Gennifer Flowers."

Bury then played excerpts of a tape of a telephone conversation between Clinton and Flowers that Flowers had released after the 1992 "60 Minutes" interview. In it, Clinton appeared to coach Flowers on what to say if asked about the affair: "If they hit you with it, just say no and go on. There's nothing they can do. If all the people who are named deny it, that's all. I mean I expect them to come look into it and interview you and everything, but I just think if everybody's on record denying it, you've got no problems."[9] Finally, Bury showed Press Secretary McCurry's response to a question about the contradiction between Clinton's 1992 public statements that the Gennifer Flowers story was not true and his 1998 admission under oath that he did have an affair with Flowers. McCurry said, "The president knows that he told the truth in 1992 when he was asked about that relationship and he knows that he testified truthfully on Saturday, and he knows his answers are not at odds."[10]

In the ensuing firestorm of media coverage, many media commentators predicted that Clinton would be forced to resign or would be impeached. Even Stephanopoulos publicly predicted resignation or impeachment if the story proved to be true.[11] Clinton stonewalled, convinced (reportedly with the help of polls from his former adviser Dick Morris) that he could not survive if he told the truth about his relationship with Lewinsky. On January 25, a Fox network television reporter asked White House Communications Director Ann Lewis point blank whether it was true that the president did not consider oral sex to be a "sexual relationship." Lewis responded categorically: "No. Sex is sex."[12] Clinton did not correct her. The next day, Clinton made his famous finger-wagging statement: "I did not have sexual relations with that woman, Miss Lewinsky."

Clinton and the New Media

The New Media (the Internet, cable, satellite technology, and the like) played an important role in shaping the Lewinsky story. The Internet broke the story and then propelled it in the coming months. As one commentator wrote shortly after the Lewinsky scandal broke, "the Web was not simply a convenient conduit for releasing an exclusive story—it was the entity that was driving the media frenzy about the alleged presidential sex scandal."[13] Even Clinton's relationship with the White House press corps had been shaped, in part, by the president's attitude toward the New Media.

Just as Franklin Roosevelt mastered the use of radio and John F. Kennedy mastered the use of television, Bill Clinton came to office expecting to master the use of the New Media. Advances in technology had dramatically changed the nature of communication by 1992. Cable, satellite technology, and the Internet all provided an unparalleled opportunity for direct communication with the American people. In the 1992 presidential campaign, Clinton had effectively followed a strategy of "narrowcasting"—using media outlets like MTV, "Arsenio Hall Show," "Phil Donahue," and Don Imus's radio talk show to transmit direct, targeted messages to particular constituencies.[14]

Once Clinton was elected, his advisers planned to expand their use of the New Media to bypass the critical filter of the White House press corps. Sidney Blumenthal, who later joined the White House as a communication strategist, touted such possibilities for unmediated communication in an article in the *New Yorker*. There he wrote that the "Old Media," such as the three big network news shows, were "anachronistic" and were "no more likely to return than are the big bands."[15] The White House seemed to agree. It created a White House Web site, making it possible for virtually anyone with a computer to download the text of Clinton's public remarks, his daily schedule, White House press briefings, and even photographs. This electronic channel bypassed the filter of reporters who used to be the only source for transmitting such material.[16] White House Media Affairs Director Jeff Eller also spoke, only partly in jest, of creating what he called "BC-TV"—the Bill Clinton Television Network—to broadcast White House events unedited.[17]

Cable outlets, talk radio, and local media also provided ways for Clinton to bypass the White House press corps. During his first two months in office, President Clinton did not even hold a full-scale press conference for the White House press corps. He did, however, hold some twenty-five sessions with representatives of local media as part of an effort to target messages to specific media markets.[18] The first lady followed a similar strategy; by mid-April of 1993, she had granted interviews to nineteen local television news anchors, but had granted only three interviews to the White House press corps.[19] Ann Compton of ABC News said that of the five presidents that she had covered, Clinton was the only one who "did everything in his power to go around, under, and away from the White House press corps."[20]

It soon became evident, however, that the White House was not the only one who could use such tactics of circumvention. Administration opponents also used the New Media to spread charges of presidential scandal and ineptitude. Talk radio, which Clinton had used so effectively in the 1992 presidential campaign, came back to haunt him as president. By 1997, news/talk was the most popular radio format in America, carried by 1,330 commercial radio stations (up from only 308 in 1989).[21] The growth was spurred by the 1987 repeal of the Fairness Doctrine, and conservative shows dominated the airwaves.

Soon they became a powerful vehicle for criticizing Clinton and spreading stories about White House scandals. Some, including the mainstream media, blamed talk radio for helping to fan the opposition that ultimately doomed Clinton's nomination of Zoe Baird for U.S. Attorney General in 1993.[22] Democrats blamed talk radio for contributing to their disastrous showing in the 1994 midterm elections, when they lost control of both houses of Congress to the Republicans.[23] President Clinton publicly suggested in 1995 that conservative talk radio had fanned the flames of societal unrest that led to the Oklahoma City bombing.[24] And Hillary Clinton dismissed the Lewinsky story in early 1998 as part of a "right-wing conspiracy," of which talk radio was a part.[25]

Likewise, the Internet altered the way that the Old Media responded to breaking news stories. The Old Media had served not only as a filter of White House news but also as a more general gatekeeper of other news. With the Internet, however, virtually anyone could post a story. Not only did the "Drudge Report" on the Internet break the Lewinsky story, but the Internet came to shape the way the media covered the scandal. Before the Lewinsky scandal most major media outlets followed an unwritten rule that they would not use their web site to break a story; instead, web sites contained information that had already been reported in other venues.[26] This changed with the Lewinsky scandal. As competing news organizations struggled to stay one step ahead of the competition, web sites became important. The first mainstream coverage of the Lewinsky scandal appeared on the *Washington Post* web site, prompting *Newsweek* to follow suit. In the drive to scoop the competition, errors were made. The *Dallas Morning Herald,* for example, posted an erroneous story on its web site that a secret service agent was an eyewitness to a presidential tryst. The editors subsequently pulled the story, but not before other news outlets, such as ABC, had reported it.[27]

Such situations prompted Cable News Network (CNN) senior analyst Jeff Greenfield to worry about what he called an "echo effect"— news organizations picking up and repeating without independent corroboration a story from a single source. Regardless of the story's reliability, the simple act of repetition by different news venues made the story seem more credible.[28] The incessant chatter of talking heads on twenty-four-hour cable news networks like CNBC, MSNBC, and Fox News further enforced the echo effect. There the story seemed to be "All-Monica, All-the-Time," with pundits endlessly repeating and analyzing the story—even if they had no particular expertise on the matter.[29] MSNBC created a nightly show called "The White House in Crisis" to discuss the scandal—even when there was nothing new to discuss.

Fox and MSNBC, both of whom joined the cable news lineup in 1996, relied heavily on talk shows to fill their air time. Talk is easy and talk is cheap, and the proliferation of these shows led to saturation coverage of the Lewinsky story.[30] They also led to high ratings. And although many of these talk shows aired on "news" networks, their approach often descended into gossip. Indeed, a Committee of Concerned Journalists issued the results of a study in October 1998 suggesting that the talking heads on these shows were responsible for the most blatant errors and distortions in the coverage of the Lewinsky scandal. For example, rumors of Clinton liaisons with other interns that would have never merited coverage by a responsible news organization were fair game for the talking heads.[31] Ironically, this saturation coverage may have ultimately helped Clinton. By the time impeachment hearings rolled around in the fall of 1998, many Americans just wanted the story to go away.

Quite simply, the New Media were changing how news was released and the rules of the game by which news organizations played. Both the Web and twenty-four-hour cable news networks quickened the pace of news reporting and increased the sheer volume of coverage of the story.

Clinton and the Old Media

Even if the scandal stories were driven by the New Media, the Old Media proved to be harsh critics of the president in the early days of the Lewinsky scandal. There is no doubt that the Lewinsky story would have created a furor under any circumstances, but the president's sour relationship with the White House press corps had festered since the earliest days of the administration and did nothing to discourage coverage of the scandal.

Problems of arrogance and inexperience badly damaged Clinton's relations with the White House press corps in the early days of his first term. Those wounds never completely healed. The Clinton White House began its first term by turning a cold shoulder, both substantively and symbolically, to the White House press corps. When Clinton took office, the West Wing of the White House was transformed overnight from a place where President George Bush had enforced a dress code (men had to wear ties, women skirts) to one where almost anything went. Those in power were young and inexperienced. As Tom

Rosenstiel has noted, Director of Satellite Services David Anderson was twenty-three years old, had spiked hair, wore all black, and had not yet finished college (he was working at night after work to finish up his degree at Oberlin). The director of Ratio Operations, Richard Strauss, also twenty-three, was finishing up his degree at UCLA at night by correspondence. Rosenstiel added that sixty-three out of the roughly 450 people who were full-time White House staffers were under the age of twenty-four. Communications Director George Stephanopoulos had reached the ripe old age of thirty-two.[32] Veteran White House reporters experienced a generation gap. Faced with gum-chewing male aides with earrings who blared rock and roll from their offices, the staid, sixty-three-year-old David Broder of the *Washington Post* said that covering the new White House was like "coming home and finding your kids got into the liquor cabinet."[33]

The extent to which these new kids on the block wanted to control the news and put veteran reporters at bay stunned the press corps. One of Communications Director Stephanopoulos's first decisions was to close off access to the upstairs foyer in the West Wing where Stephanopoulos and White House Press Secretary Dee Dee Meyers had their offices. For more than twenty years, reporters had been free to wander that foyer in search of news. They could chat informally with communications officials or poke their heads into the press secretary's office to get a quick answer to a question. It was a clear sign that reporters and officials were on an equal playing field. Now, as Ann Compton put it, the foyer was a "no-fly zone" symbolizing the hierarchical relationship between reporters and officials.[34] In the new arrangement, reporters had to wait to be spoon-fed—and the White House appeared to be making only minimal efforts to do even that. Calls from downstairs were not returned in time for reporters to meet their deadlines, and some reporters felt that even when Stephanopoulos did invite them upstairs, he did not treat them with respect.[35]

The press corps reacted with fury. Stephanopoulos, who seemed surprised by the reaction, refused to rescind his decision to shut off the upstairs foyer. He did try to increase access elsewhere, however. He assigned two communications staffers, Lorrain Voles and Arthur Jones, to the lower press room on a permanent basis to handle reporters' queries.[36] He also added an extra press briefing each day. In addition to Stephanopoulos's own midday briefing, Press Secretary Myers began briefing the press at both 9:15 A.M. and 5:00 P.M.[37] But the new measures did nothing to calm the irate press corps. They had lost their space and, with it, a kind of access that was irreplaceable. In turn, the White House lost the goodwill of reporters. "Put it this way," said Karen Hosler, Washington correspondent for the *Baltimore Sun* and president of the White House Correspondents Association, "We're not going to cut them any breaks."[38]

Early on, the Clinton White House felt that it could get away with this kind of treatment. What the White House failed to realize was that the Old Media still mattered. A 1998 Gallup Poll showed that Americans continued to get most of their news from the Old Media and, even more importantly, *trusted* the Old Media more than the New.[39] Despite all the new sources of news, Americans embraced the gatekeeping role of the Old Media because they trusted it. In the new environment, narrowcasting and circumvention of the White House press corps had its place. But the symbiotic relationship between the White House and the Old Media continued to exist, and that worked only if the White House courted the press corps and fed it information instead of snubbing it. The White House learned that lesson too late.

A study by the Center for the Media and Public Affairs showed that only one-third of the stories aired on the three major television networks about Clinton in his first six months in office were positive (President George Bush, in comparison, received 55 percent positive stories in his first year in office).[40] Public opinion polls were also troubling. Clinton pollster Stan Greenberg found that 70 percent of the American people rated Clinton in the poor or fair categories, while only 28 percent chose the excellent or good categories.[41]

By the spring of 1993, the White House had significantly revamped its communications operation. The president moved Stephanopoulos out of the communications director post (replaced by Mark Gearan) and brought in David Gergen (communications director for Republican presidents Gerald Ford and Ronald Reagan) as counselor to the President in charge of communications. Gergen reopened the upstairs foyer in the West Wing, saw to it that reporters' calls were returned before deadline, held backgrounders, and quickly arranged for the president to hold a press conference. In July 1993, a month after Gergen took over, network news coverage was 40 percent positive (up from 27 percent positive in May).[42]

Still, Gergen could not get the White House to fashion a consistent media message. Part of this reflected internal White House splits, such as the one between Gergen, who wanted Clinton to move toward the political center, and Stephanopoulos (now senior advisor to the President for policy and strategy), who wanted Clinton to articulate a more liberal message. But it also reflected Clinton's own lack of discipline in communicating. Howard Kurtz has noted that the president was "unfocused and error-prone" in his dealings with reporters and "seemed unable to leave any question unanswered, even one on MTV about his underwear."[43]

Clinton further compounded the problem. On occasion, he openly treated reporters with contempt. Like Richard Nixon before him, Clinton seemed to feel that the press were conspiring to undo him. Kurtz has written that Clinton's staff felt that if the president had an Achilles' heel, "it was his tendency to go off half-cocked about the press."[44] At times unable to control his temper in front of reporters who antagonized him, Clinton further damaged his relationship with the press corps and fostered the image that he was petty.

Out of necessity, Clinton reached out to reporters after the disastrous 1994 midterm elections and sought to mend fences.[45] The president now asked for their forgiveness. He opened up to them at informal bagel breakfasts, cultivated ties with influential opinion makers like E.J. Dionne, and scrupulously practiced his answers to questions in formal sessions with his staff before any encounter with reporters. Known as the "pre-brief," these sessions focused the president's responses, but White House aides also used them to limit public displays of Clinton's temper by allowing him to vent privately before meeting with the press.[46]

By the time Clinton won reelection in 1996, he was more focused and disciplined in his relationship with the press. He enjoyed high public approval ratings and had the potential for a successful second term. But the never ending stream of scandals would not go away. Travelgate, Filegate, Whitewater, allegations of fundraising abuses, and the Paula Jones sexual harassment suit all dogged him. And the White House press corps remained suspicious. From their years of covering Clinton, they had concluded that he was the master of what was known in the Watergate days as the "non-denial denial"—evasive answers that skirted the truth. Privately they continued to rail at his lack of candor and their belief that Clinton arrogantly felt that he could get away with anything.[47]

That pent-up hostility may have fueled the media firestorm that erupted when the Lewinsky story broke in January 1998. When the president wagged his finger and denied sexual relations with Monica Lewinsky, reporters were not convinced. Nor were they predisposed to come to the president's defense. Only when it became clear that a majority of the American people were not as concerned about the scandal as the reporters seemed to be did the Old Media reflect on their frenzy and temper coverage.

Coordinating the Message

Planning and distributing the White House message is now the job of many White House staffers and of several distinct staff units.[48] During the Lewinsky scandal, such units included the White House Press Office and the White House Office of Communications, both of which deal directly with media relations. But staff also included a wide array of other staff units ranging from an ad hoc group set up specifically to deal with damage control associated with the scandal to the Office of Congressional Relations, which worked closely with Democrats on Capitol Hill during the House impeachment debate and subsequent Senate trial.

The development of these many staff units is a relatively recent phenomenon that corresponds with the enormous growth in presidential staff over the last seventy years. During Franklin Roosevelt's first term, the entire White House staff numbered only forty-seven. By 1974, it had grown to over five hundred. If you include the Executive Office of the President, created in 1939 to give the president ongoing expert advice on a variety of topics ranging from national security to economics, presidential staff has numbered over five thousand.[49] The purpose of this staff is to help the president. But the tremendous growth of staff has also posed some problems. As it multiplied, duplication and overlap sometimes undermined its effectiveness. Internal power struggles became more likely. The chain of command became less clear. Public statements from different officials were more likely to conflict. And the media, whose penchant for dramatic stories leads to a preoccupation with conflict, were eager to focus on any apparent dissension within the ranks.[50] Such stories only increase the tensions between those at odds and make the president look like a poor manager.[51]

The president's personal staff in the White House all have a vested interest in the president's success. Yet different staff units within the White House often split badly over how to further the president's "best interest." This was apparent during the Lewinsky scandal in the split between President Clinton's legal advisers and his political advisers over how to respond publicly to the accusations. Likewise, officials from different parts of the administration represent different constituencies and may take positions that conflict. As the Lewinsky scandal unfolded, for example, the public statements of FBI Director Louis Freeh conflicted with those of the White House. Inevitably, Attorney General Janet Reno distanced herself from White House communications strategies. Clearly, the interest in maintaining the legitimacy of her office required a different communications strategy than one designed to keep Bill Clinton in office.

From the start of his presidency, Clinton had a tendency to supplement the advice of formal staff units with informal advice from a variety of sources. In the area of communications, Clinton has set up several ad hoc staff units and relied on the advice of an array of special White House counselors (ranging from David Gergen to Dick Morris), as well as former Clinton advisers and other individuals outside of the administration (such as James Carville and former White House chief of staff Leon Panetta). With so many different individuals and staff units sharing similar functions, personality splits, policy differences, and other self-interested motivations ultimately pulled at the fabric of a seamless communications strategy. These divisions contributed to Clinton's lack of focus in his first term.

The Clinton administration's initial response to the Lewinsky story again reflected a divided set of advisers who were working with incomplete information. In an attempt to coordinate a response, the White House created a special communications team to deal specifically with the Lewinsky story. That reflected the seriousness of the story, but it also reflected the White House desire to put the story on a "separate track"—to have the rest of the White House go on with business as usual. At the same time, the Democratic National Committee established an office led by Karen Hancox to help coordinate damage control.[52] Hancox worked closely with White House communications director Ann Lewis. As impeachment drew near, they coordinated public statements from a wide array of pro-Clinton spokespersons, suggesting, for example, that Ken Starr was a sex-obsessed Republican zealot and that Republicans in the House of Representatives were unfair in their partisan maneuvers to impeach the president. The coordinated line was clearly on display on December 19, 1998, the day the full House voted to impeach the president. In a morning statement to reporters, White House press secretary Joe Lockhart three times decried "the politics of personal destruction." House minority leader Richard Gephardt repeated the line that morning in a speech on the floor of the House. So, too, did the president in his Rose Garden speech after the impeachment vote.

Often, though, the president's communications advisers seemed adrift. White House press secretary Mike McCurry later admitted that he purposely stayed out of the loop so that he could truthfully respond that he did not know the answers when questioned by reporters. After leaving his office, McCurry suggested that the alternative to being out of the loop would have been to "disseminate erroneous information, because the president was obviously in denial and concealing his affair."[53] Meanwhile, the president's legal advisers were said to have stymied attempts to have the president admit his guilt and offer a full apology. And, as the impeachment process proceeded, events sometimes unfolded beyond White House control. At times the president seemed to be aided by luck as much as by any systematic strategy for coping with the scandal.

Most importantly, the president was buoyed throughout the scandal and the impeachment trial by high public opinion polls. Indeed, scandal stories only seemed to drive the president's approval ratings higher. A week after the scandal broke, President Clinton's approval rating reached 67 percent—up from 59 percent before the story broke and the highest approval rating of his presidency.[54] A surging economy no doubt helped to bolster the president's approval ratings. But there may have been more to it than that. "Just maybe," Samuel Kernell has suggested, "survey respondents discriminate between the president as a public and private person."[55] Whatever the reason for the polls results, the White House took them seriously and effectively used them in its campaign to suggest that impeachment was simply a partisan maneuver.

Throughout his presidency, Clinton has been described as a president driven by polls.[56] Some White House advisers later speculated to members of the press that the president's high approval ratings had actually lulled them into a false sense of security—especially after the November 1998 midterm elections, when Democrats did far better than expected. How, they had thought, could the House of Representatives vote to impeach in the face of such strong public opinion? But impeach it did, and, even then, the president's approval ratings just went higher. By at least one poll, it reached its highest point to date (73 percent approval) immediately after the full House voted to impeach.[57] When Clinton delivered his 1999 State of the Union address in the midst of the Senate impeachment trial, an ABC News survey showed that 77 percent approved of the speech.[58] When the Senate finally voted to acquit, it must have been mindful of the polls.

Conclusions

This brief overview of the Lewinsky scandal and the Clinton communications strategies suggests several things about the Old and New Media. First, the New Media has significantly altered the way news is reported. It has undermined the gatekeeping function of the Old Media by allowing virtually anyone to post information, speeding up the pace with which news is reported, and contributing to saturation coverage of high-visibility stories. Second, despite these developments, the Old Media is alive and well. It remains the news source that most Americans trust and that most Americans continue to rely on. Although certainly influenced by the pressures of the New Media, the Old Media has not been shunted aside. Third, the Clinton White House underestimated this continued importance of the Old Media. The White House squandered its opportunity to forge a close working bond with the White House press corps in the early days of the administration.

All of this serves as a reminder that presidents must engage in a balanced approach to communications. They cannot afford to ignore the Old Media any more than they can afford to ignore the opportunities of the New Media. Although the gatekeeping function of the Old Media may sometimes seem to be a hindrance to White House communications, presidents should remember that this gatekeeping function can also help them—and the American people—by filtering out rumor and unsubstantiated stories and serving as a tempering influence on the news.

Notes

1. ABC News, "This Week," 18 January 1998, transcript no. 98011805-jl2.
2. Howard Kurtz, *Spin Cycle: How the White House and the Media Manipulate the News* (New York: Touchstone, 1998), 291.
3. Susan Schmidt, Peter Baker, and Toni Locy, "Clinton Accused of Urging Aide to Lie," *Washington Post*, 21 January 1998, A1.
4. ABC News, "Nightline," 21 January 1998, transcript no. 98012101-jO7.
5. ABC News, "ABC Special Report," 21 January 1998, transcript no. 98012101-jl4. The PBS interview was carried live on ABC television and was also published in "Clinton: 'There Is No Improper Relationship'," *Washington Post*, 22 January 1998, A13.
6. ABC News, "Nightline," 22 January 1998, transcript no. 98012201-jO7.
7. "Clinton: 'There Is No Improper Relationship'."
8. ABC News, "Nightline," 22 January 1998.
9. Clinton's aides suggested that this tape was doctored.

10. ABC News, "Nightline," 22 January 1998.

11. ABC News, "Good Morning America," 22 January 1998, transcript no. 98012217-jl4.

12. Kathy Kiely, "Defenders Work the Talk Shows; Blue Subject Spurs Red-Hot Language," *New York Daily News,* 26 January 1998, 7.

13. David Noack, "Clinton Sex Story Forces Print Media Changes," *Editor & Publisher Magazine,* 31 January 1998, 30.

14. Tom Rosenstiel, *The Beat Goes On: President Clinton's First Year with the Media* (New York: Twentieth Century Fun, 1994), 7.

15. Sidney Blumenthal, "The Syndicated Presidency," *The New Yorker,* 5 April 1993, 42–47.

16. Richard L. Berke, " 'Hey Prez!': Computers Offer New Line to Clinton," *New York Times,* 5 April 1993, A1.

17. Blumenthal, "The Syndicated Presidency," 44.

18. Ibid., 42. Clinton's first formal televised news conference came on March 23, 1993, three months into his administration.

19. Rosenstiel, *The Beat Goes On,* 8.

20. Rita K. Whillock, "The Compromising Clinton: Images of Failure, A Record of Success," in *The Clinton Presidency: Images, Issues, and Communication Strategies,* ed. Robert E. Denton Jr. and Rachel L. Holloway (Westport, Conn.: Praeger, 1996), 126.

21. "Talking the Talk," *Insight on the News,* 9 February 1998, 9.

22. Randall Bloomquist, "The Word According to Talk," *Adweek,* 3 May 1993, 1.

23. Mark Hudis and Cheryl Heuton, "Talk Ratings Are Stronger than Ever," *Mediaweek,* 8 April 1996, 4.

24. Laura Rich, "Liberals in the Land of Limbaugh," *Inside Media,* 7 June 1995, 1.

25. Ivo Dawnay, "Fightback at the White House: The Saving of a President," *Washington Post,* 1 February 1998, 22.

26. Noack, "Clinton Sex Story Forces Print Media Changes," 30.

27. Dan Trigoboff, "The 'Source' Heard Round the World," *Broadcasting & Cable,* 2 February 1998, 62.

28. Ibid., 62.

29. Robin Pogrebin, "Lewinsky Story Feeds Cable News Networks," *New York Times,* 8 August 1998, A10.

30. Alicia C. Shepard, "White Noise," *American Journalism Review,* January/February 1999, 20.

31. Ibid., 20.

32. Rosenstiel, *The Beat Goes On,* 8.

33. Ibid., 9.

34. Burt Solomon, "How a Leak-Loathing White House Is Putting the Press in Its Place," *National Journal,* 13 February 1993, 416.

35. Rosenstiel, *The Beat Goes On,* 10.

36. Leslie Kaufman, "The Young and the Relentless," *American Journalism Review,* March 1993, 30.

37. Solomon, "How a Leak-Loathing White House," 417.

38. Kaufman, "The Young and the Relentless," 30.

39. Frank Newport and Lydia Saad, "A Matter of Trust," *American Journalism Review,* July/August 1998, 30.

40. Rosenstiel, *The Beat Goes On,* 21.

41. Bob Woodward, *The Agenda: Inside the Clinton White House* (New York: Simon & Schuster, 1994), 226.

42. Rosenstiel, *The Beat Goes On,* 19–21.

43. Kurtz, *Spin Cycle,* xiv.

44. Ibid., 69.

45. Ibid., 73–74.

46. Kurtz, "White House at War," *Vanity Fair,* January 1999, 40.

47. White House reporters, interview by author, tape recording, Washington, D.C., 29 August 1997. See also, Kurtz, "White House at War," 40.

48. See, for example, Michael Baruch Grossman and Martha Joynt Kumar, *Portraying the President* (Baltimore: Johns Hopkins University Press, 1981), and John Anthony Maltese, *Spin Control: The White House Office of Communications and the Management of Presidential News,* 2d ed. (Chapel Hill: University of North Carolina Press, 1995).

49. Gary King and Lynn Ragsdale, eds., *The Elusive Executive* (Washington, D.C.: CQ Press, 1988), 205, 208. For some of the problems associated with counting the number of staff in the White House office, see John Hart, *The Presidential Branch,* 2d ed. (Chatham, N.J.: Chatham House, 1995), 112–25.

50. David L. Paeltz and Robert M. Entman, *Media Power Politics* (New York: Free Press, 1981), 16.

51. Robert M. Entman, "The Imperial Media," in *Politics and the Oval Office,* ed. Arnold J. Meltsner (San Francisco: Institute for Contemporary Studies, 1981), 89.

52. John F. Harris, "Office of Damage Control: DNC Operation to Counter Negative Publicity," *Washington Post,* 31 January 1998, A1.

53. John Kennedy, "Mike McCurry's About-Face," *George,* March 1999, 78.

54. Frank Newport and Alec Gallup, "Clinton's Popularity Paradox," *Gallup Monthly Poll,* January 1998, 14.

55. Samuel Kernell, "The Challenge Ahead for Explaining President Clinton's Public Support," *PRG Report,* spring 1999, 3.

56. Carl M. Cannon, "Hooked on Polls," *National Journal,* 17 October 1998, 2438ff.

57. Judy Keen and Richard Benedetto, "Clinton Poll Ratings Surge," *USA Today,* 21 December 1998, 1A.

58. Jack W. Germond and Jules Witcover, "The Defendant Gave a Boffo Speech," *National Journal,* 23 January 1999, 226.

ELEVEN

Presidential Personality: The Clinton Legacy

Stephen J. Wayne

When historians look back on the Clinton presidency, they may be more fascinated by Clinton himself than by the accomplishments and failures of his administration, the impact of his foreign and domestic policy on the country, or even his impeachment and its implications for the presidency. In short, the most enduring legacy of the Clinton years may very well be his character, his style, and his resiliency in the face of the crises he has faced in office. His is a personal presidency, one that we are not likely to forget or encounter for some time.

The personal dimension of Clinton's presidency arises out of the dominance of the man himself—a president whose persona has become the overriding issue of his administration, a complex individual but also one who has been easily stereotyped by late-night humorists and political opponents, a magnet that both attracts and repels, a focus of adulation and condemnation, a larger-than-life Baby Boomer.

What factors have enabled Clinton to so dominate the news of his presidency? Has it been the triumph of his politics or of his personality? I think it is the latter. How else can we explain the survival of such a consummate politician in an antipolitical age? How else could a president whose integrity, candor, and moral turpitude have been so extensively criticized and ultimately questioned by a majority of the public maintain such high job-approval ratings throughout most of his latest five years in office? How else could a scandal-plagued president in a scandal-plagued administration continue to be well liked by so many people?[1]

To answer these questions, we have to examine the Clinton persona, particularly those aspects of his character, style, and worldview that have enabled this particular individual to generate such passions and withstand a torrent of ridicule and yet focus like a laser, grow in office, and maintain a presidential presence throughout the end of his first term and during his second term in office. What makes him tick?

A Political Character

Several of Clinton's personality features stand out: his limitless ambition, boundless energy, and intellectual prowess.

Bill Clinton is goal oriented. The goals represent steps on a political ladder that led in his own mind toward the presidency, ever since he shook hands with John F. Kennedy at the White House in 1963 as a member of Boys' Nation: band major in high school, president of his freshman and sophomore classes at college, Rhodes scholar, Yale law graduate, Arkansas attorney general at thirty, and governor at thirty-two—the youngest governor in the country since Harold Stassen of Minnesota. Defeated once, Clinton was reelected five times and achieved national prominence as leader of the National Governors' Association and head of the Democratic Leadership Conference prior to his election as president in 1992.

Clinton explains his nonstop political career as a kind of reaction to his biological father's death six months before he was born and to the precariousness of life as he saw it:

> For a long time I thought I would have to live for both of us in some ways. . . . I think that's one reason I was in such a hurry when I was younger. I used to be criticized by people who said, "Well, he's too ambitious," but to me, because I grew up sort of subconsciously on his timetable, I never knew how much time I would have. . . . It gave me an urgent sense to do everything I could in life as quickly as I could.[2]

The investment Clinton has put into his work has been substantial. He seems to be in a state of perpetual motion. Up early in the morning, jogging regularly before breakfast, round-the-clock meetings, telephone calls, numerous appointments, events topped off by ceremonies and/or political and policy discussions late into the night, reading three or four books on the side—his life is a constant whirlwind. It is almost as if he were afraid to rest.

Getting the newly elected president to take a vacation in his first year in office is a case in point. It required a herculean effort by his family and aides who saw him (and themselves) as spent and overwrought. Elizabeth Drew describes these efforts in her book, *On The Edge:*

> Hillary Clinton buttonholed Presidential advisers to tell them to urge the President to go on vacation. Aides buttonholed Hillary Clinton to tell her to urge the President to go on vacation. Gergen kept up the argument that Clinton had been overexposed on the budget battle, and that he should withdraw and come back fresh on Labor Day.[3]

The president finally agreed to do so, but not before he flew to the Midwest to commiserate with flood victims, went to Denver to meet the Pope, spoke to aerospace workers in California, attended the National Governors' Conference in Tulsa, and returned to the White House for a day of prevacation, nonstop activity. His relaxing vacation on Martha's Vineyard included daily golfing, nightly partying, and afternoon visits to the village ice cream shop. According to Drew, "He left behind many exhausted Vineyarders and not a few cases of bad nerves."[4]

Dick Morris, the political guru who planned Clinton's reelection strategy, describes the president's regular schedule as so full that "he often had no time to think or to act on his own and, unfortunately, very little time for sleep."[5] Trips from the White House would begin at 6 A.M. and last throughout the day and evening with little or no break, the president returning to the White House in the early hours of the next morning. Two- or three-day jam-packed schedules on the road were a regular occurrence. According to Morris, "Clinton willingly agreed to each new meeting and demanded even more speeches and more stops on each new trip."[6] The president would return exhausted, "a basket case" in the words of Nancy Hernreich, deputy assistant to the President and director of Oval Office Operations.[7]

Stanley Renshon, a psychoanalyst and political scientist, argues in his book, *High Hopes,* that Clinton's frantic manner is motivated by a desire for constant stimulation. "Clinton's behavioral pattern suggests that he frantically pursues not just work activity, but activity itself," that he has a fear of being alone.[8] Journalist David Maraniss comes to much the same conclusion. In describing Clinton's intense activity in high school, his public speaking, his playing of the saxophone, his position as band major, Maraniss writes, "He had always hated to be alone, and playing the sax was one of the few ways he could tolerate it."[9] Both of these psychologically oriented biographers go on to argue that the fear of being alone stemmed from Clinton's unconscious desire to avoid dealing with feelings and experiences that he had growing up in a troubled home.[10]

Whatever the reason, Clinton's energy level has been a driving force throughout his life. He outlasts others, be they campaign aides, White House advisers, or his political opponents. And when that energy is combined with his very considerable cognitive talents and political instincts, it has enabled him to outsmart, outmaneuver, and outwit his adversaries.

Clinton has applied his intellectual skills to school, where he excelled, and to his career in government. Known as a policy "wonk," he is enamored with the details of issues, thrives on debate and discourse, and likes nothing better than to confront the challenge of an intricate policy problem. He flourishes on the complexity of issues; they provide him with the intellectual stimuli he craves and obviously needs for self-fulfillment.

Intellectuality is also a tool for Clinton, a device in his seductive arsenal of political weapons, which he taps when appropriate to impress and test others. George Stephanopoulos describes his first meeting with the then-governor and presidential candidate:

> Clinton started to putter around the office, picking up books, poll questionnaires, photos, anything that caught his eye. . . . For the next half hour, I joined him on the first of countless stream-of-consciousness tours across the political landscape of his mind. He seemed to know something about everything—from the party rules for picking superdelegates to turnout in black precincts on Super Tuesday, from how the credit crunch was bankrupting small businesses in New Hampshire to how micro enterprise loans could help farmers in the Mississippi Delta—and he swooped from issue to issue without losing his thread, punctuating his soliloquy with questions for me. By the time he closed with the prediction that the nomination would be decided on the day of the Illinois primary, I was blown away.[11]

Despite his considerable problem-solving skills, his agile mind, and questioning manner, Clinton's intellectual prowess can also be dysfunctional. In the words of one of his advisers, "Clinton never stops thinking." In the words of another, "He makes a decision when he absolutely has to."[12] The presence of a mind attuned to nuance that constantly searches for new information to put into the calculus of deciding has contributed to what George Stephanopoulos refers to as "chronic bouts of indecision."[13]

And so has Clinton's overwhelming desire to please those around him. This desire is associated with the need for approval, with being liked, appreciated, and respected. If approval is the bottom line, an ultimate goal, then the right solution for Clinton is the one with which most people agree. Using polls to find out is a reality check for him, an empirical substantiation for a psychological need.[14]

Because he craves accommodation and consensus, Clinton is uncomfortable with conflict, particularly among his inner circle. The most precarious decision-making situations for him are those in which his advisers are divided.[15] Not only are situations of internal disagreement unpleasant for Clinton, they can be disabling.

Consider, for example, the president's vacillation on the economic proposals he submitted to Congress in the first year of his administration. Three groups with three differing perspectives competed for the president's attention in shaping his economic policy. Journalist Bob Woodward describes these groups as the populists who had worked on his campaign, the pragmatists who worked with the Democratic Congress, and the economic advisers who were attuned to the needs of the business and investment communities—the "bond marketeers."[16] The competing priorities, policies, and interests of these groups conflicted the president, causing him to delay decisions, reverse some he had previously made, and finally compromise again and again to achieve some kind of legislative outcome. These factors also produced emotional outbursts when the president could not get his way.

The desire for agreement, particularly in the absence of a well-defined ideological perspective, is one reason why having advisers who have strong personalities and well-defined policy and political goals, such as treasury secretary Robert Rubin, budget chief and later White House staff director Leon Panetta, and political consultant Dick Morris, has been so important for Clinton and also why these advisers have exercised so much influence on him. George Stephanopoulos, who does not fit into this category even though he had the title of senior adviser to the president for policy and strategy, describes the chemistry of one of these relationships: the Morris–Clinton connection.

> Watching Dick, I began to see what attracted Clinton to him. . . . Dick's mind was color blind. He thought in black and white, a useful complement to Clinton's kaleidoscopic worldview. . . . He offered clear prescriptions and promised measurable results. His certainty helped cure Clinton's chronic bouts of indecision.[17]

Robert Reich, cabinet secretary and longtime friend of Clinton, saw Clinton's overwhelming desire to please as a character flaw and predicted that it could be a disabler in his presidency. Writing in his diary in September 1992, Reich noted:

> Faced with genuine evil or a national crisis of undisputed dimensions, Bill will rise to it. But in the more common situation where the public is uncertain about the choices it faces and what's at stake in those choices, I worry that his leadership may fail. He'll become unfocused and too eager to please.[18]

Numerous examples from Clinton's presidency confirm Reich's insight, from the failed attempts to find a suitable attorney general and assistant attorney general for civil rights, to the vacillation and endless compromises over the components of his 1993 economic plan, to his anguish over whether to approve or veto for the third time the Republicans' welfare reform proposal in 1996, to the middle-of-the-road military solution he fashioned in Kosovo. Stanley Renshon sees Clinton's indecisiveness as a consequence of the dichotomy between limitless ambitions and the constraints of the political environment. "For Clinton, making choices means accepting limits, which is extraordinary [sic] difficult for a person with such substantial ambitions and a high level of self-confidence in his ability to accomplish his irreconcilable purposes."[19]

Ambition combined with accommodation also accounts for Clinton's tendency to promise more than he can deliver. This tendency was particularly evident in his 1992 presidential campaign, but it was also present in his first campaign for the governorship of Arkansas. Once in office, however, Clinton finds that he cannot achieve most of his policy goals unless he reduces their number and modifies their content. So he does, lending support to the accusations that he is inconsistent and unprincipled. The latter charge often sends him "up the wall." Elizabeth Drew describes such a reaction when an aide at a White House meeting criticized the president for not taking enough strong stands. Clinton responded, "Don't ever say that to me again! . . . The problem isn't that I haven't taken strong stands, . . . It's that I don't have any help around here."[20]

He then exploded at his staff:

> They treat me like a f---ing pack mule around here. They use my time poorly. They schedule me to make calls to individual members of Congress, not understanding that the role of the president of the United States is message.[21]

Situations in which ambition is thwarted by the real politick have regularly given rise to Clinton's emotional outbursts, "the purple fits" or "earthquakes" as his staff refers to them.[22] The fits occur in those situations in which Clinton goals are frustrated by others, by events that go wrong, leaks, or being blindsided. Bob Woodward describes one such situation. Upon realizing for the first time that the House's enactment of its 1993 budget resolution would cap expenditures for some of his favorite programs, Clinton exploded at the messengers of bad tidings:

> Slamming his fist down on the end of his chair, Clinton let loose a torrent of rage and frustration. He said he felt blindsided . . . Day after day, in dozens of hours in the Roosevelt Room going over the smallest programs and most trivial details, there had been no meeting, no discussion of the caps? The president turned red in the face. Why didn't they tell me? . . . that's what I was elected for . . . that is why I'm here.[23]

According to Stephanopoulos the outbursts are readily predictable. He describes "the morning roar," which "rarely signified any deep seething, just irritation at an outside event that he couldn't control, like an overcrowded schedule, a speech draft he didn't like, or almost any story in the morning paper";[24] and "the nightcap," a similar type of explosion that was usually triggered by a telephone call from a friend, a conversation with Hillary, a speech, or a remark on a talk show.[25]

The president obviously needs a target for his rage, an enemy whose fault it is. But he also wants reassurance from his friends, and if possible, a promise to fix the problem. When things do not go right, Clinton tends to see himself as victim. He rarely blames himself, however.

Clinton not only lashes out at his staff, but also demonizes his opponents. They are out to get him. Demonizing has the effect of displacing blame from Clinton to his opponents as well as providing an explanation for his failure. Of course, Clinton is not the first president to have an enemies list, but he has used that list to great political advantage.[26]

Clinton also finds it difficult to be contrite. His August 1998 response to the allegations that he had had a sexual encounter with a White House intern, a charge that he had previously denied, was circumspect, to say the least. Only before the prayer breakfast of religious leaders did he acknowledge himself as a sinner, a caricature that he did not often repeat.

Stanley Renshon suggests that Clinton's difficulties with contrition stem from his inability to engage in self-examination and his propensity to believe only the best about himself, his motives, his intent, his desires. For Clinton, being caught is being victimized, the object of a political witch-hunt by his enemies. His mother responded in a similar way to criticisms about her own lifestyle, blaming them on "various forces which tried for thirty years to destroy my career."[27]

Camouflaging his inability to acknowledge mistakes and admit wrongdoing, Clinton has combined raw charm with dogged perseverance. Those who stand in his way are chastised; the rest are wooed.

A Seductive Style

Bill Clinton is a charmer, a person who ingratiates himself with others in order to get their affection and approval. And it is not an act. It is Bill Clinton, the healer, the compromiser, the I-can-feel-your-pain kind of guy.

Clinton gives and gets much from this style of interpersonal interaction. What he gives is his undivided attention, his empathy, and his promise to help; what he gets is gratitude and political support.

Winning the approval game is a perpetual challenge, but one from which he derives pleasure. And he is very good at it. He loves to work the crowds, to befriend an audience—everyone in it if he can do so. His mother claimed that this style was a family trait.

> Bill and Roger and I are all alike in that way. When we walk into a room, we want to win that room over . . . need to win that room over. If there are one hundred people in a room and ninety-nine of them loves us and one doesn't,

we'll spend all night trying to figure out why that one hasn't been enlightened.[28]

Dick Morris also notes his client's penchant for wanting recognition and praise from those around him.

Typically, much of Bill Clinton's self-image comes from the feelings reflected by others around him. In a room, he will instinctively, as if by a canine sense of smell, find anyone who shows reserve toward him, and he will work full time on winning his or her approval and, if possible, affection.[29]

Journalist Bob Woodward observes, "Clinton was a master of sustained eye contact, hunting reaction in the eyes of an audience of one or a thousand."[30] George Stephanopoulos makes a similar observation:

When he [Clinton] was "on" before a live audience, Clinton was like a jazz genius jamming with his pals. He poured his whole body into the speech, swaying to the rhythms of his words, losing himself in a wonky melody, soaring from the text with riffs synthesized from a lifetime of hard study and sympathetic listening. If he sensed a pocket of resistance in the crowd, he leaned its way, determined to move them with raw will if sweet reason didn't work.[31]

In his book, Stephanopoulos describes a 1991 Democratic party dinner in Chicago where candidates Clinton and Senator Bob Kerrey (D-Neb.) spoke:

The Chicago crowd saw an engaged and optimistic Bill Clinton, a man who loved his work. He wooed his audience, forged a connection, and paid them the compliment of delivering a speech that didn't seem canned. Kerrey didn't work hard enough to win the room, giving people the impression that he expected them to support him because of who he was rather than what he would do for them.

After the speeches, Kerrey left right away. Clinton stayed for another reception with the local VIPs and greeted each one with a personal word while I stood off his left shoulder and collected their business cards for our field and fundraising efforts.[32]

For his whole life, getting along for Bill Clinton has meant trying to please as many diverse and often conflicting interests as possible.

Journalist Peter Applebome defines this as a "compulsive need to please, to bring people together at some hazily defined, accommodating center" as if he [Clinton] were still re-enacting in politics the role he played at home."[33] In the words of Morris, "he needed the crowds, the cheers, the mirror."[34] David Maraniss sees the crowd-pleasing behavior as a need for "happy and nonconfrontational associations" in contrast to the unpleasantness and anger he experienced at home with an alcoholic stepfather.[35]

According to John Brummett, editor of *Arkansas Times* magazine, "He tries not to say no to anyone. He has an obsession to please. For years, I've seen legislators from different sides of the same question come out of his office, all thinking he's on their side."[36]

Supporters see Clinton's seductive style as a desirable trait, responsible for his political successes. Says Betsey Wright, his chief of staff for six years when Clinton was governor of Arkansas, "Part of what attracted me to Bill is he's always been secure enough as a person to be able to listen, to be able to negotiate, to hear other points of view."[37]

Critics, however, see another side: that of a manipulative personality, a person who tries to please others to further his own political ambitions as well as to provide salve for his ego. The appellation "Slick Willie," coined by Arkansas newspaper columnist Paul Greenberg, was intended to put such a spin on the motivation behind Clinton's tendency to tell people whatever it is they want to hear.[38]

Clinton does overpromise in public, and overpromising has gotten him into trouble. Once in office, he finds that he cannot obtain his policy goals unless he modifies them. But by backing off, he is accused of being unprincipled, inconsistent, and even hesitant, reinforcing the Slick Willie image.

The compulsion to please has also led to another charge—that Clinton compromises too easily, that he can be "rolled." It has frustrated members of Congress, particularly Democrats, and led one, Representative David Obey (Wis.), to complain during the 1995–1996 budget debate, "I think most of us learned some time ago, if you don't like the President's position on a particular issue, you simply need to wait a few weeks."[39]

Compartmentalization is another stylistic technique that Clinton has used to wall off problems that threatened to derail his political career. He learned this from his mother. She told him to "construct an airtight box" when bad things happen. Hillary Rodham Clinton also gave her husband similar advice to box off the troubles and not let others interfere with his private life.[40]

To compartmentalize is to focus, and that is when Clinton is at his best. When the survivor instinct takes hold, when he is up against the wall, tottering on the brink of disaster, somehow he conjures the intellectual skills and political fortitude to survive and move on.

A Survivor Mentality

Bill Clinton is a survivor. He has the capacity to learn from experience and, for the most part, the flexibility to make adjustments when he has to do so. As first-term Arkansas governor he overpromised and, from the perspective of his electoral constituency, underdelivered. Rejected by the voters in his quest for reelection, he apologized to the people and promised them that he would listen more closely in a paid advertisement that kicked off his next (and successful) reelection campaign.

Again, as president, he overreached with his plan to end discrimination against gays in the military; his proposals to immunize all children under the age of two; his comprehensive plan to reduce the deficit in half by raising twice as much money through new taxes than from spending cuts; his and Hillary's universal health care reform; numerous other programs for education, job training, business investment; and various community development projects. Thwarted by a divided Democratic majority and a unified Republican minority, he took what he could get, compromising whenever necessary and sometimes when it was not necessary. For Clinton, half a loaf has always been better than none at all if it allows him to claim political success.

A quick study and a fast learner, Clinton gains from experience. He readily accepted Dick Morris's advice to move to the political center in the mainstream of public opinion, becoming in effect a "born-again" moderate in 1995. Similarly, in the management of his office, he began with a flat organizational structure, a weak, inexperienced chief of staff, many advisers, friends, associates, and campaign acquaintances and an open-door policy into and out of the Oval Office. This staff arrangement maximized his involvement in policymaking and agenda building but also blurred his administration's focus as the president moved back and forth from issue to issue. The chaotic staff structure and decisional processes also served to exacerbate Clinton's indecisiveness, making his decisions prone to the "who-talked-to-him-last" syndrome.

Outside criticism, mirrored by declining public approval, provided the incentive for change. After a painful and embarrassing first five months, Clinton allowed a more traditional, hierarchical advisory system with a chief of staff, weakening his personal control but facilitating a more professional staffing operation.

Despite his penchant for detailed involvement in policy and political issues, involvement that had engulfed him in trivia; a tendency to speak his mind and demonstrate his intellect and knowledge, which blurred the focus of his administration; and a constant campaign mentality that reduced the office to his size, Clinton constrained those behavioral patterns that had adversely affected elite and public perceptions of his early presidency. Policymaking became more structured, speeches became more tailored and targeted, and presidential activities were more orchestrated. Taking a lesson from the Reagan administration's playbook, the Clinton White House scripted and staged a traveling road show in which Clinton the person and politician was replaced by Clinton the president, replete in that office's splendid regalia, comforting the afflicted, defending the popular, and carrying the flag to the far corners of the world. It was a sight to behold.

A Summary: The Clinton Cycle

Throughout his public life, Clinton has repeated the cycle of excess, rejection, perseverance, and, ultimately, rejuvenation. Driven by limitless ambition and desires, Clinton says more than he should, promises more than he can deliver, or behaves in an excessive manner. Stymied by political defeat, legal constraints, and/or public admonishment, he recovers. He does so by moderating his words and actions and making compromises when necessary and carefully and consciously orchestrating his public persona to be more closely in accord with mainstream opinion and the political feasibility that it permits. But the corrective is short lived and becomes undone when ambition and desire take over again.

The roots of this character are traceable to the events of his youth, which have been reinforced by his experience in politics. After his biological father's death, Bill's mother also persevered under difficult circumstances. She sent her two-year-old son to live with her parents while she completed her nursing education. Her marriage to Roger Clinton improved the family's financial situation but also brought the alcohol-related problems of an abusive stepfather into the household. Later, Clinton's stepbrother, Roger, would also have serious drug abuse problems. These early traumas and the pain they undoubtedly inflicted on Bill Clinton's psyche help explain the young politician's grandiose ambitions, narcissism, resiliency, and the carefully honed and now instinctive coping mechanism he has developed: the seductive style that has contributed so greatly to his personal and political successes.

Notes

1. Gallup Poll trends indicate that Clinton's job approval ratings have stayed within the 60 percent range for most of his second term; his favorability ratings have been in the 50 percent range, but a majority of people question his honesty and trustworthiness, his values, and his judgment. <http://www.gallup.com/poll/trends>

2. David Maraniss, "Clinton's Life Shaped by Early Turmoil," *Washington Post*, 26 January 1992, A1, 17.

3. Elizabeth Drew, *On the Edge* (New York: Simon & Schuster, 1994), 291.

4. Ibid., 292.

5. Dick Morris, *Behind the Oval Office* (New York: Random House, 1997), 100.

6. Ibid.

7. Ibid.

8. Stanley Renshon, *High Hopes* (New York: New York University Press, 1996), 58.

9. David Maraniss, *First in His Class* (New York: Simon & Schuster, 1995), 45.

10. Renshon, *High Hopes*, 58–59; Maraniss, *First in His Class*, 30–45.

11. George Stephanopoulos, *All Too Human* (Boston: Little, Brown, 1999), 29–30.

12. Drew, *On the Edge*, 67.

13. Stephanopoulos, *All Too Human*, 335.

14. Dick Morris, *Behind the Oval Office*, 338, puts the best spin on Clinton's affinity for poll data when he writes, "Clinton used polling . . . as a tool for governing, as a technique to facilitate progress in a democracy. Polling for him was not a one-time test of opinion. It was a way of conducting an extensive dialogue with the public." Morris goes on to claim that Clinton never used polls to determine what position he should take on an issue.

15. He also had a tendency to "wing it" on occasions, using his intellectual capacities to substitute for careful preparation. Renshon, *High Hopes*, 63.

16. Bob Woodward, *The Agenda* (New York: Simon and Schuster, 1994).

17. Stephanopoulos, *All Too Human*, 335.

18. Robert B. Reich, *Locked in the Cabinet* (New York: Alfred A. Knopf, 1997), 7.

19. Renshon, *High Hopes*, 84.

20. Elizabeth Drew, *Showdown* (New York: Simon & Schuster, 1996), 19.

21. Ibid.

22. Woodward, *The Agenda*, 255.

23. Ibid., 161.

24. Stephanopoulos, *All Too Human*, 286.

25. Ibid., 287.

26. Stephen J. Wayne, "With Enemies Like This, Who Needs Friends," *Presidential Studies Quarterly* (summer 1999), 773–79.

27. Gail Sheehy, "Hillary's Choice," *Vanity Fair* (February 1999), 143.

28. Ibid, 174.

29. Morris, *Behind the Oval Office*, 11.

30. Woodward, *The Agenda*, 21.

31. Stephanopoulos, *All Too Human*, 202–3.

32. Ibid., 36–37.

33. Peter Applebome, "Bill Clinton's Uncertain Journey," *New York Times*, 8 March 1992, 60.

34. Morris, *Behind the Oval Office*, 16.

35. Maraniss, *First in His Class*, 47.

36. John Brummett, "As Governor, Clinton Remade Arkansas in His Own Image," *New York Times*, 31 March 1992, A16.

37. Bill McAllister and David Maraniss, "Clinton: An Instinctive Dealmaker," *Washington Post*, 28 March 1992, A12.

38. Joel Brinkley, "As Governor, Clinton Remade Arkansas in His Own Image," *New York Times*, 31 March 1992, A16.

39. Drew, *Showdown*, 237.

40. Sheehy, "Hillary's Choice," 141.

TWELVE

Presidential Character: Multidimensional or Seamless?

James P. Pfiffner

There is a widespread consensus in American politics that presidential character is important—just as, or more, important than intellect, organizational abilities, television presence, or effectiveness in public speaking. Character refers to the deeper roots of behavior that predispose people to act in certain ways. These character traits stem from psychological processes early in life and are formed by decisions made over a period of years. It is often assumed that character is relatively fixed in most adults and that it is not easy to change. The idea of character is often explicitly normative, that is, people of character are said to exhibit one or more positive character traits including honesty, integrity, courage, loyalty, consistency, sexual probity, marital fidelity, and so forth. Those persons of poor character are said to lack these positive traits.

Scholars have examined presidential character and its importance from a variety of perspectives, but there is no scholarly consensus on the definition of character.[1] They all have difficulty explaining the good and bad aspects of presidential behavior in terms of one definition of character or set of character traits. And no system can encompass consistently the character traits common in popular rhetoric. The consensus about the importance of presidential character combined with the lack of consensus about its definition has an element about it of Justice Potter Stewart's dictum about pornography: "I can't define it, but I know it when I see it."

Character is often used in political campaigns as a way to denigrate one's political opponent. The negative character traits are seldom explicitly stated but are understood to include things such as sexual impropriety, lying, inconsistency, and dishonesty. Given the lack of consensus on the nature of presidential character, it is tempting to say that character comprises those facets of individual personality, attitude, and behavior to which people attribute presidential success and failure.

In this chapter I will not attempt to develop a formal model of presidential character; there is not enough consensus on what character is, and the issues are too complex. But most serious treatments of character include issues of sexual fidelity and truthfulness as important dimensions of presidential character. In the first section of this chapter, I examine how sexual probity discriminates among different presidents and its effect on other dimensions of presidential performance. Presidents often lie, and in the second section of the essay I distinguish between more-serious and less-serious lies. But people who are faithful spouses and are always truthful are not necessarily the best presidents. In the final section I argue that presidential character is broader and more important than the narrow issues of sex and lying, and I examine the positive and negative aspects of three presidents—Lyndon Johnson, Ronald Reagan, and Bill Clinton—in order to demonstrate that presidential character is multidimensional rather than seamless.

Sexual Probity and Presidential Character

While there is no consensus on the exact nature of presidential character, most observers believe that it is important and that extramarital sexual behavior is relevant to it, although not necessarily the most important aspect of it. For some, the private sexual behavior of presidents should not be a public issue since it does not have to do with the performance of official duties or public policy. From this perspective there should be a zone of privacy that journalists ought to respect unless there is a clear connection with the official duties of the president. Regardless of the personal morality of the behavior this view holds, it is not the public's business to be concerned with the sexual conduct of presidents. This general norm was largely respected by the press into the 1970s.

On the other hand, the argument that sexual behavior is relevant to presidential performance argues that character is seamless. Sexual infidelity is seen as a breach of trust, and trust is seen as one of the most important dimensions of the relation of citizens to their government. If a president cannot be trusted to be faithful to his spouse, how can we have confidence that he will tell the truth to the American people? One criticism of Bill Clinton in the 1992 campaign was, "You can't be one kind of man and another kind of President."[2] This line of argument leads to the conclusion that inappropriate sexual behavior is an important element of presidential character, that its uncovering is a legitimate focus of journalistic inquiry, and that the public ought to use the information in judging a president's fitness for holding office.

Extramarital Affairs of Modern Presidents

It is worth noting that Bill Clinton is not the first president accused of sexual misbehavior. To take a prominent example in the twentieth century, President Harding was by any standard an egregious philanderer. Harding had numerous affairs with a variety of women before and during his presidency. He conceived a child with Nan Britton, and his wife almost caught them in a room near the Oval Office. He also had paid money to support a child he had with Susan Hodder. His former mistress, Carrie Fulton Phillips, blackmailed the president with his love letters to her. Secret service agents assisted Harding in his assignations with numerous women while he was in office, often at a house on H Street used for presidential parties. His friends set up secret bank accounts for payments to women threatening to reveal their relationships with him as well as for Nan Britton and their daughter. Harding's laxity in his personal behavior spilled over into the rest of his administration.[3]

Franklin Roosevelt had a relationship with Lucy Mercer Rutherford when she was his wife's social secretary and he was assistant secretary of the Navy. When Eleanor discovered the relationship, FDR broke off with Mercer and did not see her until the last years of his life. President Roosevelt also had an ongoing relationship with his personal secretary, Marguerite "Missy" LeHand, who had been with the Roosevelts since FDR had been governor of New York, and for a part of his presidency she functioned in many ways as his "wife."[4]

During World War II, Dwight Eisenhower was widely rumored to have had an affair with his driver and aide, Kay Summersby. Although they were often seen and photographed together in public, they were seldom alone together. But according to Stephen Ambrose, a sympathetic biographer of Eisenhower, Summersby and Eisenhower did have sex once, at least by the definition used in President Clinton's deposition in the Paula Jones case. But in her memoirs, Summersby said that they did not consummate their relationship sexually (that is, they did not have sex according to Monica Lewinsky's definition).[5]

According to many reports, John Kennedy was a reckless philanderer, before and during his presidency. If only some of the allegations about John Kennedy's sex life reported by Seymour Hersh in *The Dark Side of Camelot* are true, Kennedy was reckless and irresponsible in his sexual exploits while in office.[6] It has been argued that Kennedy's relationship with Judith Campbell Exner compromised Kennedy because she was also connected to organized crime figures. While there were some rumors of JKF's sexual behavior circulating while he was in office, the press was not aggressive in investigating them or in reporting on what was then considered to be private behavior.

Lyndon Johnson was said to have had a number of sexual relationships while he was president, continuing a pattern in his political life. According to biographer Robert Dallek, "throughout his Senate and vice-presidential years, he remained an exhibitionist and a philanderer who didn't mind flaunting his conquests."[7] Johnson reportedly bragged, "I had more women by accident than he [Kennedy] has had on purpose."[8] The 1970s were slack years for presidential sex scandals, with Presidents Nixon, Ford, and Carter seemingly faithful spouses. George Bush, especially during the 1992 campaign, was dogged by rumors about an alleged sexual relationship with Jennifer Fitzgerald, an aide to Bush at the Republican National Committee and when he was in China, although no improper relationship was ever proved.[9]

Judging Presidential Behavior

In looking at past presidential sexual behavior and character, it is not obvious that sexual probity is always associated with presidential competence and trustworthiness. Nor is sexual indiscretion always associated with poor presidential performance. Certainly President Harding was sexually profligate and not a particularly effective president, with his administration suffering from a number of major scandals; but Franklin Roosevelt, with his acknowledged relationships with Lucy Mercer and Missy LeHand, is generally rated as one of the great presidents. John Kennedy, while sexually irresponsible, was an effective president and is certainly one of our most popular chief executives. There was no hint of any sexual impropriety in Jimmy Carter's presidency, yet he was not considered to be more effective than FDR or

JFK. Richard Nixon was surely faithful to Patricia Nixon in the White House, yet other aspects of his character led to Watergate and campaign abuses.

Thus, while sexual probity may be an important aspect of presidential character, it does not guarantee morality or competence in the Oval Office. And sexual impropriety can be found in presidents who are clearly competent in affairs of state.

While conceding that some presidents were competent even if engaging in sexual activity outside of their marriages, we might still want to judge whether their behavior in this area was appropriate or moral. If the basis of moral judgment is that fidelity vows are broken, a surface judgment can be made with little understanding of the circumstances. In judging presidential character from the absolutist perspective that sex outside of marriage is always wrong, it should not matter whether the behavior took place before or after election. Adultery is adultery, and character is the bedrock of a person's behavior. Adultery at any time reveals flaws that, according to the absolutist interpretation, bring into question a person's fitness for office. Those who take this perspective must thus take into account how Eisenhower's pre-presidential sexual behavior might have affected his presidential character.[10]

One basis for judgment, other than an absolute condemnation of adultery or expectation of moral perfection, would be the exercise of prudential judgment and self-restraint. While conceding that we might not know enough to be able to judge the relationship between two people, we might still make harsh judgments about a president's sexual behavior outside of marriage.

Such judgment would be based on the premise that public morality, however hypocritical it might be, proscribes adultery and sexual profligacy. And it is predictable that public reaction about discovered sexual impropriety would be harsh and could threaten the reputation of a president and the administration. Given this reality of American politics, any president who violates these public norms is liable to judgment for risking his or her reputation and the success of the policy and political agenda.

The implication here is that a president ought to realize that any sexual indiscretion while in office may very well be uncovered, and if it is, much more is at risk than personal reputation: the political and policy legacy of the administration is also in jeopardy. The predictable ensuing political scandal will at the very least distract the president and at the most engulf the administration. The president will be spending time plotting with lawyers about how to confront charges rather than pursuing public policy goals.

It is from this perspective that we can judge Bill Clinton: his sexual relationship (of whatever kind) with a young woman in the White House can be judged to be reckless and irresponsible. At a personal level, Clinton's indiscretions were predictably embarrassing to his wife and daughter. In satisfying his own pleasure he undermined public trust in him, he made himself vulnerable to the distractions of defending himself, and he put at risk his political agenda and legacy.

Presidential Lies

> *"When in doubt, tell the truth. It will confound*
> *your enemies and astound your friends."*
>
> Mark Twain

In a democracy or republic based on the consent of the governed, citizens need accurate information in order to make informed decisions about elections and public policy. Thus it is wrong for public officials to lie about public issues. The following is a discussion about presidential lies that are intended to avoid embarrassment or cover up important facts in order to preserve political power or viability;[11] subsequent text will examine presidential lies concerning national security. Often presidential lies are justified on national security grounds. The assumption is that the United States exists in a potentially hostile world and that deception is necessary and justified in order to protect national security interests. But presidents are tempted to use the national security justification to excuse lies that are not necessary but merely useful to them. The distinction will be made between lies that are justified and lies of policy deception. Justifiable lies are those that are necessary to protect lives or ensure the effectiveness of national security operations undertaken to support legitimate (constitutionally acceptable) policy objectives. This justification would exclude covert policies, that is, when the government says that it is pursuing policy X when it is in fact pursuing policy Y.

Lies to Prevent Embarrassment or Cover Up Important Facts

We must admit that politicians in a democracy are in particularly difficult positions with respect to complete truth telling. In order to knit together coalitions of support, they must often present the same policy position to suit the goals of different groups. This shading of one's position can easily slide into misrepresentation or lying. Politicians are also at a disadvantage because any fact about them will be used by their opponents to their greatest disadvantage. Thus behavior that would be unremarkable in a private citizen might be used to attack a person running for office. So U.S. politicians might be tempted to deny, for instance, being gay, having had an abortion, having been treated by a psychiatrist, or having used drugs in the past for recreational purposes. Even though these denials would be lies, we can understand how a politician running for office might be tempted to feel that a lie would be justified.

A less justifiable lie is one told to cover up facts about illegal or embarrassing past official behavior. This type of lie might be justified by the teller by arguing that even though the behavior was wrong or questionable in the past, revealing it now would lead to negative political consequences. These consequences would hurt the ability of the president to stay in office and to pursue the mandate received from the voters.

Following, I examine lies that are wrong though understandable; then I consider those lies that are serious breaches of the public trust. The understandable (though wrong) lies include John Kennedy's lies about his health and George Bush's claims about his nomination of Clarence Thomas to the Supreme Court and his assertion that he was "not in the loop" during the Iran-Contra affair. More serious breaches of the public trust will include President Nixon's lies about Watergate and President Clinton's lies about his affair with Monica Lewinsky.

Less-serious Lies

Kennedy Denies That He Has Addison's Disease Presidential health is always a sensitive subject, and administrations go to great lengths to minimize any question of the president's full capacity to do the job. Rumors that John Kennedy had Addison's disease, a disease of the adrenal gland that was often fatal, swirled around the 1960 campaign. On January 19, 1961, when Kennedy was asked by a reporter if he had Addison's disease, he said, "I never had Addison's disease . . . and my health is excellent."[12] But the fact was that Kennedy had medical problems all of his life and as an adult took combinations of pills and injections daily. He had in fact been given the last rites of the Catholic Church (extreme unction) four times as an adult.[13] Kennedy was often in pain with back problems and went to great lengths to project an image of physical vigor.[14]

President Bush and the Clarence Thomas Nomination   In 1991
George Bush nominated Clarence Thomas to the Supreme Court.[15]
Bush invited Thomas to Kennebunkport, Maine, before the Fourth
of July weekend in 1991 and held a press conference to publicly
introduce Thomas. After some remarks by Thomas, President Bush
said that Thomas was "the best qualified" person for the position. In
addition, Bush said that "the fact that he is black and a minority had
nothing to do with this." Critics argue that both of these statements
by President Bush were lies.

Although Thomas began life in a poor household and very impres-
sively worked his way up the educational and professional ladders
and was on the District of Columbia Circuit Court of Appeals, his
credentials were not as impressive as were those of most Supreme
Court nominees. Thomas had practiced law only briefly a decade before and had been on the bench for less than two years. He had never
litigated a case before a jury, and on the bench he had not issued a
substantive constitutional opinion. It was apparent to all that Thomas's
being African American was key to his nomination. He was to replace
the revered Thurgood Marshall on the Court, and his race would
inhibit liberals from mounting an effective attack on his candidacy.

The reason for Bush's statement was to maintain the political viability of the nomination and to reduce embarrassment to Clarence
Thomas. If one is to criticize Bush, it should be for the nomination
itself, which, according to Bush's critics, put a marginally qualified
person on the Supreme Court. Bush's critics claimed that the nomination was cynically protected by the race of the nominee. The lies to
defend the nomination, however, were incidental to the nomination
itself, meant to avoid embarrassment. They also were transparent to
all informed political observers.

George Bush Lies about His Knowledge of Iran-Contra   During
the campaign for the presidency in 1988 George Bush was the sitting
vice president and heir apparent for the Republican nomination. One
of the issues raised in the campaign was the level of his engagement
in and knowledge of the Iran-Contra scandal. If he knew about it and
had not objected to it, he was vulnerable to criticism for having
participated in a questionably legal and probably unwise policy.[16]

With this potential vulnerability in the 1988 race for the presidency,
George Bush made several statements about his being "out of the
loop" during decision-making about the arms-for-hostages deal with

Iran. In his campaign autobiography, *Looking Forward,* he said that he had been "deliberately excluded from key meetings involving details of the Iran-Contra operations."[17]

On November 9, 1986, on *This Week with David Brinkley,* Bush said that it was inconceivable even to consider selling arms to Iran for hostages.[18] In an interview with David Broder of the *Washington Post,* Bush said, "If I had sat there and heard George Shultz and Cap express it [opposition to the Iran arms sales] strongly, maybe I would have had a stronger view. But when you don't know something, it's hard to react. . . . We were not in the loop."[19]

The problem was that Bush had been at meetings when the Iran issues were discussed and had heard Shultz and Weinberger object to the project.[20] Perhaps the key meeting was on January 7, 1986, during which Secretary of Defense Weinberger and Secretary of State Shultz objected to the arms-for-hostages policy. According to George Shultz in his memoirs, "I was astonished to read in the August 6, 1987, *Washington Post*" about Bush's statement that he was "not in the loop." "Cap [Weinberger] called me. He was astonished, too: 'That's terrible. He was on the other side. It's on the record. Why did he say that?' "[21]

Serious Breaches of the Public Trust

Nixon and Watergate President Nixon lied many times about his knowledge of the cover-up of the Watergate break-in during June 1972. For instance, on May 21, 1973, he said in a public statement that he had "no part in, nor was I aware of, subsequent efforts that may have been made to cover up Watergate."[22] He repeated similar statements often during 1973 and 1974 as he tried to avoid public disclosure of the Watergate cover-up and other illegal activities sponsored by the White House.

Perhaps the most important lie was recorded on the "smoking gun" tape from June 23, 1972—Nixon told Haldeman to have the CIA call the FBI to tell them to stop pursuing the trail of Watergate money because it would make public a CIA covert operation. Nixon told Haldeman to tell Richard Helms, " '[T]he president believes that it is going to open the whole Bay of Pigs thing up again. And . . . that they [the CIA] should call the FBI in and [unintelligible] don't go any further into this case period!"[23] The disclosure of this order to the CIA to lie to the House Judiciary Committee was the turning point in the impeachment proceedings against Nixon. The committee voted impeachment articles, and Nixon resigned before the full House could vote on them.

Nixon also lied in order to receive an income tax deduction of more than $500,000 for the donation of his vice presidential papers to the National Archives. In order to qualify for the deduction, his lawyers backdated the official documents. Nixon signed the papers, thus testifying to the false date in order to escape paying full taxes for his income.[24]

President Clinton's Lies about His Affair with Monica Lewinsky
President Clinton lied under oath as well as in his emphatic public denial of his affair; thus, his lies were much more serious than lies merely to prevent embarrassment. One of the prominent arguments in defense of President Clinton during the Lewinsky affair was that "everyone lies about sex" and that such lies about private matters are less blameworthy than other lies. One justification for failure to tell the truth is the premise that one does not have to answer truthfully questions that people have no right to ask. Part of the premise in this argument is that privacy is essential to liberty and that individuals have a right to protect that privacy. Only serious circumstances can override a person's privacy. If a person is asked about his or her sexual practices, therefore, unless there is an overriding justification for the question (e.g., a criminal inquiry), the person could be justified in lying. President Clinton might have used such reasoning to justify to himself his lying about his sexual relationship with Lewinsky.

He might also have felt that the process leading to his questioning was illegitimate. The Paula Jones lawsuit was filed at the last minute before the statute of limitations ran out, and it was financed by conservative enemies of Clinton. The lie that Clinton told was not about the Paula Jones affair but about Lewinsky. The only reason that the affair with Lewinsky was relevant to the *Jones* case was that the law had recently been changed to allow questioning of a suspect in a sexual matter about previous sexual relationships in order to establish a pattern of behavior.

Clinton may have reasoned to himself that the Lewinsky affair was not relevant to the *Jones* case, that the *Jones* case was trumped up by his enemies, and that a private, consensual affair with Lewinsky was not illegal and therefore none of their business. The House impeachment managers made a powerful argument that the system of justice depends upon the assumption of truth telling under oath and that to lie under oath is therefore an offense serious beyond any specific telling of an untruth.

Clinton's lie was wrong in several ways. Lying under oath undermines the assumptions upon which the judicial system is based and sends a message that the president thinks that the office of president is not subject to the law. In addition, Clinton cynically used others in his lie by lying to his staff and cabinet with the expectation that they would innocently repeat his lies. This violation of the confidence of his friends led to their feelings of betrayal and often to large legal fees. While we might argue that even presidents ought to have some privacy and we might deplore the tactics that Kenneth Starr used to obtain evidence of Clinton's sexual affair with Lewinsky, the president did in fact lie about it, and the lie was wrong. Whether the lies rose to the level of high crimes and misdemeanors for which a president ought to be impeached and removed from office is a separate question.[25]

National Security Lies
Some lies are legitimately justified by national security interests. First I examine a genuinely justified lie that Richard Nixon told in the 1960 presidential debates with John Kennedy and next consider the U-2 affair when the Eisenhower administration denied in 1960 that the U-2 was on a spy mission. I will then turn to the most serious type of presidential lies: lies of policy deception.

Justified or Arguably Justified National Security Lies

Nixon and Cuba   During the 1960 campaign for the presidency, U.S. policy toward Cuba was an important issue. Fidel Castro had led a revolution to overthrow the corrupt Batista regime in 1959 and had allied with the Soviet Union and other communist powers. The Eisenhower administration had been supporting and training anti-Castro exiles for a possible future invasion of the island to overthrow Castro. Shortly before the final series of presidential debates between Kennedy and Nixon, Kennedy came out publicly in favor of active U.S. intervention in Cuba and support of the Cuban anti-Castro forces saying, "Thus far, these fighters for freedom have had virtually no support from our government."[26]

Nixon found himself in a difficult situation. He knew that the government was actively involved in support of the Cuban exiles, but the operation was covert and could not be publicly acknowledged for fear of disclosing its existence and putting Castro on guard. Nixon concluded that the only responsible action was for him to attack Kennedy's proposal as being reckless and irresponsible:

> I think that Senator Kennedy's policies and recommendations for the handling of the Castro regime are probably the most dangerously irresponsible recommendations that he's made during the course of this campaign. . . . if we were to follow that recommendation . . . we would lose all of our friends in Latin America, we would probably be condemned in the United Nations, and we would not accomplish our objective . . . it would be an open invitation for Mr. Khrushchev . . . to come into Latin America and to engage us in what would be a civil war and possibly even worse than that.[27]

Ironically, and to Nixon's dismay, the eastern establishment press commented favorably on Nixon's forbearance. In addition, Nixon accurately predicted the eventual outcome of the Bay of Pigs invasion: it did not achieve its objective and it encouraged Khrushchev to place midrange nuclear missiles in Cuba a year and a half later, leading to the 1962 Cuban missile crisis.

In his first memoir, *Six Crises,* Nixon recalled his moral position: "I was in the ironic position of appearing to be 'softer' on Castro than Kennedy—which was exactly the opposite of the truth, if only the whole record could be disclosed."[28] Thus, Nixon in this situation was telling a blatant lie, saying exactly the opposite of what he believed. But from his perspective, it has to be seen as a legitimate, justified, and even necessary lie. The United States was undertaking a covert operation against what was seen as a communist enemy, and disclosure of the operation could have led to its failure. Setting aside what we now know about the Cold War and the future consequences of U.S. actions toward Cuba, we have to admit that Nixon's actions were ethical and even courageous.

Eisenhower and the U-2 Incident   In the spring of 1960 President Eisenhower had proposed to negotiate with the Russians a test-ban treaty that would end the testing of nuclear weapons, and Khrushchev had expressed interest in such a treaty.[29] Gary Powers took off in a U-2 the morning of May 1 for an espionage mission over Russia.

When the plane did not return for several days, it was presumed to be destroyed and the pilot dead because of self-destruct mechanisms built into the plane.[30]

The decision of the administration to lie about the U-2 affair was important to Eisenhower. He had told advisers in February 1960 that he would have "one tremendous asset" in negotiations about his hoped-for treaty with the Russians: his reputation for honesty. "If one of these aircraft were lost when we were engaged in apparently sincere deliberations, it could be put on display in Moscow and ruin my effectiveness."[31] Eisenhower once told a friend that if a president has lost his credibility, "he has lost his greatest strength."[32]

On May 5, Khrushchev announced that the Soviet Union had shot down an American spy plane and denounced the United States for "aggressive provocation." Eisenhower knew that the Soviets were aware of the U-2 overflights, but he presumed that Powers was dead and the plane destroyed. So he approved a statement by NASA that the plane was not a spy plane but rather a weather research plane that had been over Turkey and might have strayed into Soviet air space. Then, after the administration had lied about the plane, Khrushchev announced on May 7 that he had the pilot, Gary Powers, and wreckage from the plane. Faced with this incontrovertible evidence, Eisenhower compounded the lie by having the State Department say Powers did not have any authorization to fly over the Soviet Union.

Finally, Eisenhower had to admit publicly that the United States had been spying on the Soviet Union and that the administration had authorized the flights. Eisenhower felt personally mortified and told his secretary, Anne Whitman, on the morning of May 9, "I would like to resign."[33] He resolved to go ahead and try to salvage the summit, although by then it was hopeless, and Khrushchev walked out of the summit in Paris. Thus, Eisenhower's hopes for a test-ban treaty to crown his eight years in office were dashed, and he was severely disappointed.

The irony, as pointed out by historian Stephen Ambrose, was that the U-2 overflights were no secret to the Soviets, who had been trying to shoot them down with surface-to-air missiles for some time. Nor were the overflights secret to U.S. allies in Britain, France, Norway, Turkey, or Taiwan. Those who did not know about the U-2 flights were members of Congress and the American people. Thus Eisenhower undermined his most important asset, his "reputation for honesty," and undermined the trust of the American people in their government because he thought that there was no evidence to expose his lie.

Lies of Policy Deception

The most basic premise of democratic government is that the government ought to do what the people want and that during elections the voters get to choose whom they want to govern them. Thus, misleading the public about the direction of government policy does not allow the electorate to make an informed choice and undermines the premise of democratic government. In the words of philosopher Sissela Bok, "Deception of this kind strikes at the very essence of democratic government. It allows those in power to override or nullify the right vested in the people to cast an informed vote in critical elections."[34]

LBJ and Vietnam   It is now widely understood that Lyndon Johnson misled the American public and concealed his policy of escalation in Vietnam in 1964 and 1965. In the presidential election campaign of 1964, Johnson presented himself as the "peace candidate" in order to contrast himself with Senator Barry Goldwater who was a "hawk" on Vietnam and favored immediate and massive U.S. military action. The second reason Johnson so presented himself was that he was planning the spate of legislative proposals that would make up his "Great Society" program and wanted this to be his claim to historical fame to rival that of Franklin Roosevelt's New Deal. In short, Johnson wanted it both ways: he wanted to be seen by the political right as standing firm against the communists in Vietnam, and he wanted to pass the Great Society legislation in 1965.

One of Johnson's most far-reaching deceptions was his orchestration of the Gulf of Tonkin Resolution in August 1964. On the stormy night of August 4 the *Maddox* reported that it was under attack by North Vietnamese gunboats. The problem was that on the afternoon of August 4 the commander of the *Maddox* expressed doubts about whether an attack had actually taken place.[35] Admiral Sharp, the commander of the Pacific forces in Honolulu, told Secretary of Defense McNamara that there was a "slight possibility" that the attack had not taken place.

But Johnson and McNamara continued to act as if the attack had in fact taken place and ordered U.S. air attacks against the North Vietnamese and pursued the approval of Congress. In response to Johnson's request for support, Congress passed the Gulf of Tonkin Resolution, which was used by Johnson as a blank check for the remainder of his term to do what he thought best in Vietnam and to avoid asking Congress for a declaration of war.[36] Several days later, Johnson himself admitted to George Ball, "Hell, those dumb, stupid sailors were just shooting at flying fish!"[37] In early 1964 Johnson said "For all I know, our Navy was shooting at whales out there."[38]

In the fall of 1964 Johnson returned to downplaying any hint of an expanding U.S. involvement in Vietnam. On October 21 in Akron, Ohio, he declared, "But we are not about to send American boys nine or ten thousand miles away from home to do what Asian boys ought to be doing for themselves."[39] In October he told a group of supporters in New Hampshire that he planned to "get them [the South Vietnamese] to save their own freedom with their own men."[40]

In December Johnson authorized planning for airstrikes against North Vietnam, in part to convince the South Vietnamese that the United States would stick with them if they increased their own military efforts. In December 1964 General Harold K. Johnson predicted that it would take 500,000 men and five years to achieve victory in Vietnam.[41] In late January 1965 a Joint Chiefs of Staff study estimated that 700,000 troops would be necessary.[42]

On January 21, 1965, Johnson's first full day as an elected president, he and McNamara met with a bipartisan group of members from both houses of Congress. He misled them by presenting the bombing of Laos and covert operations against North Vietnam as being successful, and he misrepresented his military advisers' judgment about the status of South Vietnamese military readiness. He presented a much more optimistic picture than was warranted, in the judgment of military leaders. Johnson told the congressional leaders that he had "decided that more U.S. forces are not needed in South Vietnam short of a decision to go to full-scale war . . . war must be fought by the South Vietnamese. We cannot control everything that they do and we have to count on their fighting their war."[43] He did not tell them of the plans to begin bombing North Vietnam. On March 8, 1965, the first combat troops of 3,500 Marines arrived at Danang in South Vietnam.

These troops, although engaged in combat, were supposed to be assisting the South Vietnamese in defensive operations. But in April an increase of 18,000 to 20,000 Marine forces was authorized, and their mission was changed by National Security Action Memorandum [NSAM] 328, which authorized the offensive utilization of U.S. ground troops against the Viet Cong. NSAM 328 stated explicitly that the change in mission was to be kept secret: "premature publicity [should] be avoided by all possible precautions. The actions themselves should be taken as rapidly as practicable, but in ways that should minimize any appearance of sudden changes in policy . . . changes should be understood as being gradual and wholly consistent with existing policy."[44] Ambassador Maxwell Taylor sent a cable to Secretary of State Dean Rusk saying, "we believe that the most useful approach to press problems is to make no, repeat, no special public announcement to the effect that U.S. ground troops are now engaged in offensive combat operations. . . ."[45]

McNamara and Johnson also understated the needed additional financial support by $10 billion and argued that military mobilization was not necessary. Johnson refused to ask Congress for the money that he knew would be necessary to support the war effort for fear that such a request would undercut the possible passage of his full Great Society program.

By the time Johnson left office in 1969, 30,000 U.S. troops had died as well as hundreds of thousands of Vietnamese. Thus, Johnson had led the United States into a major land war in Asia in 1964 and 1965 while doing his best to conceal increasing U.S. participation. Instead of choosing to present the Congress and the public with the choice he had made, calling up reserve units, requesting adequate funds from Congress, and asking for a declaration of war from Congress, Johnson chose to pursue what he saw as the national interest in Vietnam.

Nixon and the Secret Bombing of Cambodia   The secret bombing of Cambodia in 1969 involved elaborate deception and falsification of reports.[46] The pilots of the B-52s were briefed on missions in South Vietnam, but a subset of the pilots were told that they would get special orders while in flight: they would be instructed to leave the other planes and deliver their bombs to specific coordinates in Cambodia; after dropping the bombs, they would return to their bases and report as if they had been bombing in South Vietnam. The falsified reports were the official reports that were recorded in the Air Force and Defense Department records. The secret reports of the actual bombings of Cambodia went through back channels to the White House. Not even the secretary of the Air Force knew of the secret bombings.

The question arises as to the purpose of the secrecy. Originally Secretary of Defense Melvin Laird favored making the bombing public, but he was overruled by Nixon and Kissinger—after all, the North Vietnamese knew they were being bombed, the Cambodians knew bombs were dropping on their country, and the communist allies of the North Vietnamese were informed of the bombing. The only implicated parties who did not know were the U.S. Congress and the American people. Kissinger argued that if the bombing were acknowledged diplomatically, the Cambodian government might feel compelled to protest or the North Vietnamese might try to retaliate. But Richard Nixon was more forthright in his memoirs, "Another reason for secrecy was the problem of domestic antiwar protest. My administration was only two months old, and I wanted to provoke as little public outcry as possible at the outset."[47]

Nixon's deception about the secret bombing of Cambodia was wrong because it was a legally and militarily significant expansion of the war into a neutral country (even though the North Vietnamese did not respect Cambodia's neutrality). The war at that point was controversial, and its expansion would have increased political opposition to it and to President Nixon (as did the public invasion of Cambodia on May 1, 1970). Thus, the lies and secrecy were intended to pursue a significant foreign policy change without the knowledge of Congress or the American people.

President Reagan and Iran-Contra   During the Iran-Contra affair from 1985 to 1987, President Reagan told several lies or made misstatements when he denied (to the Tower Commission) that (1) he authorized shipments of arms to Iran, (2) that arms were sent in exchange for hostages, and (3) that he knew about continuing aid to the Contras during the period of the Boland Amendment.

On January 26, 1987, President Reagan told the Tower Commission that he had approved of the shipment of TOW (tube-launched, optically tracked, wire-guided) missiles from Israel to Iran in August 1985 and of the replacement of those missiles to Israel by the United States. But in another meeting with the review board on February 11, 1987, he reversed himself. He said that he had gone over the issue with his chief of staff Donald Regen and that he had not approved of the transfer before it was undertaken. Later, on February 20, 1987, in a letter he wrote to the commission, President Reagan stated: "The only honest answer is to state that try as I might, I cannot recall anything whatsoever about whether I approved an Israeli sale in advance . . . the simple truth is, 'I don't remember—period.' "[48]

The issue was important because Secretary of Defense Casper Weinberger and Secretary of State George Shultz objected to the United States trading arms in order to obtain the freedom of hostages held in Lebanon. They agreed with President Reagan's statement on

June 18, 1985: "America will never make concessions to terrorists—
to do so would only invite more terrorism. . . . Once we head down
that path, there would be no end to it."[49]

On November 13, 1986, after the arms deals had been revealed by
a Middle Eastern newspaper, President Reagan addressed the nation
and said, "The charge has been made that the United States has
shipped weapons to Iran—as ransom payment for the release of American hostages in Lebanon. . . . Those charges are utterly false. . . . Our
government has a firm policy not to capitulate to terrorist demands.
That 'no-concessions' policy remains in force in spite of the wildly
speculative and false stories about arms for hostages and alleged ransom
payments. We did not—repeat—we did not trade weapons or anything
else for hostages."[50]

But as more information about the arms-for-hostages deal with
Iran came out in congressional hearings and testimony, President
Reagan had to admit what the evidence showed. In a March 4, 1987,
address to the nation, he said, "I told the American people I did not
trade arms for hostages. My heart and my best intentions still tell me
that's true. But the facts and the evidence tell me it is not. . . . What
began as a strategic opening to Iran deteriorated in its implementation
into trading arms for hostages."[51]

On January 26, 1987, President Reagan told the Tower Review
Board that he did not know about the diversion of funds or that
the National Security Council staff had been engaged in helping the
Contras in addition to the diverting funds.[52] After the congressional
hearing began, Reagan changed his story and said that he had been
"kept briefed" on private support to the Contras: "I was very definitely
involved in the decisions about support to the freedom fighters. It
was my idea to begin with."[53]

Thus, during the investigation President Reagan changed his story
at least three times about (1) his approval of arms to Iran, (2) whether
the arms were intended to get the hostages freed, and (3) whether he
knew about U.S. aid (other than the diversion of funds) to the Contras
during the period the Boland Amendment was in effect. If one wants
to argue that Reagan told no lies during this period, one must argue
that he was very confused about what his administration was doing
in this important and controversial area of national security policy.

I have addressed the issue of presidential lying, which is a problem
because it undercuts the democratic link between citizens and their
government. It also undermines trust in the government and all public
officials. Obvious lying also sets a bad example and may lead others

to justify their own lying. But it is the argument of this chapter that not all lies are equal. Some are worse than others. The argument that "they all do it" so there is no point in examining the issue is insidious and undermines moral responsibility. We, as citizens, have the responsibility to distinguish among different types of lies in order to decide which are acceptable and which are not.

We must also keep presidential lying in perspective. Lies are not the most important aspect of what presidents do, either in a negative or a positive sense. Lyndon Johnson's lies about Vietnam were not as damaging as the broader, flawed policies that got us into a land war in Asia. President Nixon's lies about Watergate were not as insidious as the broader aspects of his lack of scruples (e.g., using the IRS to harass his enemies, employing campaign "dirty tricks," creating the "Plumbers," wiretapping citizens without any warrant to do so, implementing the Huston plan, etc.). President Reagan's lies or misstatements about Iran-Contra were not as bad as the deliberate breaking of the law by his administration.

Character Complexity

Sexual fidelity and truthfulness in an individual are not guarantees that he or she would make a good president. Too much contemporary rhetoric deals with only character failure. In judging presidential character we ought to consider positive character traits as well as failures. I consider three presidents whose characters are complex and who have both positive and negative character traits: Lyndon Johnson, Ronald Reagan, and Bill Clinton.

Lyndon Johnson

The negative aspects of Lyndon Johnson's character are recognized in both scholarly and popular judgments. His personal behavior was often crude, and he took a domineering approach to many of his personal and professional relationships. His behavior toward women was often boorish and crude. His misleading of the American people during his escalation of the Vietnam conflict had severe consequences (some of which have been analyzed previously). But emphasis on the negative aspects of his character also obscures the positive dimensions of Johnson's character—if we are to blame his political and policy failures on his character, we must credit his political and policy victories to his character as well.

Those who knew him testified to the complexity of Johnson's personality. His White House aide, Joseph Califano, said, "The

Lyndon Johnson I worked with was brave and brutal, compassionate and cruel, incredibly intelligent and infuriatingly insensitive, with a shrewd and uncanny instinct for the jugular of his allies and adversaries. He could be altruistic and petty, caring and crude, generous and petulant, bluntly honest and calculatingly devious—all within the same few minutes." [54] His press secretary, George Reedy, said that Johnson "was a man of too many paradoxes. . . . Almost everything you find out about him you can find out a directly contrary quality immediately. . . ." [55] His biographer, Robert Dallek, summarized Johnson's contradictions: "Driven, tyrannical, crude, insensitive, humorless, and petty, he was also empathetic, shy, sophisticated, self-critical, uproariously funny, and magnanimous." [56]

His childhood, which exhibited some of the negative traits that would characterize his adult personality, also laid the experiential basis for his future commitment to policy accomplishments. In rural Texas he saw firsthand the nature of poverty and the limits it put on the lives of those caught in its grind. He also witnessed the ravages of racism on the self-esteem and life opportunities of minorities in the South. [57] Despite his own pretensions and condescension toward some of the less privileged, Johnson also was able to identify with their affliction. When he got to be president, his empathy for the less privileged and particularly for African Americans drove his policy agenda as well as his need for personal achievement.

As a southerner, Johnson was able to accomplish more progress in civil rights than a northern liberal would have been able to. He knew the South firsthand and understood intimately the nature of the prejudice and political opposition he would have to overcome if he were to succeed. One of his greatest legislative victories as majority leader in the Senate was his orchestration of the Civil Rights Act of 1957. Even if its provisions were primarily symbolic, they were an important symbolism: the first civil rights bill to be passed by Congress since 1875.

After John F. Kennedy's death in 1963, Johnson committed himself to the passage of the civil rights bill then in Congress to end segregation in public accommodations. Senator Richard Russell (D-Ga.) warned him that his championing of the bill would "cost you the South and cost you the election." Johnson replied, "If that's the price I've got to pay, I'll pay it gladly." [58]

While it was true that Johnson calculated the impact of civil rights legislation on his political opportunities and historical legacy, it is also true that he felt strongly about the issue, and his commitment to civil rights was not necessarily in his short-term political interests: It took political courage to press for historical changes in the public treatment of blacks in the United States. Civil Rights leader Andrew Young said that "it was not politically expedient" for Johnson to back the 1964 Civil Rights Bill.[59] After Johnson signed the bill on July 2, 1964, he told his aide Bill Moyers, "I think we just delivered the South to the Republican party for a long time to come."[60]

Johnson was also committed to expanding political equality to African Americans and worked to pass the Voting Rights Act of 1965, which had a huge impact on the political complexion of the South. Johnson was also responsible for the passage of the many programs created by his Great Society agenda, some of which include Medicare, Medicaid, food stamps, aid to education, public housing, environmental cleanup, and consumer protection laws.

Despite the negative aspects of Johnson's character, therefore, he must be given credit for the many positive accomplishments of his term.

Ronald Reagan

Ronald Reagan's character was closely related to his strengths and weaknesses as a politician and his successes and failures as president. One of his great attractions for the American public was his frequent appeal to traditional, American values. His American values included a suspicion of government and of national government in particular, but also a conviction that America was still destined for greatness. Part of Reagan's appeal was also that he was confident in himself and projected his optimism about the United States, if it could only be brought back to its traditional values. Importantly, he was not insecure in the way that Johnson and Nixon were.

His rhetorical abilities were impressive, in part because of the professional skills he had developed as an actor and in part because he personally believed what he was preaching. That his personal vision of the country was simple was a strength—it was easily understood and it corresponded with his own values and vision. But the weakness of his vision was that its simplicity did not always correspond with reality. His executive style was to set the overall direction of a policy but to delegate the details and implementation to his subordinates. This conforms to good management theory, as long as the executive has the knowledge of the policy and the tenacity to oversee and ensure that his subordinates are accurately carrying out the policy. But Reagan often neglected the follow-through aspect of this management approach and thus was vulnerable to his subordinates' entrepreneurial tendencies. I will examine these aspects of President Reagan's character in the context of three major policy areas: the initial economic agenda of his first year in office, the Iran-Contra affair, and the end of the Cold War.

Reagan's First-Year Budget Victories

Ronald Reagan ran for office in 1980 by arguing that the economy was a shambles. He promised to cut taxes, balance the budget, and make America strong again militarily. In addition, he appealed to social conservatives who were concerned with moral issues such as abortion, crime, and prayer in school. But after he won the election he decided to limit his policy agenda to his economic priorities and put the agenda of the social conservatives on the back burner, a wise strategic choice.[61] Reagan succeeded in increasing military spending substantially and in getting Congress to cut income taxes by 25 percent. His promise to bring the budget into balance was undercut by these two policies, and the cuts in domestic programs were not sufficient to make up the difference.

The supply-side theory that tax cuts would result in new investments and spur the economy to produce large revenue increases did not work. Thus, one of the Reagan legacies was a string of $200-billion deficits and a tripling of the national debt from $1 trillion to $3 trillion. Reagan deserves credit for his resolute leadership and political skill in pushing his initial agenda through Congress, but his failure to understand the flaws in supply-side theory or how his economic policies would hurt poor Americans made him blind to the negative aspects of his economic policies.

Iran-Contra

While Reagan's hands-off approach to management worked in his first term, in part because he chose James A. Baker to be his chief of staff, it led to disaster in his second term. Baker left the White House to become secretary of the treasury, and treasury secretary Donald Regan came to the White House to be chief of staff. Regan was a domineering chief of staff and did not have the political instincts or skills of Baker.[62] Thus, the plan for trading arms to Iran in hopes of freeing hostages held in Lebanon was allowed to go forward despite the vehement objections of Secretary of State George Schultz and Secretary of Defense Casper Weinberger.

When Lieutenant Colonel Oliver North had the "bright idea" to use the profit from the arms sales to Iran to support the Contras in

Nicaragua, even though it was forbidden by law, there was no system in place to stop him. Reagan had made it clear that he wanted the United States to support the Contras, and even though he did not specifically order North to break the law, his national security adviser, John Poindexter, concluded that Reagan would have approved the illegal aid. So Poindexter had North go forward with it but did not inform Reagan (so he testified) so that the president would have "deniability" if he were asked. The delegation approach to management thus failed to prevent disaster in this case because President Reagan had been unwilling to oversee the activities of his subordinates.

The End of the Cold War

Ronald Reagan's hostility to the Soviet Union had long been a central part of his political persona. When he came to office his actions were prudent but his rhetoric was often bellicose, condemning the "evil empire" of the Soviet Union. But when Gorbachev came to power in 1985, Reagan was able to develop a relatively trusting relationship with him and engage in a dialogue about the reduction of nuclear forces on each side. Reagan's optimism and willingness to take bold steps brought him to take seriously the possibility of deep cuts in nuclear arms and to bring Gorbachev along with him.

The deep-cuts option came close to being accepted by the two leaders at the 1986 Reykjavik summit (a possibility that alarmed the national security establishments of both nations), except that Reagan refused to consider abandoning his Strategic Defense Initiative (SDI). The plan for the SDI envisioned an antimissile system that was space based and that would enable the United States to intercept and destroy any hostile missiles fired at this country. Computer specialists concluded that such a system was technologically not feasible at that time, but Reagan believed that it could be created. Fortunately, so did the Russians. Part of the final push that led to the breakup of the Soviet Union was their expectation that the United States could develop an effective SDI and that the Russians could not afford to keep up with the expenditures necessary to counter such a system.

While Reagan might be faulted for his rigid and hostile attitude toward the Soviet Union, he must be given credit for his open relationship with Gorbachev. While the downfall of the Soviet Union was due to a wide range of historical forces related to the internal contradictions of a nation that suppressed political freedom and tried to run the economy through central control, part of the credit is due Ronald Reagan and his relationship with Gorbachev.[63]

Bill Clinton

President Clinton has been the poster boy for defective character in the 1990s. In both the 1992 and 1996 campaigns "the character issue" was raised in attacking Clinton. He picked up the nickname "Slick Willie" and he gave misleading answers (or lies) during the 1992 campaign to questions about his draft status in 1968 and 1969, his previous affair with Gennifer Flowers in Arkansas, and his indecisive statement on alleged marijuana smoking in college ("I didn't inhale").[64] But his most significant breaches of trust attributed to character failures were his affair with Monica Lewinsky while he was president and his lies in public and under oath about it.

While Clinton's weaknesses are well known, his character is not unidimensional. Insightful analysts and observers point out that strengths and weaknesses cohabit side by side in Clinton's character.[65] *New York Times* reporter Todd S. Purdum observes: "One of the biggest, most talented, articulate, intelligent, open, colorful characters ever to inhabit the Oval Office can also be an undisciplined, fumbling, obtuse, defensive, self-justifying rogue. . . . In a real sense, his strengths are his weaknesses, his enthusiasms are his undoing and most of the traits that make him appealing can make him appalling in the flash of an eye."[66] Clinton's talents and failures of judgment alternate throughout his political history. Fred Greenstein describes Clinton's leadership style as "his tendency to oscillate between an uninhibited, anything-goes approach to leadership and a more measured operating mode in which he sets attainable goals and proceeds skillfully in his efforts to realize them."[67]

Critics of President Clinton, even when admitting that he has some political skills, can find few redeeming character traits and see Clinton's policy positions as merely poll-driven opportunism.[68] But in several important policy battles, Clinton did what he judged to be best for the country despite serious political opposition, for example, the 1993 deficit reduction, the North American Free Trade Agreement (NAFTA), gun control, intervention in Haiti, the bailout of the Mexican peso, and intervention in Bosnia and Kosovo. One might criticize any one of these decisions on policy grounds, but it is hard to argue that they were all craven adherence to the path of least resistance. Thus, despite Clinton's faults, his character led him to some significant victories.

Deficit Reduction in 1993   Clinton's decision to pursue deficit reduction early in 1993 rather than the middle-class tax cut that he had promised in his campaign has been criticized as demonstrating a lack of trustworthiness.[69] Clinton decided in February 1993 that he had to abandon his campaign promise and pursue deficit reduction in his first budget. His budget combined a gas tax increase with an increase in the tax rate on high-income individuals with program cuts to achieve about $500 billion in deficit reduction over five years.[70] "Deficit hawks" in his administration who convinced Clinton that he had to do this included Lloyd Bentsen, Leon Panneta, Robert Rubin, Alice Rivlin, and Federal Reserve Board Chair Alan Greenspan. They argued that, with a projected deficit approaching $300 billion, a failure to address the deficit seriously would lead Wall Street financiers to anticipate inflation and raise interest rates, which, in turn, would slow the economy and prolong the recession. Clinton did not want to confront the deficit but was convinced that it was necessary for the health of the economy.

While some might argue that Clinton should have kept his campaign promise, it can also be argued that the deficit hawks were correct and that the economic boom of the latter 1990s would not have occurred without the 1993 deficit reduction. One might argue that it took strength of character for Clinton to change his mind in light of rational arguments that economic conditions had changed between the campaign and the spring of 1993. (The same argument can be made about President Bush's decision to abandon his campaign pledge of "no new taxes" in 1990 and achieve a $500-billion deficit reduction over five years.) Although making the initial decision was tough, it was not nearly so tough as convincing Congress to pass his first budget. Yet Clinton applied all of his political skills to win the thinnest of victories without any Republican votes. In this case, Clinton pushed the political system as far as it would go.

Peace in the Middle East Clinton's powers of persuasion were also demonstrated in negotiations over Middle East peace at Wye Plantation in the fall of 1998, when he convinced Israel's Prime Minister Benjamin Netanyahu and Palestinian Yasir Arafat to sign an agreement that neither felt was fully fair to their side and that was attacked by their political enemies in their own countries. This achievement pushed the political possibilities for peace in the Middle East about as far as they could go at that time. Clinton's abilities to empathize, his powers of persuasion, his patience, and his tenaciousness were all demonstrated in the Wye Plantation negotiations. Clinton's commitment to peace in the Middle East was recognized by King Hussein of Jordan, who left a cancer treatment center in Minnesota to help facilitate the final agreement. Hussein, who had dealt closely with presidents since Eisenhower on Middle East peace issues, said to Clinton: "With all due respect on all the affections I held for your predecessors, [I have never] known someone with your dedication, clearheadedness, focus, and determination to help resolve this issue."[71]

Confronting the 104th Congress   Another aspect of Clinton's character was the resoluteness he demonstrated when faced with the severe budget and program cuts passed by the Republican 104th Congress in 1995. The Republicans, led by Newt Gingrich, were convinced that they had a mandate from the people in the 1994 elections and set out to dismantle important elements of the federal government establishment. They proposed to eliminate three cabinet departments, cut Environmental Protection Agency funding by half, make severe cuts in Medicare and Medicaid, cut educational funding, and make cuts in other social programs.

Because President Clinton was politically vulnerable at the time, the Republicans felt they could force him to sign the budget bills in the fall of 1995. Clinton, although he agreed to move to a balanced budget, refused to go along and vetoed the bills, allowing much of the government to be shut down for temporary lack of funding. Whether one agrees that the programs were worth saving or not, it must be admitted that Clinton's actions took courage, skill, and tenaciousness.

Despite President Clinton's spectacular character failings (recklessness, lying, lack of sexual restraint), positive aspects of his character allowed him to win significant policy victories.

Conclusion

Presidential character is multidimensional. None of our presidents has been perfect; Washington and Jefferson owned slaves, Lincoln misled audiences about his stand on slavery in order to get elected. Imperfection does not mean that they were not great presidents, only that they were not perfect human beings. The implication of this argument is that character is not seamless: Presidents can act wisely in some areas and show very poor judgment in others. The sooner we can move beyond campaign slogans when talking about presidential character, the sooner we will be able to understand presidents for what they truly are and make rational decisions about what makes up acceptable and unacceptable presidential behavior.

Notes

For advice and assistance on this chapter the author would like to acknowledge Brack Brown, Tim Conlan, George Edwards, Robert Dudley, Jerold Duquette, Robert Dallek, Betty Glad, Fred Greenstein, Hugh Heclo, Scott Keeter, Burdett Loomis, John Maltese, Herbert Parmet, Priscilla Regan, Elizabeth Spaulding, Robert Spitzer, Susan Tolchin, and Roger Wilkins. The first section of this chapter is based on James P. Pfiffner, "Sexual Probity and Presidential Character," *Presidential Studies Quarterly,* fall 1998, 881–86.

1. James David Barber, *The Presidential Character,* 4th ed. (Englewood Cliffs, N.J.: Prentice Hall, 1992); Alexander L. George, *Presidential Decisionmaking in Foreign Policy: The Effective Use of Information and Advice* (Boulder, Colo.: Westview Press, 1980); Alexander L. George and Juliette L. George, *Presidential Personality and Performance* (Boulder, Colo.: Westview Press, 1998), 9; Fred Greenstein, foreword, Alexander L. George and Juliette L. George, *Presidential Personality and Performance* (Boulder, Colo.: Westview Press, 1998), ix–x; Stanley A. Renshon, *High Hopes: The Clinton Presidency and the Politics of Ambition* (New York: New York University Press, 1996), 37–38; Robert Shogan, *The Double-Edged Sword* (Boulder, Colo.: Westview Press, 1999); James Q. Wilson, *On Character* (Washington: AEI Press, 1995), 5; Robert A. Wilson, *Character Above All* (New York: Simon & Schuster, 1995).

2. Lynn Martin, Secretary of Labor for George Bush, quoted by Michael Beschloss, "George Bush," in Robert A. Wilson, *Character Above All* (New York: Simon & Schuster, 1995), 242.

3. For details and documentation of Harding's affairs, see Carl Sferrazza Anthony, *Florence Harding* (New York: William Morrow, 1998). Nan Britton wrote a book about her affair with Harding: *The President's Daughter* (New York: Elizabeth Ann Guild, 1927).

4. For a sensitive and insightful analysis of the Roosevelts' marriage and their extramarital relationships see Doris Kearns Goodwin, *No Ordinary Time* (New York: Simon & Schuster, 1994); on the role of Missy LeHand, see 20–22.

5. Stephen E. Ambrose, *Eisenhower: Soldier and President* (New York: Simon & Schuster, 1990), 102–103, 125. Summersby writes about their sexual episode in Kay Summersby Morgan, *Past Forgetting: My Love Affair with Dwight D. Eisenhower* (New York: Simon & Schuster, 1976), 268. Incidentally, Summersby included in her book a photograph of a celebration of the Allied victory over Germany in which she appeared and claims that her image was removed from some official versions of the photograph (256–57); also, according to Summersby, after they were back in the United States, Eisenhower offered to help her with a job in New York (275).

6. Seymour Hersh, *The Dark Side of Camelot* (Boston: Little Brown, 1997). For a skeptical review of Hersh see Garry Wills, "A Second Assassination," *New York Review of Books,* 18 December 1997, 4–8.

7. Robert Dallek, *Flawed Giant: Lyndon Johnson and His Times* (New York: Oxford University Press, 1998), 186.

8. Nigel Cawthorne, *Sex Lives of the Presidents* (New York: St. Martin's, 1998), 236.

9. See Herbert Parmet, *George Bush: The Life of a Lone Star Yankee* (New York: Scribner, 1997), 178–79, 239–49.

10. Those who argue that character is seamless would also have to assess Eisenhower's and Reagan's truthfulness. It may be understandable that the Eisenhower administration at first claimed Gary Power's U-2 flight was not a spy mission. But it is harder to explain President Reagan's claim to Israel Prime Minister Yitzhak Shamir on November 29, 1983, that he (Reagan) had photographed Nazi death camps at the end of World War II, when he in fact had never left the country. See Lou Cannon, *President Reagan: The Role of a Lifetime* (New York: Simon & Schuster, 1991), 486–90.

11. This chapter takes a relatively narrow approach to presidential lies, limiting the analysis to presidential statements (or statements made at the direction of the president) that are not true. Other types of deception, such as truth telling with the intent to deceive, will not be considered. This treatment is not exhaustive of all types of presidential lies or possible justifications for lies.

12. Richard Reeves, *President Kennedy: Profile of Power* (New York: Simon & Schuster, 1993) 24.

13. Ibid.

14. See Robert E. Gilbert, *The Mortal Presidency* (New York: Basic Books, 1993), 154–79.

15. This account is based on Jane Mayer and Jill Abramson, *Strange Justice* (Boston: Houghton Mifflin, 1994), 11–22.

16. On the probable violation of the Arms Export Control Act by the Reagan administrations see, George Shultz, *Turmoil and Triumph: My Years as Secretary of State* (New York: Charles Scribners Sons, 1993), 11.

17. George Bush with Victor Gold, *Looking Forward* (New York: Doubleday, 1987), 240.

18. Shultz, *Turmoil and Triumph,* 808–09.

19. Ibid., 809.

20. William S. Cohen and George Mitchell, *Men of Zeal,* (New York: Viking, 1988), 264–65. For another account of Bush's dissembling about his involvement in meetings about arms sales to Iran, see Independent Counsel Lawrence E. Walsh, *Iran-Contra: The Final Report* (New York: Times Books, 1993), 473–83.

21. Shultz, *Turmoil and Triumph,* 809.

22. Stanley I. Kutler, *The Wars of Watergate* (New York: Alfred A. Knopf, 1990), 347.

23. James P. Pfiffner, *The Modern Presidency* (New York: St. Martin's, 1998), 210.

24. Stanley I. Kutler, *The Wars of Watergate* (New York: Alfred A. Knopf, 1990), 332–433.

25. James P. Pfiffner, *The Modern Presidency,* 3d ed. (New York: Bedford St. Martin's, 2000), chapter 8; and Pfiffner, "President Clinton's Impeachment and Senate Trial," in James P. Pfiffner and Roger Davidson, *Understanding the Presidency* (New York: Addison Wesley Longman, 2000), 456–567.

26. Richard Nixon, *Six Crises* (New York: Doubleday, 1962), 353.

27. Ibid., 355.

28. Ibid.

29. Ambrose, *Eisenhower*, 507.

30. See the account by Fred Greenstein, *The Hidden-Hand Presidency* (New York: Basic Books, 1982), 253.

31. Michael R. Beschloss, *Mayday: Eisenhower, Khrushchev and the U-2 Affair* (New York: Harper & Row, 1986), 233.

32. Ibid., 252.

33. Ibid., 254.

34. Sissela Bok, *Lying: Moral Choice in Public and Private Life* (New York: Vintage Books, 1978), 182.

35. FRUS, Vietnam, 1964 V, 607–9; quoted by Robert Dallek, *Flawed Giant: Lyndon Johnson and His Times* (New York: Oxford University Press, 1998), 151.

36. The question arises as to whether President Johnson deliberately lied to the American people and members of Congress in characterizing the August 4 incident as a military attack against U.S. naval vessels. Johnson's actions can be read in two different ways. He can be seen as taking the best judgment of Secretary McNamara and Admiral Sharp that U.S. forces had in fact been attacked. But when subsequent reports came in that there was serious doubt about whether there had been any attack, Johnson pushed ahead to further his initial reaction to order retaliatory raids, to address the American people, and get Congress to pass a resolution of support for his reaction to the doubtful attack.

37. George W. Ball, *The Past Has Another Pattern* (New York: W. W. Norton, 1982), 379. For an analysis sympathetic to Johnson see Robert Dallek, *Flawed Giant*, 147–56; for a critical account see Stanley Karnow, *Vietnam: A History* (New York: Penguin Books, 1983), 367–75; Joseph Goulden, *Truth Is the First Casualty: The Gulf of Tonkin Affair* (Chicago: Rand McNally, 1969); Neil Sheehan, *A Bright Shining Lie* (New York: Vintage Books, 1988). See also Larry Berman, *Planning a Tragedy: The Americanization of the War in Vietnam* (New York: W. W. Norton, 1982), 31–34; and H.R. McMaster, *Dereliction of Duty* (New York: Harper Collins, 1997), 107–08, 121–23.

38. Goulden, *Truth Is the First Casualty*, 160.

39. David Wise, *The Politics of Lying* (New York: Vintage Books, 1973), 65–66.

40. McMaster, *Dereliction of Duty* (New York: Harper Collins, 1997), 195.

41. Ibid., 247.

42. Ibid., 261.

43. Ibid., 211.

44. Berman, *Planning a Tragedy*, 57.

45. Ibid.

46. A dual reporting system was developed. Nixon ordered that a cable be sent to Ambassador to South Vietnam Elsworth Bunker, saying that all discussion of possible bombing of North Vietnamese targets in Cambodia was suspended. At the same time he had a separate, backchannel message sent to the commander of American forces in Vietnam, General Creighton W. Abrams. Abrams was instructed to disregard the cable to Bunker and to plan for the Cambodian bombing campaign. See Seymour Hersh, *The Price of Power* (New York: Summit Books, 1983), 60–65.

47. Hersh, *The Price of Power*, 64.

48. Independent Counsel Lawrence E. Walsh, *Iran-Contra: The Final Report* (New York: Times Books, 1990), 468. When the Tower Commission was conducting its inquiry, making false statements could be punished under the criminal code (18 U.S.C. Par. 1001), but the issue was not pursued by Independent Counsel Walsh because "it was virtually impossible to prove beyond a reasonable doubt what the President remembered in January and February of 1987. Although it seems obvious that President Reagan made hopelessly conflicting statements to the Commission, it would be impossible to prove beyond a reasonable doubt that any misstatement was intentional or willful." Walsh, *Iran-Contra: The Final Report*, 469–70.

49. Lawrence Walsh, *Firewall: The Iran-Contra Conspiracy and Cover-Up* (New York: Norton, 1997) 4.

50. *Washington Post*, 16 July 1987, A15.

51. Ibid.

52. Ibid.

53. Ibid., A14.

54. Joseph A. Califano, Jr., *The Triumph and Tragedy of Lyndon Johnson* (New York: Simon and Schuster, 1991), 10.

55. Robert Dallek, "Lyndon B. Johnson," in Robert A. Wilson, *Character Above All: Ten Presidents from FDR to George Bush* (New York: Simon and Schuster, 1995), 105–06.

56. Ibid., 106.

57. Robert A. Caro, *The Years of Lyndon Johnson: The Path to Power* (New York: Alfred A. Knopf, 1995) and *Means of Ascent* (New York: Alfred A. Knopf, 1990).

58. Robert Dallek, *Flawed Giant*, 112.

59. Ibid., 114.

60. Ibid., 120.

61. For an analysis of the initial Reagan policy agenda, see James P. Pfiffner, *The Strategic Presidency: Hitting the Ground Running*, 2d ed. (Lawrence, Kans.: University Press of Kansas, 1996).

62. For an analysis of the problem of the domineering chief of staff, see James P. Pfiffner, "The President's Chief of Staff: Lessons Learned," in *The Managerial Presidency*, edited by James P. Pfiffner 2d ed. (College Station, Tex.: Texas A&M University Press, 1999).

63. See Fred. I. Greenstein, "Ronald Reagan, Michail Gorbachev, and the End of the Cold War," ed. William C. Wohlforth, *Witnesses to the End of the Cold War* (Baltimore, Md.: Johns Hopkins University Press, 1996).

64. David Maraniss, *First in His Class* (New York: Simon & Schuster, 1995).

65. For an astute analysis of Clinton and the character issue see, Betty Glad, "Evaluating Presidential Character," *Presidential Studies Quarterly* vol. 33, no. 4 (fall 1998), 861–72.

66. Todd S. Purdum, "Facets of Clinton," *New York Times Magazine*, 19 May 1996, 36.

67. Fred I. Greenstein, "There He Goes Again: The Alternating Political Style of Bill Clinton," *PS: Political Science and Politics* (June 1998), 179.

68. There are at least two justifications for paying attention to polls. In a democracy, what the people want ought to be relevant, if not determinative. Public opinion helps set the boundaries of possible action in a polity that is responsive to the public.

69. Stanley A. Renshon, "The President's Judgment," *PRG Report* vol. 21, no. 1 (spring 1998), 10. For Renshon's in-depth analysis of Clinton's character, see: *High Hopes: The Clinton Presidency and the Politics of Ambition* (New York: New York University Press, 1996).

70. For an analysis of Clinton's 1993 budget proposals and the politics of their passage see James P. Pfiffner, "President Clinton and the 103d Congress," in James A. Thurber, *Rivals for Power* (Washington, D.C.: CQ Press, 1998), 170–90.

71. Jonathan Alter, "An October Surprise," *Newsweek*, 2 November 1998, 29.

CONTRIBUTORS

Mark J. Rozell is associate professor of politics at The Catholic University of America in Washington, D.C. He is the author of numerous studies on the presidency, including *Executive Privilege: The Dilemma of Secrecy and Democratic Accountability*.

Clyde Wilcox is professor of government at Georgetown University in Washington, D.C. He is the author or editor of a variety of books on religion and politics, gender politics, and campaign finance.

Molly W. Andolina is visiting assistant professor of political science at Loyola University of Chicago. She has written on public opinion and the media.

Louis Fisher is a senior specialist in separation of powers studies at the Congressional Research Service, Library of Congress, in Washington, D.C. He is the author of numerous leading public law studies, including *American Constitutional Law*.

Michael J. Gerhardt is professor of law at the College of William and Mary School of Law. He is the author of the leading study on federal impeachment, *The Federal Impeachment Process*.

Joel B. Grossman is professor of political science at The Johns Hopkins University in Baltimore, Maryland. He is the coauthor with Charles Epp of the forthcoming book *The Judicial Imperative*.

John R. Hermann is assistant professor of political science at Trinity University, San Antonio, Texas.

Thomas A. Kazee is dean of the college and professor of political science, University of the South in Sewanee, Tennessee. His latest book on Congress is *Who Runs for Congress? Ambition, Context, and Candidate Emergence*.

John Anthony Maltese is associate professor of political science at the University of Georgia, Athens. He is the author of *Spin Control:*

The White House Office of Communications and the Management of Presidential News.

Karen O'Connor is professor and chair of the department of government at American University in Washington, D.C. She is the author of numerous studies on judicial politics and is currently the president of the Southern Political Science Association.

James P. Pfiffner is professor of government and politics at George Mason University in Fairfax, Virginia. He is the author of numerous works on the presidency, including *The Strategic Presidency: Hitting the Ground Running.*

Paul J. Quirk is associate professor of political science at University of Illinois at Urbana–Champaign. He is the author of numerous works on the contemporary presidency.

Robert J. Spitzer is distinguished service professor of political science at the State University of New York, College at Cortland. He is the author of numerous studies on the presidency, including *The Presidential Veto* and *President and Congress.*

Stephen J. Wayne is professor of government at Georgetown University in Washington, D.C. He is the author of leading works on the presidency, including *The Legislative Presidency* and *The Road to the White House.*

David A. Yalof is assistant professor of political science at the University of Connecticut, Storrs. He is the author of *Pursuit of Justices: Presidential Politics and the Selection of Supreme Court Nominees.*

INDEX